Coronavirus and Education

Khalsa College of Education
G. T. Road, Amritsar

Khalsa College of Education, Amritsar, a premier institute of Teacher Education is a unique amalgamation of professional and academic excellence. The college started its onerous journey as a B.T. Department of main Khalsa College, Amritsar in the year 1954 and subsequently became an independent college in the year 1959.

The college is offering both Under Graduate & Post Graduate courses viz. M.Ed. 2 year, B.Ed. 2 year, 3 year Integrated B.Ed. M.Ed., 4 year Integrated B.A.B.Ed, 4 year Integrated B.Sc.B.Ed & PGDCA (TE).

Accredited 'A' grade by NAAC in 2003, 2011 and 2016, the objective of the college is to prepare passionate, innovative, secular teachers for 21st century with a focus to develop their competencies and chisel their skills required to compete in the world job market.

Under the able stewardship of the Management and the Principal, the highly qualified faculty of the college are making relentless efforts to provide training to the teacher trainees to become a part of the 'knowledge generating society' by enlarging their intellectual horizon.

With a determination to synthesize precept and practice, the college promises to build a social foundation for teaching skills which will enable the students to develop their potential to the utmost. A wide spectrum of programmes paired with flexibility, experiential learning and inter disciplinary orientation emancipate our students to explore their potentialities and hone their skills for fulfilling careers.

Coronavirus and Education

Opportunities and Challenges

Editors

Harpreet Kaur
Maninder Kaur
Deepika Kohli

₹ 550
US$ 22
ISBN: 978-93-88691-90-1

First Published in India in 2021

Coronavirus and Education: Opportunities and Challenges

Published by:
SHIPRA PUBLICATIONS
LG 18-19, Pankaj Central Market
I.P. Ext., Patparganj, Delhi 110092, India
Tel.: +91 11 2223 5152; 96500 28065
E-mail: info@shiprapublication.com
www.shiprapublication.com

CONTENTS

2. Covid-19: An Opportunity to Introspect

3. Moral Responsibilities of Teachers During Pandemic

4. Social Distancing vs Wellness and Mental Health of Youth

5. Future of Education After Lockdown

6. Coronavirus and Ecological Learning

7. Impact of Lockdown on Creativity and Reading Habits

8. Covid-19 and its Future Repercussions

9. Other Related Issues

MESSAGE

The outbreak of COVID-19 has impacted nations in an enormous ways, especially the nationwide lockdown which has brought social and economic life to a standstill. These have been challenging times, which required an enormous amount of decision making, planning and understanding from all.

In this time of crisis, when people especially the students are under trauma, stress and psychological pressure, the initiative of Khalsa College of Education, G. T. Road, Amritsar to compile the ideas and experiences of the scholars and experts from across the nation to work out modalities for a new kind of education in the post COVID times is praiseworthy. The reflections from the articles will help us to re-imagine a kind of education that radiates the spirit of love, care and integral learning which is needed in the post COVID world.

I extend my warm wishes to the college fraternity for taking this tremendous initiative.

May the Institution continue its journey on the road of excellence!

S. Satyajit Singh Majithia
President
Khalsa College Charitable Society
Amritsar

MESSAGE

COVID-19 induced lockdowns and fears have triggered a full blown psychological pandemic across the country pushing people into spaces and situations they have never seen before. But there is an opportunity in every disaster, if only we know how to use it.

The ambitious lead by Khalsa College of Education, G. T. Road, Amritsar to publish the book on 'Coronavirus and Education: Opportunities and Challenges' is a great step towards compiling innovative ideas/suggestions of the educationists and scholars from across the nation. The experiences shared by the experts highlight the urgent need to understand the challenges posed by Corona Virus especially in the field of education. It will definitely help in preparing the higher education institutions to workout strategies to turn this crisis into an opportunity to reform.

I convey my best wishes to this laudable venture of Khalsa College of Education, G. T. Road, Amritsar.

S. Rajinder Mohan Singh Chhina
Honorary Secretary
Khalsa College Charitable Society
Amritsar

FOREWORD

The Corona Virus (COVID19) outbreak in December 2019 has been unprecedented. It forced most of our activities to be restricted to a great extent. Many countries declared full or partial lockdown, asked citizens to observe physical distancing, allowed work from home and closed institutions where the chances of infection to spread were high. The closing of institutions included educational institutions too, which affected globally around 1.5 billion learners of all ages. United Nations has acknowledged education as a fundamental human right. Therefore, following the ideal #LearningNeverStops, educational institutions switched to *emergency remote teaching* during this pandemic.

Institutions, teachers, parents and students adopted unique methods to emergency remote teaching. I noticed a teacher in the building next to ours used a megaphone to teach mathematics to the students residing in the building. He would first introduce the concept and then ask the students to do the exercises and indicate the answers. I noticed the parents too to come out in the balcony of their homes to be in support of their kids and the teacher. Another good example which has been in the news from Jharkhand, India where the efforts were made to teach students using loudspeakers when there is no Internet facility available. It was the time we saw innovations in transacting knowledge, keeping students engaged, carrying out assessments. Zeal was that the learning should never stop. This was the time to train the teachers for emergency remote teaching and thus volumes of webinars were offered by institutions and independent experts. Companies offered free access to their platforms and applications. Online learning platforms offered free access to their courses while waiving the fee for certification. This was the time when we noticed the changing role of parents who turned active teachers, while working from home. It was the time zoomcasting and zoombombing too emerged. Students were made to sit in front of webcam to attend the live classes. After few months resentment of students towards such webinars and online sessions started to appear.

The editors of the book *Coronavirus and Education: Opportunities and Challenges* need to be congratulated to have brought out this book at this crucial time when teaching and learning strategies are being redefined and new modes are being explored for continuity of teaching, learning and assessment. This book would be very useful to teachers, educational planners and educational technologists in realising how the challenges posed to us by COVID-19 can be addressed, what new opportunities are available to us. This also shares good insights into how the philosophy of care and empathy should need to stay on the top of agenda as that is what the learners need in this time of crisis.

Ramesh C Sharma
Ambedkar University, Delhi, India

PROLOGUE

Time and again, mankind has to face various types of challenges, several disease outbreak have happened in the past and numerous lives have been lost to it. In 2020, we went through just another such phase and as saying goes "This too shall pass", similarly the havoc created by the COVID-19 too will be a thing of past. Till that time we will have to adjust our lives according to it.

During these challenging times of global pandemic when we need to stay motivated all the times and keep making efforts in the right direction (while maintaining utmost precautions every time), it has been a big challenge for educational institutions to impart and continue with the studies. The disruption in the delivery of education is pushing policymakers to figure out how to drive engagement at a scale while ensuring inclusive e-learning solutions and tackling the digital divide. In this time of crisis, a well-rounded and effective educational practice is what is needed for the capacity-building of young minds. It will develop skills that will ensure their employability, productivity, health and well-being in the decades to come, and contribute towards the overall progress of India.

In this time of crisis, the gigantic initiative taken by Khalsa College of Education, G. T. Road, Amritsar to publish a book 'Coronavirus and Education: Opportunities and Challenges' is commendable. The book will provide reflections on developing a multi-pronged strategy which is required to manage the crisis and build a resilient Indian education system in the long term.

I convey my best wishes to this significant venture.

Prof. Amit Kauts
Dean
Faculty of Education
Guru Nanak Dev University
Amritsar

PROLOGUE

I am delighted to write message for the book *Coronavirus and Education: Opportunities and Challenges* which is a valuable guide for all the stakeholders in education to reshape the education system during the Covid-19 pandemic as well as post pandemic.

I believe that sharing knowledge enriches the learning communities and this book is a piece of knowledge that is going to be a great source of new learning both for present and perspective educators. Being member of the peer review committee of the book I found it to be very useful, relevant and productive in present educational scenario. This book refreshes my personal teaching experiences during this pandemic in a completely new educational setup.

Covid-19 the unprecedented global issue faced by world economy has shaken the education system to its core. The complete closure of educational institutions hampered the complete educational process worldwide. Being an educator, we found this situation very vulnerable. The Question before us was 'how to ensure the continuity in teaching learning process?' But the manner in which education system prepares itself to face this challenge is really commendable. Being the only viable solution in such a scenario, E-Learning solutions took place of traditional learning in no time. In 27 years of my teaching experience, it is for the first time that I witnessed completely the digitalized system of education. Transformation of face to face classroom teaching learning to virtual learning, paper based assessment system to online assessment and introduction of E-learning tools which were initially considered as an ornamental alternate solution has now became new normal for both the students and educators. Nevertheless, the pandemic has compelled the educational thinkers to rethink the traditional educational system. This book provides a useful compilation of educational tools, approaches, strategies, and devices developed during this pandemic. A complete range of innovative and improved teaching learning strategies for planning, designing and developing teaching learning programs has been discussed in this book. All such changes that have taken place were developed as a solution to face the challenges laid down by pandemic but these are not going to fade away post pandemic. The manner in which technology has entered into our present educational system, it will have long lasting impact. Introducing Digital education, MOOCs, E-learning to Indian Education systems were considered as an alternative to mainstream education but now all these are important features of our education system.

This book will surely prove to be a very useful resource as it goes well making readers aware of not only the new learning opportunities that have emerged during pandemic but also the challenges associated with those opportunities.

This book is a productive resource for educators, students and researchers and everyone related to education field by providing insights into a new perspective on educational solutions evolved especially during this pandemic and secondly, the challenges that need to be encountered to make such solutions more useful. Throughout the book, the authors set out to make the content accessible to readers by presenting ideas in form of questions, adding graphics and providing practical suggestions. The description completely from such an author who has personal teaching experiences would provide invaluable knowledge which is worth the value of the book.

Overall, this well organized, clearly described, practically oriented book is a must buy not only by learners and teachers but also by educational institution to make a productive addition to their academic libraries.

Best wishes!

Prof. Deepa Sikand Kauts
Head, Department of Education
Guru Nanak Dev University
Amritsar

PREFACE

The lockdown, the restrictions, the confinement, the paranoia — Covid-19 spawned situations that had no precedence. The virus not only tested immunity, but also the elasticity of human ties. As a vaccine shot becomes a reality, lifting the pandemic's occupation of the mind-scape is the big challenge.

In the initial weeks, an unsuspecting populace treated it more like a holiday—not going to work, no school, spending time with family. The pause provided the much-needed break everyone had yearned for at some point of the time. However, reality soon set in that the pandemic and the 'pause' is here to stay and no one knows for how long.

At this moment of the pandemic, when our mental landscape is severely wounded and chronic uncertainty is the order of the day, college and university students, needless to add, are deeply worried about the state of education, their life trajectories and future prospects. Possibly, they need a healing touch, or an innovative and ethically enriched engagement with their teachers and mentors. They need to contemplate, understand the changing world around them, and redefine themselves to make sense of the new reality.

In this time of crisis, a multi-pronged, well-rounded and effective educational practice is what is needed for the capacity building of young minds. It will help to develop skills that will enhance their employability, productivity, health and well-being in the decades to come.

At this critical juncture, when the crisis is forcing teachers to reinvent their roles from that of transforming information to enabling learning, Khalsa College of Education, G.T. Road, Amritsar invited the ideas and experiences of the research scholars, teachers, teacher educators, administrators and experts from across the nation to work out the modalities to overcome the learning crisis we are already facing and to get back on the path of faster improvement in learning through hi-tech and low-tech sources.

The views, perceptions and thoughts of experts have been compiled and presented in an edited book *Coronavirus and Education: Opportunities and Challenges*.

The book provides a mosaic of articles on the Covid-19 pandemic. The perceptions and thoughts given by the academicians, experts and scholars on various sub-themes clearly indicate that the pandemic has surely led to a 'new normal' in our lives. The articles reflect that Covid-19 has made us realise values and systems, some of which can be termed as traditional, concerning hygiene, health, education and even society and communities in which we live. The pandemic has perhaps enforced conduct that requires the use of new techniques and technologies with the widespread adoption of old but otherwise normal systems and practices, which were lost in our pursuits to grow, perhaps unknowingly. The pandemic has driven us to the new world of work and living. In many ways, it has also helped us to re-imagine kind of education that radiates the spirit of love, care, integral learning and prudence in life, which is needed in the post Covid-19 world.

We would like to thank S. Satyajit Singh Majithia, President and S. Rajinder Mohan Singh Chhina, Honorary Secretary, Khalsa College Charitable Society, Amritsar, Punjab for supporting us during the journey of completing this special volume. Further, we would like to extend our thanks to the Peer Reviewers and all the authors for contributing their scholarly papers and support in bringing out this book. Last, but not the least, heartfelt gratitude to Shipra Publications, for their timely work. We are grateful to all who extended every feasible help to bring out this edited book.

Dr. Harpreet Kaur
Dr. Maninder Kaur
Dr. Deepika Kohli

1

ROLE OF DIGITAL EDUCATION DURING AND AFTER COVID-19

1

BLENDING OFFLINE & ONLINE CLASSES: A SILVER BULLET IN COVID TIMES

Harpreet Kaur (Dr.)

Now-a-days touch has become a taboo & life sustaining "breath" brings with it risk to life. Humanity is living on the edge. Living in the times of Covid-19 is never going to be the same as life before the pandemic. Giving the steady surge of infections, it will take a while to reach a stage that can be called life after the corona virus. Until a vaccine is found and the virus is dealt with, we will have life alongside the corona virus. One should press the reset button instead of pressing the pause button. Both our minds and modes of living need a reset.

A recent post-corona virus survey by PEW research centre revealed that 91% of Americans have said that virus has changed their lives in varying degrees, 86% prayed for an end to the virus, 77% did not want to eat out at a restaurant again. This is the invisible impact of virus across the globe.

Experts and government official say that the fight against the corona virus is a long haul. Since the vaccine may take some time in coming the confidence to reset life to deal with the virus should guide people as they await the next set of rules. The contour of the society will depend on the curve of infections and the conduct of people. Whatever the case, there is no doubt that the rules in all the domains viz: social, economic, political and educational domains have to be reset. Of course, now the comfort of being in the presence of others is forcibly replaced by that of absence, life has to adjust accordingly. While ensuring social distancing, we need to stay connected in a meaningful manner and support each other in every way.

With the corona virus induced life style stretching to almost eight months and crowded spaces continuing to be potentially hazardous for an intermediate period, the education sector is facing some unique challenges as the academic calendar zooms past.

A recent nationwide survey which covered 12,000 respondents in cities like Bangalore, Mumbai, Chennai, Kolkata, Hyderabad, Delhi says 15% of parents are considering home schooling as one of the options. According to the survey, 92% Indian parents are unwilling to send their children to school when they reopen, 50% will monitor for a month before sending their wards to schools, 21% want to avoid sending them to school for at least 6 months.

Principal (Offtg.) Khalsa College of Education, G.T. Road, Amritsar

Post corona virus, class rooms have been replaced by homes, seminars are morphing into webinars, meetings are no more physical. A really digital life is emerging though the issues related to equitable access to the tools still exist.

Both educationist and students are trying to make good use of the time at home by logging into online classes. Efforts to tackle the technology hurdles, have not borne the deserved results. Majority of the students have not been able to attend the classes, because of lack of necessary tools (smart phones, laptops, bandwidth and internet) particularly in rural remote areas.

India has already been experiencing a substantial deeply entrenched learning deficit. ASER 2018 reports that less than one-third of children in class 3, and half of children in class 5 are able to read a class 2 level texts which the pandemic will further exacerbate.

Between the two extremes of the elite private and government schools lie many low cost private and public schools which suffer from varying level of deficiencies in education, technology and pedagogy. As per UNESCO's estimate over 280 million children in India have been impacted by school closures due to Covid-19. The School Education Quality Index (SEQI) Report 2019 by NITI Aayog indicates that in states such as Kerala too, the elementary schools do not have computer aided learning and even in the best performing states such as Tamil Nadu, secondary schools do not have computer labs. Additional factors such as unavailability of separate rooms for children as well as noisy surrounding in homes cannot be ignored.

The survey included private schools too. The usual explanation of poor students in cities and rural areas not having computer/smart phones/smart mobile and high speed broadband has often been cited for the inability of government schools to get on to the blended online learning. Although over the years, there has been a push by the government to vast technology enabled learning, self learning online portals like Swayam, e-pathshala and Diksha have come up and school books are available online. Doordarshan, too, has started special education broadcasts which are also available on YouTube. Government school teachers use WhatsApp to send small videos and exercise sheets. In May, Centre launched e-vidya campaign to unify digital/online/on air education efforts. Yet the effectiveness of these interactions in enhancing learning outcomes remains uncertain. Research says that the academic content delivered through a passive one-way communication does not engage a student's curious mind, although learning can lead to improved cognitive outcome.

But given these extraordinary times where physical presence is not possible, the blended online delivery of school lectures by teachers remains the most effective way. Results from J. PAL's Educational Technology Evidence Review from 126 studies on the Role of Technology in Education indicate that blended learning i.e. combining online and in-person instruction can deliver as good an outcome as in-person class experience. So the teachers must be trained in the technology enabled active learning pedagogy.

The state may have, a component for technology enabled learning as part of the SSA and Rashtriya Madhyamik Shiksha Abhiyan for IT, infrastructure, devices, teaching learning material, teacher training and engaging quality teachers in the districts. If what gets measured gets done, the NITI Aayog and Ministry of Human Resources development will have to increase weightage for computer aided learning and computer labs in SEQI, which allocates 10 out of nearly 1,000 grade points. Given that technology tools often make it possible to collect data on how something is working, the National University of Educational Planning and Administration could be asked to undertake evaluations, which will help policy makers and administrators to make better decisions regarding investment in technology related problems.

Of course, in India, where the availability of quality teachers, away from capitals/ districts/ headquarters and especially in subjects such as mathematics and sciences, remain a challenge, blended online learning certainly has a distinctive advantage of removing the physical barrier between places where teachers are available and where they are needed.

It can also help take education to girls, to those from marginalized sector and those in remote areas. It may not solve the problems of the school education system, which no doubt, require incentives for schools and teachers, autonomy to Principals, well functioning school management committees, teacher accountability and management system including transparent transfer policies. However, it could address India's most persistent challenge of ensuring quality education in government schools and take us closer to Sustainable Development Goal of ensuring inclusive and equitable quality education.

Moreover, it must be ensured that the students regain the lost ground, states must invest in pedagogical and technological tools, assess students' needs and equip them with foundational skills. The parents and the community must be involved and a continuum of learning opportunities should be established because there could be closure in future too. To accomplish this task teachers should invest in their development that will help fast track the learning recovery pass.

While online education is providing a critical service in these times, it is not a silver bullet. A blend of offline and online learning should be the part of the future plans also. We should not forget that the transition from brick and mortar schools, technology based learning has its challenges like unequal access to devices and internet connection, inadequate space at home to do online schooling, teachers lacking the training in delivering online classes, short supply of customized online content and the impact of continuous online exposure on health. These realities must be acknowledged.

It is also important to remember that education is not about teaching only, it is also about learning, interactions and developing soft skills among the students and also a social capital, which only brick and mortar schools can provide.

When we shift to online education, more attention needs to be paid on how we impart it. Online education can happen in two parts. Students can go through the digital resources made available to them at leisure and at their own pace. They can also interact with teachers in real time live online classes, discussing what they have already studied from guided online resources. In the second part, the teachers can play an important role. The teaching can be made enquiry or discovery based through inclusive and active involvement of students. Moving to online classrooms gives us the opportunity to create "non didactic flipped class rooms" as students are expected to attend these after having gone through the pre lecture materials. This is what we also call blended learning. We could have done this in the physical classrooms too, but we missed the bus riding on outdated practices. But nothing should stop us from implementing a flipped classroom online mode now.

References

Mundayoor, S. (2020). Before online classes, lessons on a TV screen. *The Sunday Express*, p. 9.

Chandran, S.R. (6 August 2020). Tap Tech Giants to Bridge Digital Divide in Education. *The Tribune*, p. 7.

Mishra, Ashok (2 July 2020). Covid-19: How tech can ensure equity in education. *Hindustan Times*, e-paper.

Sisodia, M. (6 June 2020). Covid-19: A Historic Opportunity to redefine the Indian School System. *Hindustan Times*, p. 12.

2

ONLINE EDUCATION DURING COVID-19: PROS AND CONS

Navdeep Kaur (Dr.)[1] and Maninderpal Kaur[2]

A substantial number of pandemics occurred in different times globally, including cholera, plague, dengue, smallpox, influenza, severe acute respiratory syndrome (SARS) and tuberculosis, which had an effect on various spheres of human life including Education. Influenza pandemics outburst for about three times in a century since 1500 A.D., brought extreme devastation for mankind globally.

1. Assistant Professor, Department of Education, GNDU, Amritsar

2. JRF, Department of Education, GNDU, Amritsar

Covid-19, an infectious disease emerged from coronavirus, has a vast impact on the sector of education. On March 6, 2020, 26 nations among three continents, had announced school closures (UNESCO, 2020). Twenty six countries have closed educational institutions nationally while 13 countries have taken steps at local level, by 'shut down' their schools, to check the spread of Covid-19 and this shut down will hamper the education of 291 million and 471 million children and adolescents respectively.

A number of socio-economic challenges arise as an output of school closures results from Covid-19, involves student debt (Jamerson, Josh, & Joshua, 2020), digital learning (Karp & McGowan, 2020), food insecurity (Cecco, 2020) access to childcare (Belinda, 2020), healthcare (Feuer, 2020) homelessness (Ngumbi, 2020), housing (Barret, 2020), internet (Jordan, 2020) and disability services (Alex, 2020). School closures are a means of social distancing and can be used as a medium to lessen social contacts and disease transmission.

Consequently, an emergency policy initiative called 'Suspending Classes without Stopping Learning' was launched by Ministry of Education in many countries including China, to convert teaching-learning activities into digital education at the time of school closures. Since this initiative has been adopted during a pandemic outbreak, therefore the meaning, implementation procedures and process would remain ambiguous.

The main purpose of 'Suspending Classes without Stopping Learning' is to enhance student's learning through the mode of digital education and eliminate the need of offline teaching-learning activities to check the spread of Covid-19 (Ministry of Education of the People's Republic of China, 2020a). The main aim of this initiative is the collection of all teaching resources at national and local levels and to make provision for high quality digital education learning resources for all students and to support teachers' online teaching and students' online learning activities (Ministry of Education of the People's Republic of China, 2020a). Thus, it is essential for all educational institutions to build up their curriculum stronger and to develop innovative teaching strategies (Toquero, 2020).

Digital education or online learning being a subset of distance education is always concerned to provide those educational experiences, which are flexible and can be accessed at any time and at any place. The increased use of technology in an educational setting enhances learning within an environment of high standard course design that offers students the flexibility of place, pace and time and stresses on various learning styles (Huang, Chen, Yang, & Loewen, 2013).

Online learning can be defined as learning experiences in synchronous or asynchronous environments utilising various devices (e.g. smart phones, laptops, tablets, etc.) with internet access. In such type of learning, learners can learn and interact with tutors and other colleagues at any time and place (Singh

& Thurman, 2019). In online learning, students can access learning material in a variety of formats (e.g., video, audio, document, etc.). In addition, they can also organise, direct and assess their own learning with the help of an instructor. These interactions happen within a community of inquiry, implementing different internet-based synchronous and asynchronous activities (video, audio, computer conferencing, chats, or virtual world interaction). Synchronous learning is a well-designed structured learning strategy, in which the courses are scheduled at allotted time and in live virtual classroom settings. Consequently, learners get advantage from real-time interactions with teachers and their classmates and also get quick messaging and feedback when required (Littlefield, 2018). While in asynchronous learning, learners do not get instant feedback and messages and they also do not have opportunities to interact with their tutors and colleagues directly in live mode. They avail the learning content through various learning management systems or forums (Littlefield, 2018). These synchronous and asynchronous online environments develop collaborative and social skills as well as inter-personal relationships among students.

Prerequisites for Successful Implementation of Online Education

From the view point of conduction of online education on a big scale, online education should increase 'Disrupted Classes, Undisrupted Learning' on the following mentioned factors: (a) trustworthy communication infrastructure; (b) appropriate digital learning resources; (c) friendly learning tools; (d) efficient learning methods; (e) instructional organisations; (f) better support services for tutors and students; and (g) close rapport between governments, enterprises and schools.

- *Trustworthy Network Infrastructure*
  Trustworthy network infrastructure is crucial for conducting various teaching-learning activities, e.g. synchronous cyber teaching using video conferencing, asynchronous cyber learning by availing or downloading digital learning resources, and collaboration with colleagues through social software, etc. To provide reliable communication infrastructure, the following strategies can be adopted:
  - Mobilisation of all telecom service providers to enhance internet connectivity for online education, specifically for the remote areas.
  - Boosting the server bandwidth of tertiary educational institutions and schools to make provisions of flexible online learning and teaching experience for thousands of learners without any kind of interruption.
- *Appropriate Learning Tools*
  The appropriate selection and utilisation of learning tools is very important for students to find out and attain information, construction of

knowledge, cooperation with colleagues, for the expression of understanding and evaluating learning effects in clear ways. So, more importantly, learning tools should be easy and quick to: (a) assist teachers to manage resources and students efficiently, (b) help learners to take participation in learning activities effectively, (c) students and teachers can interact virtually, (d) assist schools, parents and teachers to organise school-home interaction timely. During lockdown Zoom, Google Hangouts, Skype meet up, Google classrooms, LMS, ICT, YouTube, etc. were the various tools utilised by faculty for the conduct of teaching-learning activities through online modes. Some of the educational institutions also organised faculty development programmes online to boost up positivity among faculty during this period.

- *Appropriate Digital Learning Resources*
  With the integration of ICT in education, a variety of digital learning resources such as Massive Open Online Courses (MOOC's), online video micro courses, simulations, graphics, models, e-notes, e-books, e-library, animations, etc. have made learning more accessible, interactive and contextualised. Whereas, the appropriate selection of digital learning resources should be according to the design of online learning activities. Ozdemir and Bonk (2017) asserted that it is a difficult task to find out high-quality educational resources for millions of students. So, it is the primary duty of teachers to select qualitative learning resources to use by referring to well-known national and international repositories. Student's involvement has always been a challenge, whether studying synchronously and asynchronously. During the lockdown, teachers were astonished to see the attendance of students in online learning. It increased dramatically. Different initiatives were taken by Ministry of Human Resources Development (MHRD) and by educational institutions, such as beginning of free Swayam courses and online free courses respectively. E-library and E-books were also provided to students to increase their learning.
- *Instructional Organisation of Learning*
  A variety of teaching-learning activities can be utilised in online environments to make flexible instructions, e.g. lecture, case study, debate, discussion, student-led discovery, experiential learning, academic games or competitions, brainstorming, drill and practice are the varied instructional methods used by a tutor (Petrina, 2011). Different social organisational approaches should be utilised in online contexts to make learning flexible, such as independent study, cooperative learning, and collaborative learning (Promethean, 2017; Petrina, 2011).
- *Better Support Services for Teachers and Students*
  Efficient support services are the key to success of qualitative online education. These support services are of two types: support services for

teachers — online teaching, and support services for students — online learning. These services can only be availed in collaboration with the government, educational institutions, enterprises, families and society.

- *Technical Services for Teachers*: It is a fact that most of the teachers are new to synchronous and asynchronous modes of learning and they are incapable of utilising these learning modes, so there should be more efforts to increase teacher's online teaching ability. Teachers of the day should be trained to make use of synchronous cyber learning software, utilisation of learning management system and the implementation of learning activity design.
- *Learning Supports for Students*: Support services for students increase their effective learning and personality development. Effective learning includes the harmonious development of individuals, enhances student's cognition, knowledge, skills, the consciousness of rules, integrity, perseverance and innovation. Support services involves the creation of personalised learning systems for students, utilisation of cloud classrooms to provide e-textbooks to students, to broadcast courses and study material through TV channels, to meet the requirements of students living in remote areas, where there is no provision of internet access. To quote an example here, China is using 'Classroom on Air' platform to provide support students living in underdeveloped areas. On this platform, students can access study material offline conveniently and can manage their learning through asynchronous mode of learning.

- *Close Rapport between Governments, Enterprises and Schools*
  As students are learning online, so there should be close rapport between governments, enterprises and schools to strengthen good quality learning material, to conduct varied learning activities and for getting better outcomes. This collaboration has the following features: flexible teaching, self-regulated learning, and open resources, scientific and technical support. In the present scenario, government should pay more attention to make coordination with different stakeholders and it should also build its policies for education carefully and considerably.

Difficulties in the Implementation of Online Education

In spite of careful planning and arrangements made by the government and the appreciated efforts done by other stakeholders in society, including educational institutions and families, the implementation of online education, is facing the following listed problems:

1. *Online education is restricted by infrastructure*
   Online teaching-learning platforms like Cloud Classrooms, Rain Classrooms are normally over-crowded, results in network crashes due

to teaching needs and personnel visits. Besides this, variations in information technology infrastructure among regions are also noteworthy. The network access in remote areas is insufficient, which leads to educational inequity. As per a survey conducted by CCTV (CCTV News, 2020b), approximately 2% of learners have no access to online live teaching in China. Even many of the children, who live in mountainous areas, have to walk so far to locate places with good bandwidth signals (Sohu News, 2020).

2. *Online teaching resources are not completely efficient and proportionate*
Before the pandemic outbreak, the online courses only acted as minor replacements to offline education. Moreover, there was existence of regional differences, inter-school differences and subject differences, in the quantity of selected quality courses (Fang, 2018). Besides this, a large number of teachers had limited knowledge and use of online resources, but during this pandemic, teachers were forced to copy offline teaching-learning material to the network space, without making suitable adaptations.
3. *Effectiveness of online education depends upon teacher's online teaching ability and experience*
It cannot be denied that the success of online education depends upon the teacher's ability to conduct online teaching. But, many of the teachers are unable to manage online education as there is a lack of skills among teachers to handle online teaching. Although many governments have made arrangements for teachers training, but this training was not sufficient to enhance their skills. Further, many of the teachers do not have positive attitudes towards the inclusion of online teaching-learning in education. They are not in favour of integration of technology to education due to their pessimistic view point (Zhang et al., 2015).
4. *Distractions and difficulties in finding suitable learning spaces at home*
It is not easy for teachers and students to teach and learn at home. Due to school closures, most of the teachers are busy at home to perform their household chores like to look after toddlers. As a result, they have less time to conduct their professional duties. Apart from this, many houses do not have sufficient space, where the students can learn online. Either they have to learn in the living room or in the bedroom, which causes distractions during their studies.
5. *Ambiguity regarding the best teaching mode and pedagogy for online education.*
Although the governments, parents, schools and teachers are doing their best to make effective use of online education, but the success has not been achieved yet due to uncertain decision that which teaching

method and pedagogy is best for online education. Whether it should be conducted synchronously or asynchronously.

Suggestions for Further Improvements in Online Education

1. It is mandatory on the part of governments that they must develop the educational information superhighway and must assess its functions, as well as make sure that it will fulfill the demand for online teaching during emergencies. Further if required, legal regulations must be adopted to prioritise the educational use of high-quality broadband. Moreover, there is a need to enhance the speed of technology iteration and maximise the technical application of online education programmes.
2. Teachers should be equipped with standardised home-based teaching equipments, specifically with standardised electronic devices to complete the requirements of online teaching and individualised tutoring remotely. Moreover, proper consideration should be given to learners' need for basic learning equipment.
3. In the modern technical era, it is mandatory for every teacher to have sufficient knowledge and skills concerned to adoption and usage of online platforms for high-quality teaching and learning. Thus, efforts should be made for professional development of teachers by getting legal, financial, and administrative support from governments.
4. Research should be encouraged in the areas of online education nationally, for the innovation of novel online teaching-learning strategies and platforms. Apart from the government, the role of social organisations and educational institutions itself is of paramount importance in conducting research.
5. Furthermore, in-depth investigations should also be conducted to make provisions for student support. On the behalf of result of these investigations, schools can take decisions of counseling services for students with learning difficulties during the pandemic and help learners' successful re-adaptation to offline school education after the pandemic.

Conclusion

In a nutshell, it can be said that there is a long history of pandemics occurred globally on different times, which had impact on various aspects of human life including education. Recently, the world is passing through a critical situation due to Covid-19 pandemic. School closures are one of the outputs of this outbreak nationally and regionally. So, many countries are trying to maintain undisrupted learning through the mode of online education, which is conducted synchronously and asynchronously. There are number of prerequisites for the successful implementation of online education such as adequate infrastructure, provision for learning tools and digital learning resources, support services for teachers and students and so on. However, lack of trained teachers, poor bandwidth networks, non-availability of learning resources and others are some of the problems in the way of online education. Besides this, these problems can be tackled by creating a close contact between government, schools, teachers and society and with the use of in-depth investigations and through the professional development of teachers.

References

Alex, W. (2020). National Public Radio News. Retrieved from National Public Radio News Website: http://www.npr.org/sections/coronavirus-live-updates

Barrett, S. (2020). Coronavirus on campus: College students scramble to solve food insecurity and housing challenges. CNBC.

Belinda, L. (2020). Coronavirus Forces Families to Make Painful Childcare Decisions. *Time*, 88-93.

Bender, L. (2020). Key Messages and Actions for Covid-19 Prevention and Control in Schools. Retrieved From http://www.unicef.org/romania/documents/key-messages-and-actions-covid

Cecco, L. (2020). Retrieved from Schools Race to Feed Students amid Coronavirus Closures: http://www.npr.org/

CCTV News. (2020b). How to Help the Poor Students Get the Online Courses. https://toutiao.china.com/shsy/gundong4/13000238/20200304/37868320_2.html

Feuer, W. (2020). WHO officials warn health systems are 'collapsing' under coronavirus: "This isn't just a bad flu season." CNBC.

Fang, Xu. (2018). Empirical Analysis of Affirmation of National Boutique Online Open Courses. *China Higher Education Research*. 7, 94–99. (In Chinese).

Gostin, L.O., Tomori, O., Wibulpolprasert, S., Jha, A.K., Frank, J., Moon, S., Dsau, V.J. (2016). Toward a Common Secure Future: Four Global Commissions in the Wake of Ebola. *PLoS Med*, 13(3), 55-59.

Huang, R., Chen, G., Yang, J., & Loewen, J. (2013). The New Shape of Learning: Adapting to Social Changes in the Information Society. In R. Huang & J. M. Specter (Eds.), *Reshaping Learning* SE – 1, 3–42. Springer Berlin Heidelberg. https://doi.org/10.1007/978-3-642-32301-0_1

Jamerson, K., Josh, M., & Joshua, B. (2020). Student-Loan Debt Relief Offers Support to an Economy Battered by Coronavirus. *Wall Street Journal*, 99-96.

Jordan, C. (2020). Coronavirus outbreak shining an even brighter light on internet disparities in rural America. *The Hill*.

Karp, P., & McGowan, M. (2020). Clear as mud: schools ask for online learning help as coronavirus policy confusion persists. *The Guardian*, 261-307.

Littlefield, J. (2018).The Difference between Synchronous and Asynchronous Distance Learning. https://www.thoughtco.com/synchronous-distance-learning-asynchronous-distancelearning-1097959.

Meng, L., Hua, F. & Bian, Z. (2020). Coronavirus Disease 2019 (Covid-19): Emerging and Future Challenges for Dental and Oral Medicine. *Journal of Dental Research*.

Maurice, J. (2016). Cost of protection against pandemics is small. *The Lancet*, 387-412.

Ministry of Education of the People's Republic of China. (2020a). Guidance on the Organization and Management of Online Teaching in College and Universities during the Epidemic Prevention and Control Period. http://www.moe.gov.cn/srcsite/A08/s7056/202002/ t20200205_418138.html

Ngumbi, E. (2020). Coronavirus closings: Are colleges helping their foreign, homeless and poor students? *USA Today*, 11-14.

Ozdemor, O., Bonk, C. J. (2017). Turkish Teachers' Awareness and Perceptions of Open Educational Resources. *Journal of Learning for Development*, v4 n3 pp. 307-321.

Petrina, S. (2011). InstructionalMethodsandLearningStyles. InAdvancedTeaching Methods for the Technology Classroom, 91–122.https://doi.org/10.4018/978-1-59904-337-1.ch004 Promethean. (2017). Collaborative learning vs. cooperative learning: what's the difference? https://resourced.prometheanworld.com/collaborative-cooperative-learning/

Riou, J.A., Hauser, M.J., Counotte, & Althaus, C.L. (2020). "Adjusted age specific case fatality ratio during the Covid-19 epidemic in Hubei, China, January and February 2020."' MedRxiv.http://www.medrxiv.org/content//10.1101/2020.03.04.20031 104v 1.

Rewar, S., Mirdha, D., & Rewar, P. (2015). Treatment and Prevention of Pandemic H1N1 Influenza. *Annals of Global Health*, 81(15), 645-653. http://dx.doi.org/10.1016/j.aogh. 2015.08.014

Sohu News. (2020). Hey, You Look So Nice When Study Hard. http://www.sohu.com/a/376997735_166723

Singh, V. & Thurman, A. (2019). How Many Ways Can We Define Online Learning? A Systematic Literature Review of Definitions of Online Learning (1988-2018). *American Journal of Distance Education*, 33(4) 289306. https://doi.org/10.1080/08923647.2019. 1663082.r1

Toquero, C. M. (2020). Challenges and Opportunities for Higher Education amid the Covid 19 Pandemic: The Philippine Context. *Pedagogical Research*, 5(4), em0063. https://doi.org/10.29333/pr/7947

UNESCO. (2020 updated March 11). "Covid-19 Educational Disruption and Response." Education in emergencies. United Nations Educational, Scientific and Cultural Organization (UNESCO). http://en.unesco.org/themes/education-emergencies/coronavirus-school-clos

Wilder-Smith, A., Chiew, C. J., & Lee, V. J. (2020, March 5). "Can we contain the Covid-19 outbreak with the same measures as for SARS?" Lancet Infect Dis. "http://doi.org/10.1016/S1473-3099(20)30129-8"9-8.

W.H.O. (2011b). Comparative Analysis of National Pandemic Influenza Preparedness Plan. Geneva-Switzerland: WHO.

Zhang, Y., Xiaoli, L., Fulan, F., Zhou, P. & Bai, Q. (2015). Factors Influencing on Teachers' ICT Application Level of Primary and Secondary Schools: An Empirical Analysis Based on the 14 cities of X Province. *Modern Educational Technology* 25, 44–50.

3

ROLE OF DIGITAL EDUCATION DURING AND AFTER COVID-19

Ram Mehar (Dr.)

Introduction

As of 18 May 2020, roughly 1.725 billion students are influenced because of school terminations in response to the Covid pandemic. As per UNICEF monitoring, 153 nations are presently executing across the nation terminations and 29 are actualising nearby terminations, affecting about 98.5 per cent of the world's understudy population. Eight nations' schools are right now open (UNICEF, 2020). In India, till 25 July 2020, the Ministry of Health and Family Welfare has confirmed a total of 1.44 million cases of Covid-19, 918 K recoveries and 32771 deaths in the country. The Covid-19 has resulted in closure of schools, colleges and universities which led to the dramatic change in educational sector. It is a crucial time for education sector as all the institutions are closed and this closure is disrupting the education of more than 285 million young learners in India (Choudhary, 2020).

Due to Covid-19 all the educational institutions in India have been temporarily shut down to control the spread of this deadly disease. Now the question is how the learners would be able to make up with these situations as the educational system of the country is structured with the definitive schedules. Alternative methods of teaching such as digital learning can be a useful means to ensure learners' access to learning activities during the period of Covid-19. Digital education is urgently needed to keep up with the development of the world of education which is supported by information technology leading to the digital era both in process and content. Indian universities and colleges have now recognised the importance of e-learning and online programmes and the crisis presents a range of opportunities for fast-forwarding their digital transition. Many institutions are utilising government's integrated learning platform SWAYAM and Direct to Home education channels SWAYAM PRABHA. Many institutions offer classes through Google Meet and Zoom.

Digital Education

Digital education is basically the innovative use of digital technologies and tools during teaching-learning process. It is also termed as Technology Enhanced Learning (TEL) or e-learning. The Internet is becoming the actual medium of interaction, communication and collaboration and the working

Associate Professor, Department of Education, USOL, Panjab University, Chandigarh space within which learners and teachers engage in "unique and irreplaceable learning opportunities" which may only exist in online environments. Digital education means digital learning. It is a type of learning that is supported by digital technology or by instructional practice that makes effective use of digital technology. Digital learning occurs across all learning areas and domains. Digital education gives win-win opportunities for all, at one side schools, colleges and other institutions find the rapid rise in enrolments and added revenue because of digital education and, on other side, students view this as a flexible and alternate option allowing them to study as per their convenient time and pace. Teachers and professors too find it convenient to prepare their teaching plans aided by digital technology. Teaching and learning becomes a smoother experience as it includes animations, gamification and audio-visual effects. Exploring the use of digital technologies provides educators the opportunity to design engaging learning opportunities in the course they teach, and these can take the form of blended or fully online courses and programmes. New developments in science and technology, media revaluation and internationalisation of education and the ever expanding competitive environment are revolutionising the education scene (Chouhan, 2016).

Components of Digital Education: Primarily Digital Education has three components:

(i) The content
(ii) The technology platform
(iii) The delivery infrastructure

Role of Digital Education in India During and after Pandemic

With technology changing at a rapid rate, innovative ways of obtaining and sharing information, knowledge are being developed and applied to the higher education setting. With all of these changes, it becomes even more important for colleges and universities to find ways to improve the quality of online learning to maximise learning, including effectively aligning technology with course content and instruction. Blended learning today is viewed as a mature educational concept but still in need of effective redesign. The use of Technology to facilitate better learning and training is gaining momentum worldwide, reducing the temporal and spatial problems associated with traditional learning. Despite its several benefits, retaining students in online platforms is challenging (Panigrahi, Srivastava & Sharma, 2018). Digital literacy is one component which makes a child responsible for how they use technology to interact with the world around them, what are the new knowledge gaining areas that they can be well-versed with, etc. Also there are so many online websites that have competitions which are knowledge gaining platforms for kids where they can compete as well as learn intellectually (Daga, 2016).

The corona virus pandemic has exposed the unpreparedness of many education institutions in India to migrate to online education. When the virus first hit India, the government was scrambling to figure out how best to handle the myriad of challenges it would pose on the socio-economic growth of the country. Government had to temporarily close educational institutions in an attempt to control the spread of Covid-19. Since then, India has recorded 1.44 million cases of Covid-19 with 32771 deaths and 918000 recoveries. Due to lockdown, all schools, colleges and universities have closed their campuses. Covid-19 pandemic has resulted in total closure of schools in about 192 countries all over the world with 91.4% of the total number of enrolled learners in these countries temporarily forced out of school (UNESCO, 2020). Long periods of learning would be lost for as long as the closures lasted. Schools and colleges losing long periods of learning due to Covid-19 outbreak can result in both temporal and permanent damage on educational system. The temporal damage includes disruption of curriculum which could take a long time to be recovered while the permanent damage includes the fact that some learners may never return to school even when the outbreak is ended (Kekic & Miladinovic, 2016).

Undeniably, the closure of educational institutes created an unpredicted pressure on the system to take the responsibility of the education of nearly 315 million children across the country. The concept of learning has changed overnight and in these times of crisis, digital learning has emerged as an indispensable source of education. Nevertheless, recent developments indicate recognition that education has experienced a significant shift. The leadership and managers of education institutions across India have become fully aware that empowering students to prepare for a future where pandemics such as Covid-19 and other disruptions might become a part of our daily lives also means embracing change in learning and teaching. Digital technology is providing all sorts of learning opportunities for the students across the country and enabling the teachers to create virtual experiences.

To cope up with this situation, schools and colleges are finding various ways to lessen the disruptive impact of Covid-19 on the education of the students. Initially, the teachers and students were not able to understand how to move on in view of a sudden emergence of a crisis that compelled to close down the institutions. Now, all the universities, colleges and schools moved on to online courses to engage the students from their homes to some extent. The concept of *work from home* has found greater relevance in such situations as it *ensures productivity, in case of industry (especially for the IT sector), and equally effective for the academics* (Choudhary, 2020). For bridging the digital divide and empowering teachers/learners to harness information and communication technologies for their empowerment through knowledge, the need of the hour is to provide digital literacy to teaching learning community in education system. Digital learning has the potential to overcome the inadequacy of qualified teachers in rural India. Live online tutoring, live streaming videos and virtual classrooms are some of the online learning solutions for such problems. E-learning is looked upon as a best substitute for effective and organised classroom teaching. Computerised Assessment of learners' academic performance becomes easier to the instructor especially for the courses where the enrolment is large (Thanji & Vasantha, 2018).

All round the world, school, colleges and universities have now recognised the importance of digital learning and online programmes, and the crisis presents a range of opportunities for fast-forwarding their digital transition. Many institutions are utilising the government's integrated learning platform SWAYAM and Direct to Home education channels SWAYAM PRABHA. Many institutions offer classes through Google Meet and Zoom (Mathews, 2020). Further, regulators like AICTE and UGC have been incessantly trying to mitigate the impact of aberrations caused by lockdown by launching MOOCs. According to the then Union Minister of Education Ramesh Pokhriyal in an interview with *The Times of India*, the number of hits in the past few weeks on key online portals like SWAYAM PRABHA, Virtual Labs, FOSSEE, E-Yantra, and Spoken Tutorials has gone up five times since the lockdown. However, the absence of robust digital architecture, net connectivity, availability of resources, and lack of digital awareness remains the last mile bottleneck for the effectiveness of such endeavours. Faculties of various schools, colleges and universities are making use of various applications such as Zoom, Google classroom, Skype, etc. to teach contents to the students. Students are also participating because in these applications two-way interactions between teacher and students are possible.

There are many platforms created to enable online education in India. These are supported by the Ministry of Human Resource Development (MHRD), the National Council of Educational Research and Training (NCERT), and the department of technical education. There also are initiatives like e-PG Pathshala (e-content), SWAYAM (online courses for teachers), and NEAT (enhancing employability). Other online platforms aim to increase connectivity with institutions, and accessibility to content. These are utilised for course materials and classes, and running of online modules. They include the National Project on Technology Enhanced Learning (NPTEL), National Knowledge Network, (NKN), and National Academic Depository (NAD), among others.

Distance learning, under the conditions of the pandemic-dictated confinement, pushes us to reflection and convinces us of its importance; even those teachers who had been the most reticent about new technologies have been very supportive and strongly involved. On the other hand, the new generations of students are familiar with these digital tools that they particularly appreciate and enjoy using and thus adapted well and rapidly (Bentata, 2020).

Challenges in Implementing Digital Education

Some of the major challenges digital education in India is facing are:

(i) *Internet connectivity issues*: One of the primary difficulties for digital education in India is poor web connectivity in provincial zones and some places of urban regions. Dominant part of populace across India has still no access to web and a huge populace in country zones is as yet unskilled in the field of digital innovation. More Innovations are required in making the digital education increasingly interactive and robust.

(ii) *Shortage of trained teachers*: A major obstacle in the use of digital education in rural area is the lack of knowledge and skills. There is a shortage of teachers, formally trained on digital technology. In some of the academic institution in rural areas, school teachers and college professors are not interested in using digital tools for conducting classes. They feel that a lot of information is explained to the students at one go through the digital medium and they prefer traditional teaching methods of chalk and blackboard. In rural areas, primary teachers and senior teachers are reluctant to get trained and adopt digital technologies for digital education in school because they are of the view that these disruptive technologies are out to replace them permanently (Gupta & Gond, 2017).

(iii) *Students' interest related challenges*: One of the biggest challenges, teachers are facing is how to keep students on board and also how to avoid their distractions from other social networking sites during the learning period.

(iv) *Dialect and content related issues*: Dialects is one of the principles hindrances for the advancement of digital education in India, there are a few unique dialects in various states and pushing all the digital content in all these local dialects sometimes gets hard for the agencies or teachers.

(v) *Insufficient funds*: Digital education involves effective and efficient usage of appropriate and latest hardware and software technology available in the market. In developing countries like India, digital technology implementation into education systems is a difficult task as it requires huge funds and infrastructure. Through Digital India programme, the government has promised availability of funds for technology implementation but lack or insufficiency of finances leads to redundant and obsolete infrastructure and equipment in rural schools (Gupta & Gond, 2017).

(vi) *Poor maintenance and up-gradation of digital equipment*: In rural areas maintenance and up-gradation of digital equipment is one of the major challenges. This is largely due to budgetary constraints by government. The digital education projects in rural schools are not self-sustainable. At initial stage various projects have been launched by government for the development of digital education, but later, they have not been taken due care for the maintenance of digital equipment which is affecting the digital education development in rural areas.

These are the basic challenges which the students and teachers are facing these days. Institutes should work upon these issues so that online learning can be done easily without any interruption.

Possible alternatives or solutions for implementation of Digital Education:

- Since technology has become a part and parcel of lives of individuals, it becomes imperative for the teachers to be comfortable in its handling in education system as well. The teachers may utilise them in the instructional materials as per individual differences.
- Refresher programmes need to be organised from time to time so that they become comfortable with using technology. As per National Policy on ICT in School Education, teachers need to participate in selection and critical evaluation of digital content and resources. They need to be encouraged to develop their own digital resources, sharing them with colleagues through the digital repositories.
- With the help of power supply, digital skills of teachers and students, internet connectivity, it is necessary to explore digital learning, high and low technology solutions, etc.
- Students those are coming from low-income groups or presence of disability, etc. distance learning programs can be included for them.
- To provide support for digitalisation to teachers and students.
- The necessity to explore digital learning platforms.
- Edtech reform at the national level that is an integration of technology in the present Indian education system.

In future of Indian education system, blended learning, virtual classroom, online courses will take important place to cater to the needs of the changing scenarios. Virtual access is achieved through Internet / Intranets. Techniques such as e-mail, web notices, discussion forums and video conferencing allow a student to access information without visiting the physical location of delivery. A typical interactive e-learning system will have these characteristics and thus demonstrates the paradigm shift. The institutes need to work on the upgradation of the courses and provide the various opportunities to cope up with the demands of the skilful resource development.

Conclusion

The sustenance of good education is fundamentally dependent on the health of learners and healthy learning environment. Covid-19 pandemic affects the health of anyone infected with the virus and sometimes can result to loss of life

(UNESCO, 2020). In order to ensure the safety of learners, schools are closed together with other socio-economic activities in most countries. The lockdown of schools regionally in many countries and locally in some other countries all over the world predicated on prevention of the spread of Covid-19 is a threat to the future of many children mostly in developing countries where schools are not equipped with technology-based instructional materials due to the economic backwardness in these developing nations. Due to temporary termination of educational institutes, students are facing problems in education. To cope up with the present challenges in education, government and educational institutes are shifting the traditional classroom teaching to online learning. Various online platforms are being used for the same purpose. Indian government should work on the various online platforms and also make important recommendations in educational policies so that blended learning can be included as an important part of curriculum. It is important that government agencies should *invest in research and development (R&D) to find out technological ways to achieve digital learning* rather than cutting expenses.

Education sector in India has seen a series of rapid expansion in last couple of years which helped to transform the country into a knowledge heaven. Government of India has also taken major Initiatives for the development of digital education in India like opening of IIT's and IIM's in new locations as well as allocating educational grants for research scholars in most government institutions. The Government of India has further announced plans to digitise academic records such as degrees, diplomas, mark sheets, migration certificate, skill certificate, etc. from secondary to tertiary-level institutions into a National Academic Depository (NAD). The study highlighted the different challenges of digital education in India during Covid-19 era. Government of India needs to take the required measures to overcome these challenges for the development of digital education in India.

References

Bentata, Y. (2020). Covid-19 pandemic: a true digital revolution and birth of a new educational era or an ephemeral phenomenon? *Medical Education Online, 25*, 1-2. Retrieved on July25, 2020 from https://www.tandfonline.com/doi/pdf/10.1080/10872981.2020.1781378?needAccess =true

Chauhan, P. (2016). Challenges Facing the Current Higher Education System in India. *International Journal of Engineering Technology Science and Research*, *3*(4), 53-60.

Choudhary, R. (2020). *Covid-19 blessing in disguise for Indian education sector.* Retrieved on July 21, 2020 from https://eduvoice.in/covid-19-blessing-in-disguise-for-indian-education-sector/

Daga, V. (2016). *Importance of digital education for children in India.* Retrieved on July 25, 2020 from https://techstory.in/digital-education-children/

Gupta, R., & Gond, R. (2017). A study on digital education in India: scope and challenges of an Indian society. *Anveshana's International Journal of Reasearch in Regional Studies, Law, Social Sciences, Journalism and Management Practices, 2*(3), 12-18.

Kekic, D., & Miladinovic, S. (2013). *Functioning of educational system during an outbreak of acute infectious diseases.* Retrieved on July 25, 2020 from https://www.researchgate.net/publication/309728224

Mathews, E. (2020). India's higher education and Covid-19: Responses and challenges. *International Higher Education, 102*(Special Issue), 22-24.

Panigrahi, R., Srivastava, P. R., & Sharma, D. (2018). Online learning: Adoption, continuance, and learning outcome-A review of literature. *International Journal of Information Management, 43*, 1-14.

Singh, G. (2016). Challenges for teachers in the era of e-learning in India. *International Journal of Multidisciplinary & Allied Studies, 3*(2), 14-18.

Thanji, M., & Vasantha, S. (2018). *Effectiveness of online learning methods offered by educational institutions: A learner's perspective.* Unpublished Doctoral Thesis, Pallavaram, Chennai: Vels Institute of Science, Technology & Advanced Studies. Retrieved on July 27, 2020 from https://shodhganga.inflibnet.ac.in/handle/10603/274565

United Nations Education Scientific and Cultural Organization (2020). Covid-19 educational disruption and response. Retrieved on July 20, 2020 from https://en.unesco.org/covid19/educationresponse

4

ROLE OF DIGITAL EDUCATION AND COVID-19

Sangita Sharma

Introduction

In modern advanced technology and digitalisation era, e-learning is a blessing and plays a significant role in the development of an individual as well as the future of the country. The impact of Covid-19 on education is the shift from conventional learning mode to online learning mode. Even before Covid-19, there was a high growth and adoption of technology in education field, with global EdTech investments reaching US$18.66 billion in 2019 and the overall market for online education is projected to reach $350 billion by 2025. There has been a significant rise in the usage of learning apps, virtual tutoring, and video conferencing mode during Pandemic. In response to significant demand, many e-learning platforms are provided in social media apps and websites like ZOOM App, Google Meet, E-Pathshaala, Telegram, Classroom,

Assistant Professor in Economics, PCM S.D. College for Women, Jalandhar

BYJU's, YouTube, Facebook, WhatsApp and numerous websites. An online teaching and learning plan includes teaching pedagogies, devices, solutions, communication skills, and strategies supporting online or blended learning in the Education community.

Now in Covid-19 Pandemic situation, India has the new and latest e-learning modes in the education sector those are being used by advanced countries from pretty long period of time. Some of these are E-learning, Distance education, Gamification, Open Educational Resources, Cloud based e-Learning, Big Data in E-Learning, Massive Open Online Courses, Micro learning, Mobile Learning, etc.

Digital Education in Developing Nations

The United Nations recently reported that 166 countries have closed schools, colleges and universities to control the spread of the Corona virus disease. One and a half billion children and young learners are affected, constituting 87 per cent of the enrolled population. With limited exceptions, colleges and schools are now closed countrywide across Africa, Asia, Latin America, putting additional burden on education systems in developing countries (J.thomas, 2020).

Challenges Faced in Digital Education System in Developing Nations

1. Adjustability Chaos

Shifting from traditional classroom teaching and face to face interaction to computer-based learning in a virtual classroom makes the learning experience entirely different for students. Their aversion from classrooms to computers does not permit them to adapt to the online learning environment, whereas it takes time for them to get used to Course Management Systems (CMS) and the modes of computer-based education. While passive learning and notes taking are prevalent in a traditional classroom, online discussions or creating a web page demand springing into action. Students find it very difficult to adapt and accept the new learning technology having the traditional mindset of classroom learning. However, after understanding the benefits of e-learning may change their mindset and better prepare them for face to face learning with an open mind and heart.

2. Technical Constraints

Online courses require high bandwidth or the strong internet connection but many students are not provided with these facilities, and thus fail to move on with their virtual classmates. Their weak computer system makes it hard to pursue the Course Management System and their learning experience becomes troublesome. Sometimes, many of them have to leave campus as they find it difficult to keep in tune with the technicalities of the chosen course. Some of them do not even have own computers and seek help in Learning Resource Centres for technical assistance. The only solution to this problem is to have knowledge about kind of technological support they will need for a certain course before enrolling in it and properly equip themselves for the successful completion of the course.

3. Computer Proficiency

Although majority of students are generally technical savvy and thus able to manage computers well, but still lack of computer education is a major challenge among students today. The students find it difficult to operate basic apps and even programmes such as MS Word, PowerPoint whereas the online courses require technological proficiency as an essential requirement, as it enables the student to manage their assignments and coursework in an organised manner without struggling. Basic courses in computer literacy enhance students' knowledge in the field; having a fundamental knowledge of computer hardware would help them to participate in online classes without interruptions and hindrances.

4. Time Management: A Big Hurdle

Lack of a schedule, too many distractions, misuse of discussion forum and multitasking can lead to poor time management. Another factor that may lead to poor time management is the lack of a designated work space. Time management is a difficult task for E-Learners, as online courses require a lot of time and regress work. Moreover, mostly people prefer online learning programmes at their pace and time flexibility, but they hardly have the time to attend the courses due to everyday engagements.

5. Lack of learners' motivation

Self-motivation is an e-Learning essential requirement; however, many online learners lack it, much to their surprise. After enrolling in distance learning courses, many learners lag behind and nurture the idea of giving up, as problems in handling a digital medium also seem insurmountable. Students are to be motivated to follow new educational patterns and to fully equip themselves to face future challenges in their careers and education. Positive attitude towards the changed scenario in education system is to be built to face the challenges in online teaching. Awareness among student is to be created that it is essential to learn the online mode of learning to reap the benefits in the career building (Kumar, 2015).

How to Overcome above Challenges

1. Self-Motivation: The only solution

One of the most common e-Learning challenges that e-Learners must overcome is an overall lack of self-motivation. To overcome this hurdle, it is important to make the e-Learning course as engaging and inspiring as possible. Even topics those are dry or boring have the potential to become exciting and effective if these are made relevant and interesting for the learners.

2. Proper Time Management of the Learners

In this day and age, it seems that everyone is running short of time. There are not enough hours in the day, and there is not any room in the schedule for learning. Many people are reluctant to take an e-Learning course because they think that they won't be able to go at their own pace or that it will require a great deal of their time. It can be overcome by ensuring that e-Learning course can be in bite–sized chunks that can be accessed whenever and wherever learners are ready to learn.

3. Learners are to be Technical Savvy

All of the learners are not having the latest and greatest technical gadgets and they are not technical savvy. And the truth is that there is no reason to be! This perception is yet another e-Learning challenge. However, this can be overcome by ensuring that e-Learning course is available on a wide range of devices and platforms, and that it is in fact easy to navigate. 94% of faculties have integrated iPods, Phone into their courses, and 87% of students agree that technology has been instrumental in their success at the educational institutions.

4. E-Learning Must Offer a Solid Support System

It is a general misconception that e-Learning courses offer no support to their learners. This prevents many students from enrolling, although they are highly convinced and motivated to learn. To overcome this eLearning challenge, it is to be ensured that a solid support system is available for all learners. Learners should be offered FAQ (Frequently Asked Questions) that can help to resolve any common issues, and the facility of email or instant message support for more complicated questions or concerns should be provided, Peer collaboration should also be encouraged. A forum can be setup where learners can communicate with one another if a problem arises, or learners can be divided into groups and regular feedback can be taken. The learners can work at their own pace, while still being able to benefit from the experience and skills of their online peers, even if they happen to be in other regions of the world (Pappas, 2014).

Opportunities Available in Digital Education System in Developing Nations

- It is obvious that e-learning is growing very fast and it gives a chance for learning to everyone. Most e-learning platforms are not time specific, thus no matter where one lives, or what time of the day or week best suits to the calendar, one's able to join. It provides the opportunity to the students to study at their own pace and a facility for teachers and educational institutions to reach much wider viewers. E-learning gives an opportunity to study even at night, if student prefers to do so. All that is required is a computer/ smart phone/ Tab, a good Internet connection and the enthusiasm to learn.
- Due to ease of accessibility of information, people with high mobility due to busy schedules are able to access study materials at their own pace and time as they are well equipped with modern, electronic tools which are the pre-requisite of online learning. Some educational sectors also provide resources and services freely on digital platforms.
- E-learning gives the opportunity to different learners including those who are unable or unlikely to join traditional classroom learning to have access to quality education. The colleges and schools are facilitating learning to convenient locations which is accessible to all sort of people by expanding the basic infrastructure including computers and internet services.
- E-learning also promotes equality. It becomes easy for all to access the study material irrespective of caste and creed, age factor, occupational structure, geographical areas, gender and economic status even those students who are introvert in nature can communicate with teachers and students in e-learning mode by face to face learning (Ofori, 2017).
- Broadcasting lessons through radio or television communication devices may help to reach isolated students without internet access. These initiatives can be set up quickly, at large scale and with little investments.
- In India, many digital platforms for education purpose are used like DIKSHA, ZOOM and WHATSAPP. These platforms have created a community of practice over recent years, hosting lesson plans and supporting materials uploaded by teachers and curated by a central authority.
- Teachers will have the opportunity to test out different online learning solutions and understand how technology can be used to foster deeper student learning.

Digital Education in Developed Nations

Learning is the key to success and growth in the life of not only an individual, but also an organisation and nation through which new technologies are learned and innovated. Learning is made easier and comfortable through e-learning mode. The most of the e-learning activities are done in the workplace and home. The advanced countries consider the development of e-learning as the responsibility of government and not only of the concerned institutions. The important reason behind the increasing number of e-learning courses offered in the higher education institutions is the decrease of support mainly, financial support of the government to the institutions. Although advanced countries emphasise e-learning, the educational institutions are more concerned about their teaching pedagogies and does not completely rely on the technology.

Challenges Faced in Digital Education System in Developed Nations

The major challenge in developed nations lies in the framing and implementing the strategies those are developed in order to sustain in the global competitive market. There is lack of integration between the teacher, student and technology. Another challenge that the developed countries are facing is high dropout ratio. To overcome the above challenges, the e-learning course should be framed according to the students' perception. Developed countries face very few challenges as they are well equipped with latest infrastructure and updated knowledge about the technology.

However, educational institutions also face a variety of institutional, teachers and student-related impediments for successfully implementing, maintaining and growth of online programmes.

1. Steady Decline in College Enrollment

First, there has been a steady decline in college enrollment. Reasons for declining college enrollments include: (a) increasing cost of a college education, (b) Lack of trust about the incremental value of higher education, (c) decline in the percentage of timely degree completion, (d) unwillingness to travel long distances, (e) increasing cost of commuting, (f) unwillingness to incur long-term debts, and (g) social concerns, such as perceived insufficient institutional support for low-income, minority, and foreign students, and peers from different backgrounds, culture, or interests.

2. Institutional Factors

- Besides the challenge of declining enrollments, there is the challenge of change in student profile. Research shows that students in above 25 years of age category will increase. Hoover suggests that the solution involves creative thinking such as exploring educational programmes to attract international students, implementing online or blended courses that could help reduce commuting costs and student travel time, and accelerating graduation rates, especially for students working full time.

- Institutional factors such as lack of understanding of online pedagogy and online learning styles, lack of administrative support for online education and for marketing the programme, number of students enrolled, faculty qualifications, tuition fees, and length of the programme.

Opportunities Available in Digital Education System in Developed Nations

The opportunities available to the higher education institutions in developed countries are solely due to equipment of technology infrastructure resources like computers, electricity, internet, etc. The success of implementation of the online learning depends on the support extended from top management, financial support, faculty involvement, technical skill and technology support. There are vast opportunities for e-learning in developed countries since they use them at all levels of education. (Naresh B, 2015)

While the market for more online programmes with global coverage appears to exist, adequate planning and implementation of best practices and innovative strategies is necessary for higher education institutions to successfully introduce and expand online education. To implement a successful online programme, or launch a successful online course, the program/course being offered needs to harness innovative technology in such a way that improves student learning beyond traditional mode of classroom teaching. Any online programme or course should provide extra benefits to its various stakeholders: students, faculty, administrators, and employers over and above traditional programme or course.

Comparison of Digital Education in Developed and Developing Nations

The developed *countries* follow two types of approaches towards e-learning environment. They are substantive and instrumental. The developing countries also follow two types of approaches towards e-learning environment similar to those of developed countries, but they are more effective in developed countries due to high level of infrastructural facilities. The practices those are adopted by the developed countries are active and substantive modes whereas developing countries adopt only prominent or dominant modes of practices. The challenges and opportunities those are faced by developed and developing countries are almost similar. The developing countries are facing many challenges like lack of technology support, infrastructure and support from the government during Covid-19 Pandemic. On the other hand, in developed countries, there is a lack of motivation and active participation on the part of the students. When we come to the opportunities front, the developed countries have more opportunities in the resource professionalism, and the developing countries have availability of ICT.

Digital Education Before and After Covid-19

Before Covid-19

The countries were mainly dependent upon traditional systems of education which is face-to-face and classroom teaching with chalk and duster.

- Teachers can see students' body language to see if they understand the material.
- Traditional textbook curriculum was taught.
- The teachers delivered most of the curriculum.
- Suited more for younger students.
- Access to campus activities and services.

After Covid-19

After Covid-19 pandemic, all the countries changed the mode of teaching learning platform. They all are now adopting online platform which is the need of the hour and which is major shift from teaching culture to Learning culture.

- Learners will be empowered to learn in flexible timings, often collaborative ways, both online and offline classrooms at their own pace. They will be able to watch their own interests and vision.
- Teachers will have access to each and every student, how well each of their students is progressing — academically and emotionally — so they can devise new strategies and offer required assistance to each student to move ahead.
- Parents will be better connected to, and involved with their child's education with certainty, detail, and confidence.
- More one to one interaction with the students.
- Student Access 24*7.
- Student work at own pace.
- More flexibility in schedules for students.
- More resources for students on the web.
- Suited for students of all ages.
- Access to endless material.

Conclusion

Digital Education enhances the student knowledge, efficiency and productivity. Along with involving the students in course work, digital tools and technology will improve critical thinking and analytical skills (Education, 2017). Multiple resources including 'online-lectures', online videos, PowerPoint presentations and readings; interactive online explorations must be there. But we cannot ignore and forget the students who do not have access to all online technology. These students are less affluent and belong to less tech-savvy families with financial constraints; therefore, they may lose out when classes occur online. They may lose out because of the heavy costs involved in digital devices and internet data plans. This digital divide may widen the gaps of inequality. As per the World Economic Forum, the Covid-19 pandemic has changed the way of receiving and imparting education. Some innovations and changes are required to find solutions for arising problems in education system. Teachers have become accustomed to traditional methods of teaching in the form of face-to-face classrooms lectures, and therefore, they are reluctant in accepting and adapting any change. But amidst this crisis of pandemic, we have no other options left other than adapting to the dynamic situation and accepting the tremendous change. The unanticipated, forced absorption of learners into virtual learning during this period of Covid-19 has proved that the education sector is thrown into disruption. Education is going to be digital in the immediate future and with the latest and right infrastructure and policies in place; we would be better prepared to handle this situation (Cathy Li, 2020). It will be advantageous for the education sector and could bring a lot of magical innovations.

References

Cathy Li, F. L. (2020) The Covid 19 Pandemic has changed education forever. https://www.weforum.org/agenda/2020/04/coronavirus-education-global-covid19-online-digital-learning/

J. Thomas, C. (2020). Coronavirus and challenging times for education in developing countries.https://www.brookings.edu/blog/education-plus-development/2020/04/13/coronavirus-and-challenging-times-for-education-in-developing-countries/

Kumar, S. (2015). Common Problems By Students In e-learning.https://elearningindustry.com/5-common-problems-faced-by-students-in-elearning-overcome

Naresh B, D. S. (2015). Challenges and opportunities of e-learning in Developed countries.https://www.researchgate.net/publication/282286273_Challenges_and_Opportunity_of_E-Learning_in_Developed_and_Developing_Countries-A_Review

Ofori, D. N. (2017). Opportunities of e-learning in developing countries: Case Ghana. https://verkkolehdet.jamk.fi/ev-peda/2017/09/26/opportunities-of-e-learning-in-developing-countries-case-ghana/

Pappas, C. (2014). Top 5 Most Common e-learning challenges and How to overcome them.https://elearningindustry.com/5-common-elearning-challenges-overcome

Rana, P. (2020). Covid-19 Impact on Education Sector:Adopt Digital Way. https://yourstory.com/mystory/impact-covid-19-education-sector Education

5

ONLINE TEACHING DURING COVID-19: PROS AND CONS

Sharanjit Kaur

Introduction

Educators and students all over the world are going through a phase quite unknown to them due to the rapid spreading of the corona virus. Within weeks, students saw a drastic change in education which they have been experiencing continuously for years (Vnaya, 2020). Covid-19 has radically reshaped the way in which global higher education is delivered. As a result, universities are rapidly shifting how they communicate and operate to meet the evolving needs of students and staff (Symonds, 2020). In this period, online teaching has become a critical lifeline for education, as institutions seek to minimise the potential for community transmission. Technology can provide teachers and students with access to advanced resources far beyond textbooks, in various formats and in ways that can span time and space. Further, in response to the closure of educational institutes and to avoid total curriculum disruption till Covid-19 pandemic lasts, universities introduced technology-based pedagogy and the use of different types of media like Zoom, Google classroom, Google meet, Facebook live, Video- conferencing etc. to deliver the online lectures and to ensure that learners must have access to learning materials while staying home through Online teaching mode. There are primarily two types of online teaching (UrbanPro, 2014):

i. ***Synchronous:*** This type of teaching involves a real time online teaching experience. This involves time-bound sessions in which both the teacher and the student will be online at a given time, such as instructor-led online classes.

ii. ***Asynchronous:*** In this type, courses are not conducted in real time. It ensures that there should be an engagement between the teacher and the student according to their convenience. *Recorded training sessions* are a good example of such teaching.

Benefits of Online Teaching

Some of the prominent benefits of online teaching during the covid-19 pandemic are as follows (UrbanPro, 2014):

1. *Time and Location Flexibility*: Using the virtual classroom allows the teacher to take classes with students from different time zones, without needing to travel. Because of this, smaller specialised classes are more likely to have enough students to be feasible especially in the event of

Khalsa College Girls Senior Secondary School, Amritsar

Covid-19 crisis. Online teaching is a boon, where classes can be taken in evenings or on weekends. Often, the instructor will lecture from anywhere, regardless of where the students are situated. This ensures that teachers and students from a different location can interact with each other by online teaching.

2. *Convenience for teachers and students*: Online teaching does not require any travelling overhead. A teacher can teach right while sitting at his/her home during this period of lockdown due to corona pandemic. Thus, online teaching could be viewed as a work from home with flexible curriculum.
3. *More Teaching Opportunities*: The education platform, without any time and location limitations, clearly paves the way for substantially more opportunities for teachers than conventional classroom teaching. Teaching through an online network allows the professor the opportunity to communicate with students located in a diverse geographical location. The Ed-Tech platforms allow students to learn at their own pace. Each student is able to receive more attention to clear their doubts and help them learn better. This provides teachers with relatively more opportunities to teach and explore.
4. *Administration*: The flexible timings and schedule of online classes call for utmost self-discipline and time management skills that some students might lack. A proper timetable needs to be set and implemented to ensure that the student is not lagging behind and is able to retain momentum and learn. Online teaching also helps in a better administration. We can easily imagine the logistical challenges that teachers face in the conventional classroom than when they teach online. Like classroom education, a teacher does not need to keep track of all the students. This decreases the administrative overhead while improving the concentration and performance of a teacher during Covid-19.
5. *Better Organisation*: The significant benefit of online education is that it is well planned, preventing mismanagement. A majority of online teachers report that online teaching tools have increased their overall efficiency during the lockdown period. This is because they are able to organise the course better and are also able to automate certain activities like periodic tests, quizzes, scoring, etc.
6. *Diverse Teaching Experiences*: The online method of teaching offers an instructor the ability and experience to interact with students from diverse fields, backgrounds and cultures. Online teaching can thus take the teaching experience from a regional level to national level, and even further to an international level by organising online classes through different platforms during the lockdown pandemic situation.
7. *Easier Access and Sharing of Information*: It is evident that any study tool or information in a digital format is very easy to access and share. While teaching online, one takes help from digital libraries, search

engines and also social media channels for searching, accessing and sharing resources and information. In India, during this pandemic situation resulting in schools and colleges closing, students and teachers alike have turned to ed-tech platforms to help maintain the academic momentum and many organisations have come forward for the help of teachers and students where they have allowed the free access to their sites free of cost.

8. *Student Engagement*: During Covid-19, online teachers report that online teaching incorporates more engagement between student and the teacher. Unlike the interaction in a classroom of numerous students, an online medium provides them with a closer one-on-one session. Also, the shy and non-participative students, who were not comfortable participating in classroom discussions, are obviously more likely to participate in an online class.
9. *Increased student learning*: Online teachers also reveal that students typically do better and often show more interest in discussions during an online course. According to a recent survey conducted by a group of online teachers, 90% of them indicated that online teaching helps them remain more connected to students and also provides them the opportunity to understand each student better.
10. *Professional Satisfaction*: Given all the prime advantages of online teaching like flexibility, convenience, ease of access and sharing, etc., an online teacher is professionally satisfied. Since online education has brought about a revolution in the education sector, being part of it could be of great benefit to any teacher.
11. *Teaching an online course can help you be a better teacher*: In traditional classrooms, you go by a strict course, and it can be very hard to be aware of everything that goes on in your students' lives. Virtual classes give you an open window to your pupils, and lets you know who is actively participating and who is not. It will make a lot easier to reach out to students who need your support.
12. *Brings great opportunity for feedback*: Teachers can post online surveys asking how they are doing and on what they can improve on to make the online teaching more interesting, informative and inspirational? As a teacher, you can also give your students feedback on their performances and participation in online classes during the lockdown situation.

Limitations of Online Teaching

The Internet has fundamentally changed how we interact with each other and how we access, exchange and promote information. Along with the fruitful benefits of online teaching there are a number of cons, limitations and problems being faced by the teachers while teaching online during this covid-19 pandemic. Some of them are as follows (McIntyre, Watson, & Mirriahi, 2015):

1. *Access to technology*: In some instances, students and teachers may be limited in their regular access to reliable or appropriate technology. Several people may be sharing a computer or mobile device within one household, or may rely on using computers on campus or in a public place (e.g. public library, Internet cafe, etc.). Students or teachers may also only have limited access to required software as their membership is very expensive.
2. *Access to the Internet*: Not all students and teachers have regular or reliable access to the internet. In certain cases, internet access may be restricted to dial-up speed, or there may be restricted monthly use on the internet, which may restrict their ability to access the information.
3. *Ability to use technology*: Some technologies and tools require training. In certain cases, advanced training may not be readily accessible to students or teachers. Teachers without peer help for their online projects can be a lonely and insulating experience.
4. *Overloaded Information*: In many instances, the amount of information, 'how to' guides, help and resources provided online can have a tendency to become overwhelming and confusing if not properly managed. It can be challenging for students and teachers to see which ones are appropriate or significant.
5. *Teaching online means a lot of hard work*: Many believe that teaching online is not nearly as time-consuming as teaching in the classroom. The opposite turns out to be true for most. Taking the time to create an online course takes a lot of time, as the lesson may not translate well from a lecture to a more interactive point of view.
6. *Students do not always complete assignments at the same time*: This means that as an instructor you must be in constant communication with your pupils. That in retrospect is not a bad thing, but, when you continuously check your inbox, this can get time consuming. As well as keep up with the student's frequent messages which may or may not understand the assignments.
7. *Students may not have access to individual pieces of technology*: Now most students are indeed much more tech savvy than before. However, not everyone has access to the latest tech. This means that you should not use video and audio effects to make your website attractive and appealing. Though all these features are good but can cause frustration and hindrance among the students as they try to learn.
8. *Assignments can take longer to complete*: Most tasks that take a simple classroom period to complete take much longer to complete virtually. That is because students typically discuss these assignments together

in the classroom environment and might not be online at the same time for discussion. This takes the conversation process entirely to the side, enabling your students to consider these issues on their own. Furthermore, it typically takes a lot longer for students to discuss the activity over the Internet because they have to do a lot of reading and writing.

9. *Online teaching can make you feel isolated*: While teaching online, you usually do not meet with your fellow instructors and students in a classroom setting. This can cause trouble talking to your fellow teachers about what works best and does not work at all. Usually, the only way to overcome this is by using online chat groups that are made for online educators (Urgentessaywriting, 2016).

Online teaching is new for most of the teachers and professors especially for those who belong to public sector institutes or who do not have the previous experience and exposure of online teaching. They are facing so many problems in conducting online teaching during this lockdown situation due to Covid-19. So, here are some quick tips to make online teaching better, from an expert in online learning (Lee, 2020):

1. *Record your lectures – do not stream them*: When students struggle with internet access or are unwell, they will miss a live streaming lecture. Instead, film videos and give them to your students, so they can watch them in their own time.
2. *Show your face*: Research has shown that lecture videos showing the faces of teachers are more successful than pure scripted slideshows. Intersperse your slides with video of yourself.
3. *Keep videos short*: Videos longer than 15 minutes can cause problems with slow downloading and learning interruption. If you have more to say, please record two or three short videos.
4. *Test out slides*: Before shooting your lectures, make sure you check the slides on your mobile so that all text can be read on small screens. Font sizes, colours, template designs and screen ratios can be double-checked. Most students will be using their smartphones to access online learning.
5. *Use existing resources and make sure they are open access*: It is unrealistic to expect that you, on your own, will produce a semester's worth of high-quality videos. You can use the pre-developed online resources and provide clickable links to students. The use of open resources helps to keep students from having trouble accessing them. If all of your suggested resources are not available, you will receive an inbox full of student emails and inevitably waste all of your troubleshooting time. Spending a few extra minutes to carefully check for fully open access resources will save you from a later headache.
6. *Give specific instructions*: When you suggest online media, which runs for longer than 15 minutes, students will be put off watching.

Alternatively, recommend the exact sections they need (e.g. 13:35 to 16:28) because this will make students more interested. If you have more than two tools, mark them in the order that you want students to address them. Easy numbering, based on the level of difficulty or value of each resource object, can be of great benefit to your students.

7. *Provide interactive activities*: Most learning management systems, such as Moodle, Edmodo and Blackboard, include a range of functions to create interactive learning activities such as quizzes. Instruct the students with step-by-step guide for creating them and use those which are widely available online.
8. *Use auto-checking to measure attendance*: If you tell students that their attendance will be measured by their participation in a quiz, it will increase compliance. Nonetheless, you would not have time to review all of them, so use the automatic screening and grading features of your learning management systems.
9. *Don't hide your feelings*: Online teachers' emotional openness is a great instructional strategy. Tell your students that you are teaching online for the first time, and that you are learning while teaching. Ask them to motivate you, to remind them that you would do your best to encourage their learning as well. They are going to be compassionate because they express the same feelings, so you are going to be set up for success.
10. *Repeat*: Online students do not like frequent changes in their learning style. They are happy to repeat the same process and behaviours. When you discover a teaching style that works for you, feel free to repeat it every week until you are back in your classroom.

Conclusion

Online Teaching has become a hot trend in lockdown situation to deliver uninterrupted learning material and to take care of the academic needs of the students. Digital teaching experience, unlike conventional classroom experience, consists of a variety of computer-assisted teaching procedures involving certain programming devices and applications. While there are positive and as well as bad aspects of online teaching, it can be a very satisfying work to help you develop some viable skills. By being an online instructor, you can learn how to be more organised, manage your time better, become more comfortable with technology, learn software skills and will become an influential writer. There are some challenges of online teaching like extra hard work, requirements of equipment, problem of equality and equity, unaffordable for children of poor families, etc. However, if the teacher overcomes all these cons then he will be able to learn new skills which will of better help in the classroom along with the advancement in career and personality. With the lockout resulting in the closure of schools and universities, students and teachers have switched to ed-tech networks to help sustain academic momentum.

References

Lee, K. (2020). Coronavirus: 14 simple tips for better online teaching. Retrieved on July 25, 2020 fromhttps://theconversation.com/coronavirus-14-simple-tips-for-better-online-teaching-133573

McIntyre, S., Watson, K., & Mirriahi, N. (2015). Learning to Teach Online-Evolving approaches to professional development for global reach and impact. *e-Learning Excellence Awards 2015: An Anthology of Case Histories*.

Symonds, Q. (2020). *The impact of the corona virus on global higher education*. Retrieved July 25, 2020 from https://www.qs.com/portfolio-items/the-impact-of-the-coronavirus-on-global-higher-education/

UNESCO (2020). *Covid-19 Educational disruption and response*. Retrieved on July 25, 2020 from https://en.unesco.org/covid19/educationresponse

UNESCO. (2020). *Adverse Consequences of school closures*. Retrieved on July 25, 2020 from https://en.unesco.org/covid19/educationresponse/consequences

UrbanPro. (2014). Top 10 Benefits of Online Teaching. Retrieved on July 25, 2020 from https://www.urbanpro.com/online-tutoring/top-10-benefits-online

UrgentEssayWriting. (2016). Pros and cons of online education for teachers. Retrieved on July 25, 2020 from https://www.urgentessaywriting.com/blog/pros-and-cons-of-online-education-for-teachers

Vnaya. (2020). *Impact of coronavirus on education sector*. Retrieved on July 25, 2020 from https://www.vnaya.com/impact-of-coronavirus-on-education-sector/

6

COVID-19: HIGHLIGHTER FOR THE DIGITAL DIVIDE IN INDIA

Avneet Kaur (Dr.)

Introduction

The *Digital Divide* refers to the gap between those able to benefit from the internet and those who are not (*Smith, 2002*).

The term "digital divide" refers to the gap between individuals, households, businesses and geographic areas at different socio-economic levels with regard both to their opportunities to access information and communication technologies (ICTs) and to their use of the Internet for a wide variety of activities (OECD, 2001).

Assistant Professor, Khalsa College of Education, Amritsar

Implications of the Digital Divide

Various implications of digital divide as mentioned in the Civilsdaily (2020) are as given below:

- *Political:* In the age of social media, political empowerment and mobilisation are difficult without digital connectivity.
- *Governance:* Transparency and accountability are dependent on digital connectivity. The digital divide affects e-governance initiatives negatively.
- *Social:* Internet penetration is associated with greater social progress of a nation. Thus, digital divide in a way hinders the social progress of a country. Rural India is suffering from information poverty due to the digital divide. It only strengthens the vicious cycle of poverty, deprivation, and backwardness.
- *Economic:* The digital divide causes economic inequality between those who can afford the technology and those who cannot.
- *Educational:* The digital divide is also impacting the capacity of children to learn and develop. Without Internet access, students cannot build the required tech skills.

Digital Divide and Education in India

India has the world's second-largest school system, after China. In order to avoid community transmission during Covid-19 crisis, the educational institutions were closed and online platforms were used to complete the syllabus of various classes. The exams were also conducted by the various schools and universities across the country using online platforms. However, this practice has affected a major student population of our country. The pandemic has not only caused the wide rift in educational inequality to balloon but also exacerbated existing disparities.

The divide exists despite the rise in the number of wireless subscribers in India over the past few years. According to the monthly report released by the Telecom Regulatory Authority of India (TRAI) on 29 June 2020, the country had over 1,160 million wireless subscribers in February 2020, up from 1,010 million in February 2016. This is a rise of 150 million subscribers in five years, or 30 million per year. The growth has been evenly distributed in urban and rural areas, with the number of urban subscribers increasing by 74 million (from 579 million to 643 million) and rural subscribers by 86 million (from 431 million to 517 million). But this growth only indicates the rise in basic telecommunication facility. Services such as online classrooms, financial transactions and e-governance require access to the internet as well as the ability to operate internet-enabled devices like phones, tablets and computers. Here the urban-rural distinction is quite stark (Pandey, 2020).

The situation of India's education sector is deteriorating rapidly, which is reflected in the data collected by the NSO. Published as Household Social Consumption: Education in India Report, covering 64,519 rural households from 8,097 villages and 49,238 urban areas, this survey covered qualitative and quantitative aspects related to educational attainment of household members and educational services used by them. According to this survey, 4% of rural and 23% of urban households possessed computers and 24% had internet access. Larger states like Uttar Pradesh, Tamil Nadu, Karnataka and Andhra Pradesh have less than 20% internet connectivity. As far as society and nation building is concerned, literacy and education are powerful force multipliers which enhance the success of all other developmental efforts. Despite initiatives like Broadband Policy, 2004, the digital chasm separating the privileged from the deprived remains the same and its effects have intensified amidst Covid-19. Since all the classes are being held online, lack of internet connectivity or compatible devices has become torturous for the students, sometimes escalating to suicides (Bajpai, 2020).

A total of 320 million learners in India have been adversely affected and transitioned to the e-learning industry, which comprises a network of 1.5 million schools. An NSSO 2014 report highlights that 32 million children were already out of school before the pandemic — the majority of them belonging to the socially disadvantaged class in the country (Modi & Postaria, 2020).

A larger percentage of digital divide has been observed in rural and urban areas. According to the 75th round of National Sample Survey conducted between July 2017 and June 2018, just 4.4 per cent rural households have a computer, against 14.4 per cent in urban areas, with just 14.9 per cent rural households having access to the internet against 42 per cent households in urban areas. Similarly, only 13 per cent people of over five years of age in rural areas have the ability to use the internet against 37 per cent in urban areas (Pandey, 2020).

Not only in the case of rural and urban population, rather a significant digital divide has been observed in case of male and female population in India. According to the Internet and Mobile Association of India, for example, male users account for 67% of India's online population; women account for just 29%.

Problems Faced by Students While Using E-Learning Platforms

- *Lack of electricity*: According to the nationwide survey which was conducted by the Ministry of Rural Development in 2017-18 shows that 16.3% of households use electricity for 1 to 8 hours a day, 33.2% of households use 9-12 hours, and only 47.1% of households use electricity for more than 12 hours a day. Thus, the shortage of electricity creates a problem for students to keep their electronic gadgets charged before the online class.

- *Lack of gadgets*: Various surveys conducted during lockdown show that most students are from families that have only one mobile phone. The earning member of the family has to carry the phone while going out to work. In a family that has, say, three children, how does one decide who gets to attend classes, assuming the phone is accessible.
- *Lack of internet connectivity:* Internet connectivity and signal issues are the most prevailing problems faced by students while attending online classes. Students are very often heard telling their teacher that he/she is not audible, or the teacher's screen shared is not visible. Parents struggling to earn two meals for their family find it difficult buying expensive data packages for good internet connectivity.
- *Not all subjects can be taught online:* Subjects such as mathematics and science which demand interactivity cannot be taught with ease. The laboratory classes of certain subjects are being missed and students are at a loss.
- Non-availability of trained teachers for conducting a virtual classroom: Many teachers in the school do not have laptops and are also not familiar with the hardware and software tools to be used for conducting an online class. To make complete digitisation of education especially in rural areas, this ratio needs to be improved and a large number of skilled and well-trained teachers are required so that each and every student receives complete attention even during an online class.
- *Non-availability of standardised content for regional languages:* Children studying regional languages are at a disadvantage as there is not much standardised content available yet online for them.
- *Increased screen time:* The increased screen time has reduced the physical activity of school students. Parents are concerned about too much overall screen time of their children.
- *Parents and students need time to learn the use of new applications:* Parents and students have not been exposed to this new system of learning and take time to adapt to the new form of education.
- *Lack of discipline:* Teachers during online classes find it difficult to control their students in virtual environment as they find some of the students having their breakfast during their class.
- *Fear of being judged:* Some teachers feared being judged by parents while teaching online. It is definitely a new experience for the teachers too. They get nervous of being watched by parents and other family members constantly.
- *Non-availability of books:* Many students do not have the new textbooks and the teacher is the only source of learning and reference.
- *Online Distractions:* At times, while the class is going on, the students get distracted towards other websites too. They mute themselves

and switch off their cameras during class and surf internet for other purposes. At times, they are even found chatting online with their friends.

- *Lack of supervison:* The teachers find it difficult to keep on checking the students who are still connected once the attendance has been marked. At times students do not respond to the questions asked during the class. Also, supervision is a problem where both the parents are working and the kids are left under the care of old grandparents or caretakers.

While the government endorses India as the flag-bearer of the digital revolution and acknowledges that it is a diverse and multilingual country, as supported by the New Education Policy 2020, e-learning platforms cannot replicate the various dialects, varied contexts and different lived experiences that are brought together by physical classrooms. If e-learning is the "new normal", the policy must go further to address the feasibility of digitalisation to ensure equity and quality in education. If the Indian education system aims to transit to online learning in the future, it must emphasise policies that bridge the digital divide and move the country closer to achieving the Sustainable Development Goals.

References

Bajpai, R. (OxHRH Blog, September 2020). *Right to Education & Emergence of a Digital Divide in Digital India.* https://ohrh.law.ox.ac.uk/right-to-education-emergence-of-a-digital-divide-in digital-india/

Civilsdaily.com (2020). *Digital divide in India.* https://www.civilsdaily.com/news/ covid-19-lockdown-highlights-indias-digital-divide/

Modi, S. & Postaria, R. (2020). *How Covid-19 deepens the digital education divide in India.* https://www.weforum.org/agenda/2020/10/how-covid-19-deepens-the-digital-education-divide-in-india/

OECD (2001). OECD Communications Outlook 2001, Paris. http://www.oecd.org/dataoecd/38/57/1888451.pdf

Pandey, K. (2020). *Covid-19 lockdown highlights India's great digital divide.* https://www.downtoearth.org.in/news/governance/covid-19-lockdown-highlights-india-s-great-digital-divide-72514

Smith, C.W. (2002). Digital corporate citizenship: the business response to the digital divide. Indianapolis: The Center on Philanthropy at Indiana University

7

DIGITALISATION OF TEACHING DURING COVID-19 CRISIS

Jaspreet Kaur

Introduction

As schools, colleges and all institutions of the world are closed due to the pandemic of Covid-19, it is necessary to ensure that learning must be continued. The corona virus spread its emerging effect in the education system around the world. Now it is clear that society and students needs flexible and elastic education system, moving from offline system to the online mode. Before Covid-19, teachers had to create their "physical classrooms" and trained their students with little bit online system. Current situation demands to offer students educational facilities anywhere and anytime. For this, universities and institutions are moving more and more towards online learning and e-learning. It also requires resources regarding e-learning, staff readiness, students' accessibility and motivation. Offline to online teaching refers to the pencil and paper versus laser and screen. Offline and online both modes of teaching are having their respective benefits and challenges in the teaching-learning environment. Transferring the classroom to the online platform was a new experience for all the teaching staff and also for the students. Everyone assumes that it is easier to teach online. Offline teaching involves traditional forms of education and also requires students to develop a sense of discipline and responsibility. Students also learn how to behave in the classroom and also to follow directions. Teachers assign tasks, homework, quizzes and other more projects. All of these require responsibility of students to prepare for the assignments. Now whole learning is shifted from offline mode to online. Online teaching is a method of delivering educational information via internet, instead of physical classroom. There are very wide range of strategies, technologies and tools available for the teachers who can use formative particle in their classroom. Offline to online teaching offered many things to teachers and students nowadays: convenience, user-friendliness, accessibility to anywhere at any time. Teachers also interact with the parents of the students with the use of virtual classroom and online tools to develop an engagement between the teachers and students. So in the current situation of lockdown it is mandatory to teach the students with online methods of teaching to ensure regular studies and also taking into account that safety must not be compromised.

Assistant Professor, Khalsa College of Education, Amritsar

Offline Teaching

Before Covid-19, the education was purely offline teaching. Students and teachers come to schools or colleges on daily basis with an arranged schedule decided in advance. In an offline mode, schools or colleges usually involve having students for an entire school year and teachers also become familiar with their students. Teachers know all the needs and cognitive levels of their students. The students are required to travel to the particular location, lecture hall, college or classroom to attend the classes every day. Offline Education means a student needs to go in a school, in a classroom, and attend a class face to face with a teacher where the doubts and queries of the students are cleared immediately by their teachers.

Benefits of Offline Teaching

The process of learning is not isolated. There is an instructor or a teacher who is physically present whole time to answer or clear the doubts of students. Students and teachers can also exchange their views in real time classroom in an effective way. Students also share their views and knowledge with their fellow students. In offline mode, the students also know how to behave in the classroom and are more disciplined.

Online Teaching

The Corona pandemic has made a global impact in the past months and continues to hit most of the sectors and education sector is one of them. During Covid-19, students and teaching staff are not allowed to go to schools and colleges. Students across the world were losing their valuable time due to this lockdown period. This situation has forced the staff and authority to shift their paradigms from offline to online teaching. Online Education is a very flexible learning system that allows students to study solely via the internet on their own computer at home, or wherever they see fit. Basically, student-teacher face to face meetings are not required, allowing students to study anywhere in the world.

Benefits of Online Teaching

Time and location flexibility: A teacher can choose to teach at any time that suits him/her. Online Teaching is a boon, where classes can be taken in evenings or on weekends. There is no time wastage, unlike the traditional classroom teaching where a teacher has to travel all the way to a coaching centre/institute for taking classes. Also, the teacher can teach from anywhere, irrespective of the location of students. This means that teachers and students from diverse locations can connect together through Online Teaching.

Affordable: Online education is affordable for almost all students. It reduces travel expenses, uniform expenses, etc. It requires an internet connection on your device. Almost everyone is having a Smartphone and can attend the online class on phone itself. There are several types of Online learning programmes where students meet their teacher for class through software such as Skype or Zoom and the same is free of cost.

Convenient: Online classes are convenient for both the teachers and students as they attend the class at any time and at any place as per their choice. Students can take online classes around their existing responsibilities and commitments and can learn at their own footstep. A teacher can teach right while sitting at his/her home. Online teaching could thus be perceived as a work from home with flexible schedules and time. The material can be stored and used for the future use. Some videos of lectures have the facility of downloading and re-viewing. So, if there is any doubt, the same can be repeated several times without any distraction.

Easier access and sharing of information: It is obvious that any study resource or information in digital format is very easy to be accessed and shared. While teaching online, one can take help from digital libraries, search engines and also social media channels for searching, accessing and sharing resources and information.

*Available 24*7*: The teachers and the students can interact with each other at any time because if the student cannot understand the concept and topic during the lecture, he or she can record the whole lecture and learn again and again.

Social distancing can be exercised: Due to the Covid-19 social distancing and self-isolation are more important to stay safe from this pandemic. Online teaching facilities can provide good quality education in the comfort of staying in their homes.

Personalise attention: Online teaching increases the engagement between the students and teachers which increases the personalised attention to the students. The students can easily communicate with their teachers and vice versa.

Reduce writing: While learning through online mode there is less need of documentation which reduces the work of writing because in online mode the data and the documents can be saved in the drive.

Move from teacher-centric education to student-centric education: Online teachers report that online teaching incorporates more engagement between student and the teacher. Unlike the interaction in a classroom of numerous students, an online medium provides them with a closer one-on-one session. Also, the shy and non-participative students, who are not comfortable with participating in classroom discussions, are obviously more likely to participate in an online class.

More transparent: Pedagogy in digital education is an important link between course content, educationists, technology and course-takers. But it is a fact that technology-based education is more transparent and does not make difference in front versus back benchers or girls versus boys.

More teaching opportunities: An education medium without any time and location constraints obviously paves the way significantly to more opportunities for the teachers, as compared to the traditional classroom teaching.

How Online Teaching is Different from Offline Teaching?

The online mode of education emphasises an interactive environment. In this environment the instructor, i.e. teachers and the students both require to take the active role during the lecture. This environment is designed to stimulate the dialogues between the instructor and the students. It requires a stable internet connection and a quite professional space to conduct classes. The online work environment also involves the interactive teaching tools and softwares to set up communication between the teachers and the students. Also Online teaching does not require any travelling overhead. A teacher can teach right while sitting at his/her home. Online teaching could thus be perceived as a work from home with flexible schedules.

Tools for Teachers to Create Digital Learning

The lockdown has accelerated adoption of digital technology. Business houses, educational institutes, analytics, computer, data management methods and online education solutions have been forced to work in tandem and improve the quality and delivery time to handle such situations. This is an ideal time to experiment and deploy new tools to make education delivery meaningful to students who cannot go to campuses. It is a chance to be more efficient and productive while developing new and improved professional skills/knowledge through online learning and assessment. We have many internet tools, apps, and digital platforms that help the teachers to teach their students in this pandemic time. Some of them are already known and used many of times like:

WhatsApp: WhatsApp is a free, multiplatform messaging app that lets you make videos and voice calls, send text messages, and more. First of all, it stimulates collaborative work and achieves the exchange of content both between the institution and the students. For example, sharing audio lessons, sending PPT materials or documents, etc. It is also possible to share video content. A more personalised follow-up to the student's educational process is facilitated. Facilitating virtual meetings avoids locative physical availability and, therefore, training, meetings, etc. can be carried out.

Google classroom: It is a free web service developed by Google for schools that aim to simplify creating, distributing, and grading assignments. The primary purpose of Google Classroom is to streamline the process of sharing files between teachers and students. Google Classroom integrates Docs, Sheets, Slides, Gmail, and Calendar into a cohesive platform to manage student and teacher communication. Teachers can create, distribute and mark assignments. Teachers can monitor the progress for each student by reviewing revision history of a document, and after being graded, teachers can return work along with comments.

Zoom app: Zoom app is a cloud based video conferencing platform used for video conferencing, meetings, audio conferencing, webinars, and live chat. Teachers can take Synchronous online class sessions, where everyone joins a Zoom meeting at a scheduled time. It is one way to create engagement when students are remote, but Zoom can also be used to support other teaching and learning scenarios. Zoom can be used on laptops, desktops, tablets, Smartphones and even desk phones, giving students many ways to access the class session.

Telegram: Telegram is a freeware, cross-platform, cloud-based instant messaging software and application service. The service also provides end-to-end encrypted video calling, file sharing and several other features. It lets teachers and students to access messages from the multiple devices. This service is mainly known for the security and the speed. It also provides the facility to make the groups of students and create channels where the unlimited number of users can join your channel services. Teacher can provide e-content to the students, make voice or video and audio communications together with experts from all over the world. Thus, each teacher or the faculty member can use the Telegram programme to serve his teaching material to his students; he can employ it in accordance with the special educational conditions so as to achieve the greatest benefit in the educational aspect. Many other digital learning tools are also used, like: WebEx, Microsoft team, e-pathshala, Google drive, Google meet, etc.

Conclusion

We all know that Covid-19 pandemic has affcctcd the whole educational system worldwide. For this, online education is more acceptable approach. Online teaching has made a great impact in the lives of teachers and students. It improves the interaction between the students and teachers. The quality of education has improved by online teaching and learning. Online teaching could thus be perceived as a work from home with flexible schedules and time. By all the counts and with the proven results, there was a paradigm shift from offline to online teaching during Covid-19 crisis.

References

Mahajan, Sanjeev. (2020). Paradigm Shift from Offline to Online Teaching: Readiness Among Teachers of Higher Educational Institutions.

Bartley, S.J., Golek, J.H. (2004). Evaluating the cost effectiveness of online and face-to-face instruction. *J EducTechnol Soc*. 7(4):167–175.

Muilenburg, L.Y., Berge, Z.L. (2005). Student barriers to online learning: a factor analytic study. *Distance Educ.* 26(1):29–48.
Leisi, Pei & Hongbin, Wu (2019). Does online learning work better than offline learning in undergraduate medical education? A systematic review and meta-analysis, Medical Education Online, 24:1, DOI: 10.1080/10872981.2019.1666538
Liguori,E.,Winkler,C.(2020)FromOfflinetoOnline:ChallengesandOpportunities for Entrepreneurship Education Following the Covid-19 Pandemic. Entrepreneurship Education and Pedagogy. 3(4):346-351. DOI:10.1177/2515127420916738
https://visme.co/blog/online-teaching-tools/
https://creately.com/blog/education/online-teaching-tools/

8

COVID-19: ROLE OF DIGITAL EDUCATION

Rajwinder Kaur

Introduction

Covid-19 has thrusted digital technology and education into the spotlight. At the moment, it is difficult to think about anything other than how to cope with the immediate difficulties thrown up by school closures, university shut-downs and the pivot to online teaching and learning. The lock down in many countries has sped up the adoption of digital technology in every profession and online education solutions have been forced to work in tandem and improve in quality and delivery time to handle such situations. This is a perfect time to experiment and create new tools to make education delivery meaningful to students who cannot go to campuses. It is an opportunity to develop new and improved professional skills/ knowledge through online learning and assessment. The Covid-19 has resulted in shut-down of educational institutions all across the world. Globally, over 1.2 billion children are out of the classroom and this data varies from country to country. So the education system has changed dramatically, with the distinctive rise of e-learning, whereby teaching is undertaken remotely and on digital platforms.

In this time of crisis, a well-rounded and effective educational practice is helpful for the capacity-building of young minds. It will help to sharpen the skills that will drive their productivity, employability, health, and well-being in the years to come, and ensure the overall progress of India for solving the

---

Assistant Professor, Khalsa College of Education, G.T. Road, Amritsar

present situation due to this pandemic. Online digital learning programmes give a great opportunity to avail high-quality learning internet connectivity.

In India, although this transition has been smooth for most private universities, the public ones are still adapting. With this rapid shift away from the classroom in many parts of the globe, some are wondering whether the adoption of online learning will continue to persist post-pandemic, and how such a shift would impact the worldwide education market.

Even before Covid-19, there was already high growth and adoption in education technology. Some believe that moving toward online learning, with no training and without proper preparation, will result in poor user experience that is not useful to sustained growth, others believe that a new model, which is called hybrid will come out, with significant benefits. Wang Tao, Vice President of Tencent Cloud and Vice President of Tencent Education says, "believe that the integration of information technology in education will be further accelerated and that online education will eventually become an integral component of school education". There have already been useful transitions amongst many universities.

Online digital learning programmes give a great opportunity to avail high-quality learning internet connectivity. Ministry of Education, the National Council of Educational Research and Training (NCERT) and the Department of Technical Education are created on different platforms to provide online education in India. There also are initiatives like e-PG Pathshala (e-content), SWAYAM (online courses for teachers), and NEAT (enhancing employability), MOOCs and Moodles as learning platforms. These are used for running of online modules. A few initiatives are SWAYAM online courses for teachers, UG/PG MOOCs for non-technology courses, e-PG Pathshala or e-content containing modules on social science, arts, fine arts, natural and mathematical science, CEC-UGC YouTube channel, Vidwan — a database of experts who provide information to peers and prospective collaborators, NEAT — an initiative by AICTE based on the PPP model to develop the employability skill among students, in collaboration with Education Technology Companies and National Digital Library (NDL), a repository of learning resources with single window facility. With this, the boundaries of the classroom are extending. With online education, the restrictions to studying only the classroom material and enrolling only in a specific course is out of date. With the help of Open Educational Resources and MOOCs, the student enrolled in his/her home state university can also be a part of the other course running online by a world class university, for multiple purposes or based on interest in the specific skills set. Due to this, the classroom size has spread beyond the horizons, which develop a number of challenges for the instructors to handle the class. The major challenges created by this changing scenario of education require immediate measures to ensure continuity of learning in government schools and universities. Open-source digital learning solutions and Learning

Management Software should be adopted so that teachers can conduct teaching online. The DIKSHA platform, with reach across all states in India can be further strengthened to ensure accessibility of learning to the students. It is also a fact that use of technology in education is resulting in different concepts in the system, for instance, the move from teacher-centric education to student-centric education.

Although these many efforts are being made for the effective and smooth running of online education still there are many difficulties and challenges which all the stakeholders of education have to face, as a survey by IIT Kanpur revealed that 9.3 per cent of its 2,789 students were not able to download material sent by the institute or study online. Only 34.1 per cent of them had internet connection good enough for streaming real-time lectures. Another survey conducted by Local Circles among 25,000 respondents found that only 57 per cent students had the required computer, internet, and printer at home to attend online classes.

Most educators from different institutions agree that for standardised online education platforms, there is a need for large scale investment and not using apps and Google hangouts only; for training both students and teachers. Others emphasise the necessity to introspect on the nature of these platforms and how these platforms are helpful for students to be taught using different online tools and methods, while keeping accessibility and equity challenges in mind. There is also the need to understand all this across academic disciplines and institutions.

Role of Digital Education for Students and Teachers

- The ability to learn using different online tools and methods.
- No disruption in learning because of the pandemic.
- Listening to recorded and live conversations and working at their own speed.

Online education, a result of the digital world has brought a lot to the learning table at all levels of education, beginning from preschool up to higher level institutions.

Schools have always used educational apps or digital learning as a supplementary tool and also used them at the time when students have difficulty in content. However, the current situation has accelerated the adoption of technology and experiment with online learning and measured its success.

As digital educational development continues, it also emphasises the digital divide in India. Students from border districts and those belonging to poor areas lack the infrastructure and the means to reap the benefits of online learning. Greater influence of telecom networks and rolling out 5G services will give a huge impact to this sector. India is going to witness a 50% increase in students over the next 15 years and although it has many universities and colleges, only few have the facilities to match this surge of students in the future. Online education could be a logical solution to accommodate this problem. Indian government, for the first time, is allowing Indian universities to offer online degrees which previously was limited to foreign universities. Now, to encourage and widen the access to higher education, this restriction has been lifted from 20% to offer 100% courses online.

Education is going to be digital in the future and with the proper infrastructure and policies. We would be better prepared to handle it. However, the education community is beginning to start thinking beyond the current upheavals, and consider the post-pandemic implications for digital education.

With a rapid increase of mobile internet users in India, which is expected to reach 85% households by 2024, technology is enabling access and personalisation of education even in the remotest parts of the country. This can totally change the schooling system and increase the effectiveness of learning and teaching. Many districts have initiated innovative, mobile-based learning models for effective delivery of education. Use of technology in education is resulting in different concepts in the system, the move from teacher-centric education to student-centric education.

Impact of Digital Education on Education Process

Through digitalisation of the learning experience, both teachers and students are able to improve their skills, with a common goal to create a more engaging and effective education process.

1. *Boosting Digital Equity:* Digital equity in education means that all students can have access to learning resources in an easier and less expensive way than the traditional one. With the help of digital transformation, students can check out only one device — a smartphone, a tablet or a laptop — to access many different contents at school, at home, wherever they are regardless of their economic status.

With digital transformation, there is no more need to collect so many heavy books and also with one click the content can be shared among students.

2. *Customised Experience:* Developing the digital transformation process in schools means allowing students to access the benefits of customisation, access heavy curriculums to shape their future. Today, special programmes and tests are able to suggest what courses a learner should take based on the courses he previously completed, his scores and his aptitude.

3. *A Worldwide Audience:* Digital education helps to break the geographical and cultural boundaries, allowing teachers to bring the knowledge beyond the classroom and provide knowledge to a worldwide audience. Students from all around the world can attend and watch lessons, help to develop the global conversations through so many different points of view on the same topic, with the result of an enriched educational experience.

Asynchronous classrooms allow students to "go to school" whenever they need. This gives the opportunity to graduate students to access advanced information for their thesis and research in the exact moment when they need it the most.

4. *Modular Learning:* With the help of digital transformation, the schools build learning modules in a faster way. Educators can prepare their courses and programmes using the best content previously developed by other colleagues, from their same department but also from other institutes.

With the help of *"digital abstraction"* of content, educators can solve the problem to create a variety of effective learning materials that have to fulfil the broad range of needs for different competencies, difficulty levels, roles and departments. Moreover, thanks to digital tools, educators can measure how students learn most effectively, developing the learning modules to new evidence-based aspects.

5. *High-Quality Educators:* Teachers can join online professional learning communities to ask questions and share tips with the colleagues, staying connected and animating the common goal to create an evolved, high-quality standard of education.

Conclusion

A complete revolution, in the way we learn today, has been brought about by digital learning. Every student gets in contact with a world-class education, which is not easy to provide education by the traditional blackboard method of teaching. This new mode of learning is more interesting, personalised and enjoyable. It is also cost-effective and students get to learn in their comfort zone. All over the world, online education has met with some success. In the case of India, we still have a long way to go before digital learning is seen as mainstream education, because students living in urban areas have the facilities for providing digital education, but the students of rural areas do not have the required infrastructure or also they are not financially strong to avail the digital education. Successful delivery of education is also in question because learning at the level of higher education and learning at the kindergarten/school level can be different. If we further put the light on the educational material, digital education will have a limited scope as compared with the written and handy material which is provided in an educational institute. Moreover, the authentication of the educational material is at stake. But at the same time, there is a main disadvantage as exams have to be postponed because examinations cannot be conducted online. It is not only just the question of imparting continuous and uninterrupted learning during the outbreak of Covid-19 pandemic but also the most important challenge for the instructor is to focus on the overall elements of a well-developed course.

References

Cathay, L.(2020). The World Economic Forum. https://apolitical.co/en/solution_article/covid-19-has-changed-education-forever-heres-how

Tao, W.(2020). Empowering education through artificial intelligence. https://www.weforum.org/agenda/2020/04/coronavirus-education-global-covid19

Gonsalves, Ti. (2020). Education in the time. https://www.ndtv.com/education/hrd-minister-launches-india-report-on-digital-education-during-covid-19

Deka, M. (2020). HRD Minister Launches India Report On Digital Education During Covid-19. https://www.ndtv.com/education/hrd-minister-launches-india-report-on-digital-education-during-covid-19

Choudhary, R. (2020). Covid-19 Pandemic: Impact and strategies for education sector in India. https://government.economictimes.indiatimes.com/news/education/covid-19-pandemic-impact-and-strategies-for-education-sector

Spencer,G. (2020). Schools after Covid-19: From a teaching culture to a learning culture. https://apolitical.co/en/solution_article/covid-19

http://www.educationinsider.net/detail_news.php?id=1326

https://en.unesco.org/covid19/educationresponse

9

THE FUN THEY HAD: A STORY FROM TEXTBOOK – ITS RELEVANCE DURING COVID-19

Aiman Nafis[1] *and Vidyapati (Dr.)*[2]

Introduction

Covid-19 is the reality at present, which we have globally acknowledged as the pandemic. This pandemic period has been witnessing a real shift into almost every field of human endeavour. The education sphere has also responded to this reality in the form of online learning. How much we teachers are prepared for online learning? How can we teachers gear up for it? These are few questions lingering in teachers' mind. When we are still in the phase of making sense of Online Learning in the era of Covid-19, the story "The Fun They Had" which the researcher had read both as a student and as a teacher came

1. Former Assistant Professor, Rajat Women's College of Education and Management, Lucknow

2. Head and Dean, Faculty of Education, Ewing Christian PG College, Prayagraj

striking to the mind. The story is set in the year 2157, and we are 137 years behind it. Still, it is amazing and intimidating how Covid-19 has forced us to take a leap in faith regarding online learning. Interestingly, the researcher finds Class IX NCERT English textbook Chapter One named *The Fun They Had* by Issac Asimov to be in tune with our present condition. The above-mentioned questions worked as driving source to look for meaning of online learning for a teacher. The objectives of the study are as follow:

1. To analyse the Class IX NCERT English textbook chapter 'The Fun They Had' in the present context of Online Learning during Covid-19.
2. To study the relevance of the chapter for a pedagogy in the present context of Online Learning during Covid-19.

Review of Related Literature

Pawagi (2018) has analysed the story from technological view; he opined that the story has been a total fault by the writer who constructed it out of complete fantasy without planning or even thinking about any sensible possibility. He pointed out some areas where he believed there is quite some conflict with what we can really anticipate in the future. The present paper studies the story from educational perspective. Interestingly Pawagi has recently added an edited version entitled 'Covid-19 and Reflection' where he reanalysed the story from present context of Covid-19. He said that though one could not agree with the exaggerations of this story, there is one deeper meaning and that is the reality of isolation. Shrek (2017) has also done critical analysis of the story and he was amazed how well the author predicts the future. He mentioned that the story was written in 1951 before personal computers were around. He believes that the author wrote this story to warn us about the use of technology in education. He commented 'perhaps in the future, children really will be taught by mechanical teachers!' The same doubt was also raised by Pawagi when he says that although mechanical teachers are far from reality, the depth of the message, the future of education and its consequences run deep. Bharti (2020) reported that school goers have converted rooms of their house as a classroom and they called it as "HouSchool". They attend the school daily as per schedule dressed in school uniform. However, their parents pray that their innovation does not stay for long.

Methodology Used

Qualitative content analysis was used to conduct the study. It is "a research technique for making valid inferences from texts (or other meaningful matter) to the contexts of their use". According to Krippendorff (2004), it is an

Presentation of Data

Meaning Unit	*Condensed Meaning Unit*	*Sub Categories*	*Categories*	*Themes*
MARGIE even wrote about it that night in her diary…when they read it the first time. (1st paragraph p. 5)	The date shows that the story is set in future in 2157 i.e. 137 years from now. Margie and Tommy are two characters introduced. It depicts a world where real books (printed form) are totally replaced by e-books.	Futuristic story Real book is a prized possession as it is used to preserve knowledge.	Future learning system. Print media verses online media.	Traditional form of learning is totally replaced by Online mode.
"Gee," said Tommy, "what a waste …. What's it about? "School." (2nd paragraph pp. 6)	This futuristic world is all pervasive by information, where children are finding hard to believe the once existence of book as a source of information.	For Tommy and Margie's information changes constantly and conserving anything for generations is completely out of question.	The book's location in the attic indicates that it has lost it worth as an educational resource.	Online learning is all pervasive by information.
Margie was scornful. "School? What's there to write about school … sent for the County Inspector. (3rd Paragraph pp. 6)	Margie was totally taken by surprise that a book can be written about school which is for her the most boring subject.	Margie hates her school because of her mechanical teacher who was continuously taking test.	Mechanical teacher.	Margie hates school.
He was a round little man with a red face…and the mechanical teacher calculated the marks in no time. (4th Paragraph pp. 6)	Margie dislikes her classes: same routine daily, same screen which always displays lesson and questions. Homework schedule is also very tiresome.	Being upset by Margie's poor performance, her mother called a mechanic to fix a mechanical teacher.	Books and teachers have been discarded in favour of digital alternatives. Lost meaning of Homework.	Machine impersonal and unfriendly and the work to be repetitive and taxing.
The Inspector had smiled after he was finished … anyone write about school (5th Paragraph pp. 7)	The County Inspector sympathisised with Margie and encouraged her by patting on the Margie's head and fixed the faulty robotic teacher.	The kindness of the County Inspector shows how important human contact is to a child's development.	Margie's disappointment after a man leaves shows how much she fears the drudgery of learning.	Importance of Humane touch in making learning meaningful.

Meaning Unit	*Condensed Meaning Unit*	*Sub Categories*	*Categories*	*Themes*
Tommy looked at her with … gave them homework and asked them questions (6th Paragraph pp. 8)	Tommy explains Margie that it is not the usual one but a different kind of school with real human teachers "man".	It is difficult for Margie to believe that humans could also have a potential to teach.	She has grown up in a world where machines can provide virtually unlimited information.	The mechanised education system in the children's world has not only robbed them of fun but also the ability to believe in human potential.
A man isn't smart enough … were the same age (7th Paragraph pp. 8)	Tommy informs her that there used to be separate building called school where all kids from the neighbourhood would go together and study together.	Margie finds it difficult to imagine the possibility of going to school with other children but is nevertheless fascinated by the idea.	Teacher's and students' lively feedbacks are important for evaluation of learning. Sharing of personal experience.	Mechanised method of schooling isolates children. Online learning is learning alone.
But my mother says a teacher has to be adjusted…you after school (8th Paragraph pp. 8)	Tommy and Margie were completely engrossed in reading about real school when they were called up for joining their own individualised school.	Margie does not want to go to school as the learning is drudgery and regular.	Margie has no conception of how schooling might have been different in the past.	Children were reluctant to go personalised schooling.
"May be," he said nonchalantly…homework in the proper slot (9th Paragraph pp. 8)	Margie has fixed time, place and teacher for learning. Home assignment has to be submitted before the new lesson starts.	Irrespective of Margie inattentiveness; Mechanised teacher continues to teach.	Rigid, non-creative, fixed system.	Online learning turns to be isolating and unfulfilling.
Margie did so with a sigh… the fun they had.(10th Paragraph pp. 8)	Margie is completely lost day-dreaming about the old school which is lively, full of laughter, play, work and study together with the other students and their true relationship with the real teacher.	Margie finds herself longing for the kinds of schools that used to exist, where she could learn from human teachers and be in company of friends.	Children power to imagine.	Fun Learning.

orderly reading of a text or other symbolic matter and presented in the form of conceptual and relational analysis rather than frequency expressed as numbers or percentage. Here the text "The Fun They Had" by Issac Asimov is analysed in reference to pedagogy in the context of online learning during Covid-19. The procedure followed was decontextualisation where condensed meaning unit is developed. It is a process of shortening the text while still preserving its meaning. Second step was recontextualisation where the original text is read alongside the condensed meaning unit to describe it more specifically as codes. Next step was categorisation where codes are sorted. In other words, it is grouping together of similar codes into categories. Finally, compilation was done to figure out the themes, the content underlying meaning.

Findings

Shut down into our homes and presenting classes cling to our computer screens. Our students attending classes alone without classmates, our situations are not very different from Margie and Tommy. The story "The Fun We Had" is relevant than ever. Future is here as we are ahead of time. The Covid-19 has worked as a push factor for Virtual learning. The themes emerged in the study was the failure of 'Mechanical teacher', which was designed to be more efficient and personalised than a real teacher. Margie dislikes the lessons provided by the mechanical teacher as it leads to boredom and a lack of personal connection with the teacher and other students. The mechanical teacher falls short to provide meaningful learning despite being a personalised instructor. It points out the bleak consequences of virtual education that has forgone books and real human teacher.

The story warns teacher not to rely too heavily on technology, otherwise the learning will become impersonal. We are already witnessing too much information influx in 21st century. The teacher needs to remember the difference between information and education. Margie's mechanical teacher lacks the ability to interact with the students and tend to pour information devoid of any emotion. The chapter is very relevant in today's time of pandemic; technology cannot and should not replace teachers. We should try to exploit the technology to human use and not the vice versa. The latent meaning of the chapter is that we should believe in human potential more than anything else. Teacher should be humane and reflective and not mechanical. Students learning should be made fun by interactive session with teachers and other classmates. The chapter also shows how homework has lost its purpose for Margie. It is really tiresome if we look from students' perspective as classwork is also being done in a home so it raises the question of feasibility of homework. Margie and Tommy belong to Upper Primary level of education where children learn mainly by exploration. Therefore, we as a teacher could draw a bigger lesson that in this Covid-19 era of self-isolation; it is a responsibility of a teacher to avoid routine, drudgery and impersonal form of teaching.

This chapter included in NCERT English textbook for Class IX will now be read and taught with an altogether new perspective of Covid-19. The students and the teachers will be able to relate to the chapter as they are experiencing a world where computers are playing a major role. The story will now be interpreted more from factual outlook rather than science fiction. Now the children ironically need not imagine school of future as they are already living it. Teachers need not necessarily explain the idea of virtual classroom and virtual reality as Covid-19 has turned the idea into a real existence.

Conclusion

'The Fun They Had' was published in 1951. The writer reported later that the story was just drafted for a friend but actually turned out to be biggest surprise in his literary career. Indeed a surprise for the readers too as who could have imagined that futuristic online learning as the only mode of learning feasible in 2020. We can reminisce about the "The Fun We Had" in attending school together with our friends. But what about little kids who are thrust in this uncertain world. We believe every teacher would benefit from reading this story. It is both a great science fiction and a lesson to learn for pedagogy. We hope for our normal days to return but till then these virtual classes are new normal. We can use it as an opportunity to exploit the use of technology in education with the caution of never to be a mechanical teacher.

References

Bharti, M. (2020). School closed due to pandemic, Lucknow boys make classroom at home. Retrieved on July 19, 2020 from www.ndtv.com

Chapter 1 NCERT. Retrieved on 10 July, 2020, from http://ncert.nic.in/ncerts/l/iebe101.pdf

Krippendorff (2004) in Bengtsson, M. (2016). How to plan and perform a qualitative study using content analysis https://www.sciencedirect.com/science/article/pii/S2352900816000029#:~:text

Pawagi, M. (2018). The Fun They Had: Review from a Technological View. Retrieved on July 16, 2020, from https://medium.com/technifity/the-fun-they-had-review-from-a-technological-view-6b90cd5c225d

William, S. (2017). Story Review the fun they had. Retrieved on July 12, 2020, from https://www.edb.gov.hk/attachment/en/curriculum-development/resource-support/net/handout%201.17-%20story%20review%202b.pdf

10

TEACHING-LEARNING DURING AND AFTER COVID-19

Priyanka Aeri (Dr.)

Introduction

In the time of Corona, there has been rapid expansion of digital education. An increasing number of students slowly but steadily are moving towards online digital courses in almost every field including business, arts, medical, engineering as well as programming languages and technical tools. Also commonly known as eLearning, digital classrooms have been coming up rapidly in all streams around the world. Not only digital learning is a vastly advanced technological medium but it also provides the learners with a great deal of flexibility, allowing them to study at any time from any place at their own convenient speed without worrying about timetables and schedules. The students, for the first time, also have the liberty to choose what they want to learn and what they don't. This advantage has made digital learning hugely popular, not only among engineering students but also students involved in other fields. There are a few basics which, when applied to digital learning classrooms, improve student engagement as well as their interest. These basic principles are applicable to all kinds of digital learning courses be it language skills, process training skills or even soft skills, etc.

Enhancing Effective Digital Learning

In the wake of Corona Virus Pandemic, it has become imperative to introduce digital education in colleges, universities and in schools to walk with the call of time in field of education as well to fight with Corona which spread dangerously in all parts of the country. It brought chaos to the entire world and created terror among the entire humanity. No medicine to cure and/or to stop the community spread of the disease was available. However, vaccine was introduced in the beginning of 2021.

The impact of the disease attacked all the sectors and the education at all levels is also not remained untouched by this virus. During the sessions normally ending in March and re-opening in July every year remained disrupted. No conclusive decisions could be taken at any level as to how to manage the education in classes. To end the academic session of 2019-20, some Boards were able to conduct the exams and successfully declared the results and higher-level education started online classes so that social distancing is maintained to avoid any risks. The result and role of online education are yet to be consolidated.

Education genre is face to face interaction between students and the teacher. The teacher vibrates the class on the subject in his/her lucid style, full

---

Assistant Professor, Kamla Nehru College for Women, Phagwara

of knowledge expression and devotion to ensure that each and every student of class understand what she/he is preaching on the subject.

The educationists and the policy makers are of the opinion for educating through online mode, that is Digital Education, during and after Covid-19 till the situations of pandemic is controlled. The gathering of any type is completely banned during the virus situation and students of all classes are future of the country and society, so it is imperative to safeguard them at any cost.

The country is now number one in technology and computer sciences, so are the students through available websites on smart phones and on laptops and desktops at home and at classes. Even the kids are being introduced successfully to have access to computers and other components of new technology. These are the reasons which can lead to a system of digital education at all levels till the situation is normal.

It would be pertinent to mention that within the lockdown period many institutes, schools colleges adopted and commenced online education earnestly. And the teachers and the students, all are becoming familiar to the systems and are also changing styles so as to reach to students properly.

Such a major shift is a challenge in school education as well in higher education. While forming this policy, so far the importance of rural education from primary level to secondary level are neither being discussed, nor being considered as to how to cope with the situation of the poor and rural population as the Covid-19 spreading in villages also due to migrations of people from urban areas. It is critical situation now at all stages of categories, viz. rural, semi-urban, urban and metropolitan. It is to be ensured that each student is having fair access to online systems and computers.

While at the first stage of implementing the online education, there are mixed reactions from the students of higher education. Some are happy as they enjoyed the lockdown period at homes with passing time on computers and learning, whereas others have negative view that it is more time consuming to understand the subject in comparison to class, where they have freedom to interact with the lecturer/professor. But these petty problems would be solved in due course after the implementation of digital education.

The transition from conventional to online education is clearly evident. Laptops, mobiles and e-learning are now part of everyday education as more and more centres are available in semi-urban, urban and metros with full-fledged online books on all subjects and students are benefitted with such new ventures and are learning a lot through this media. But this would be restricted to class students and will not be available to mass students which they are gaining in the classrooms at one shot of time period of the class. The teachers, the students and many are excited about learning, yet *they* feel restricted *in the way they can use* their *new* knowledge *to* encourage *methods and format* change *in* their schools, colleges and universities.

By all means, content knowledge and methods and theory of knowledge are necessary to help students to understand scientific concepts. For this, the contemporary education system is to be continued simultaneously because of clearance of doubts in the minds arisen during online education process. Direct dialogue with the students is most essential as during discussions new topics and themes come out which may help additions in any subject.

The state of education in India is dismal especially in rural areas. This sector is currently facing grave challenges such as outdated teaching methods, shortage of teachers as qualified teachers from urban areas are not interested to work in rural areas. The ratio of student-teacher is also poor due to poverty level and child labour for earnings in rural areas. However, with the digitalisation of education, students in educationally backward areas are being taught with the help of the latest teaching tools and methodologies such as LCD screens, videos etc. The technology is also helping teachers to connect students even in remotely spread areas across several locations at the same time.

As the pandemic has prompted teachers, students and institutional heads and the management to innovate and adapt online formats, they are entering amazingly in a new world of virtual lectures and classes. Teachers are more concerned because it takes time to follow new systems and to drop the old traditional methods, but many agencies of survey in educational field have concluded that more and more teachers and professionals are learning fast to be conversant with the new methods. On the other side, the class students are already well conversant with the technology and are having aptitude of learning through digital education, their life is already techno-based due to smart phones and availability of various subjects on Google. So they are in favour of digital education as they will be free from the boredom of attending colleges and classrooms.

The most significant effect of changes would be for technical education, medical education and for lab-practicals which are compulsory for science and other technical subjects. For this also, new modality is to be adopted in due course so that students are not deprived of opportunities.

In all, new methods are to be researched and adopted for the smooth education system as it is feared that corona pandemic may continue for quite a long time. No boundary line can be drawn for the end of this life-taking disease.

But the system would hamper the interest of various institutes who have large establishments investing heavy funds for comfort of the students and teachers. Nowadays the maintenance of such big establishments is very costly affair and if the new digital education system is enforced, it would badly affect the economic viability of the institutes and as a result they will have to lay off many appointed teachers and professionals and replace them with new technologists and teachers with essence of speech. Many other odd questions and problems would arise in due course of time.

The other factor is of availability of speed and continuation of internet facilities. Improvised systems and equipments will require, meeting both the ends and for that sufficient funds are to be made available. It would also be seen that with the introduction of digital education how many students would be covered in accordance with the economic resources.

It may deprive many brilliant students of higher studies due to requirement of system and gadgets. Can we arrange the classes in colleges and universities by providing limited number of seats with availability of access to the computers at the seats and the professor/lecturer delivering the lecture as per the existing systems?

Although the system is already in vogue of distant education learning, popularity of e-classes, e-learning and e-books but looking over to the number of students at the country level the same may not be easily available to all.

It is also not clear what would be the impact of post Covid-19, what would be life style, whether it would go for good and how the people would face the post Covid-19 situation. There are so many questions which have no answers at present and so according to the emerging situations we have to format the educational system also with so many challenges and determinations with positive approaches in all walks of the life. At the end, it is prayed that the world peace is sustained with good health and energy resulting into progressive life.

References

https://www.weforum.org/agenda/2020/04/coronavirus-education-global-covid19-online-digital-learning/

https://www.washington.edu/teaching/topics/engaging-students-in-learning/teaching-with-technology-2/

http://www.bristol.ac.uk/digital-education/guides/coronavirus/

https://www.fau.eu/2020/06/05/news/studying-during-the-coronavirus-pandemic/

11

COVID-19 AND DIGITAL EDUCATION: THE NEW NORMAL

Anju Tyagi (Dr.)

Introduction

An unprecedented change in education due to closure of schools, colleges and Universities since the beginning of Covid-19 crisis has deprived the children and youth of opportunities for development and improvement through classroom education. This crisis is proving larger than any war in human history and is a challenging time not only for the students but also for teachers. Students are deprived of the opportunities for growth and development whereas teachers are in the state of discombobulation and stress as they are unsure of their obligations and how to maintain connection with the students

Teacher, Air Force Junior School, New Delhi

scholastically and emotionally. Educational institutions are the hubs of social activity and human interaction in any society. With the closure of these hubs, social contact finds no place that are essential to learning and development. Assessments and examinations are thrown into disarray.

This crisis has changed the concept of education overnight. Digital learning and online education have emerged out as the only solution to this problem. Digital learning has proved itself as an indispensable resource for education as it has proved to be catering to the needs of students and also providing them opportunities of remote learning across the globe. It is also equipping the teachers to create virtual experiences in their noble profession.

The vast development of internet and related technology, over the years, have made online education an acceptable process of learning. But, despite several renowned platforms, it was still not the primary choice for students or mainstream academic institutions. Then the Covid-19 outbreak happened.

There has always been the shout out for digitalisation of education, infusing information and communication technologies, virtual classrooms in India. But for a developing country it seems to be literally impossible to change the century old systems of education as around 68% of its population live in villages. Digital education has been much underutilised option in education system.

Corona pandemic has escalated the use of online digital education at lightening pace. Digital education acted as a silver lining among the dark clouds of pandemic. A new roadmap of education has ushered. E-learning courses, pre-recorded sessions, live virtual classrooms have evolved at an unprecedented rate. And people have enthusiastically embraced this new model of studies in every facet of life. Keeping the students' safety in mind and their academic concern, most of the educational institutions have taken the initiative to provide the facility of virtual classes to fill the gap of learning. Adoption of online education platforms have been helping the institutions to keep the classes going without a halt. Institutions started giving training to their teachers and students to use technology to facilitate virtual classes and to keep the learning process on the go. Indisputably, this is a very crucial time for students, teachers and parents. So, the budge is intended at easing the pressure on students and facilitating them to use their time valuably without compromising on the quality. To make learning process more effective, educational institutions are providing pre-recorded videos of lessons to the students in which topics are explained extensively and that can be viewed by the students multiple times according to their own understanding and learning pace. Ironically, the whole education sector has shifted to digital mode with both human and technical support.

Now, this major shift has left us brooding over the major questions: Is it temporary or permanent? Is it a boon or bane? Is it beneficial or challenging?

As we all know every aspect has two sides, it also does have both of them.

Positive Aspects of Online Learning

There are substantial benefits of online/ digital learning:

- Online learning gives the freedom to learn anywhere and beyond geographical boundaries without any hassle and long travels.
- Internet is the repository of knowledge. Anyone can dive deep in this ocean of facts, information and explanations.
- Online learning is flexible with easy operations. All digital learning content is created keeping user experience a primary focus. You can conquer the world with flexible visual learning at your own time and schedule.
- The current wave of digital education offers prospect for experimentation and for envisaging new models of education and new customs of using the face-to-face learning time.
- Children comprehensively use their senses to become skilled at, making learning enjoyable and efficient through the use of technology.
- Online learning will help countries better understand the potential of digital learning solutions and bring communities, homes, and schools closer together.
- Online learning inspires the teachers to make the most of digital advances. Teachers will have the chance to test out different digital learning solutions, and comprehend how technology can be used to foster deeper student wisdom. They need to be encouraged to reflect resourcefully about their role as facilitators of student learning, and how technology can prop up them in doing so, and how they can unite their expertise as a profession.

A Few Challenges

There are few challenges in order to settle into this new normal.

- Logistical arrangements are needed for online learning, e.g. steady network connectivity (especially in rural/ remote areas), a smart device, etc.
- Complete perseverance and determination by the authorities to see it through.
- Discipline and self-motivation on the part of the students to engage themselves actively in the course.
- Many parents cannot afford to buy multiple devices for themselves and their children.
- Many people find it difficult to go online because they don't know how to do it.
- There can be a significant gap in opportunities and resources between those from privileged and disadvantaged backgrounds.
- Increased screen time has led to stress issues among the students.

- Sometimes teachers could find it difficult to establish a rapport between them and the students.
- Disorientation in values among the students in the lack of face-to-face learning process where teachers could counsel them.
- A range of collaboration tools and engagement methods are needed that promote "inclusion and personalisation".

Conclusion

Online learning is here to stay. Whether as a mainstream learning channel or not, you can utilise this advanced learning mode with little effort today. The efforts by the governments across the globe to ensure sustainability of learning are revamping the entire education system. Integration of information technology in education will be further accelerated and that online education will eventually become an integral component of school education. However, access to devices and connectivity will have massive impact on socio-economically backward category. Education systems have to ensure equal access to learning and resources to all. Technology is leading a pedagogical change while addressing issues that affect learning, teaching and social functionalities. Technology can, therefore, be seen as a tool, a catalyst for change. We hope that this dreaded pandemic is controlled soon, but until normalcy returns, it is digital learning that will bridge the gap between teachers and learners. Transition to online learning could prove to be the catalyst to create a new, more effective method of educating students if implemented skillfully with strategic planning. Schools and organisations must be prepared for the new normal for the proliferation of learning process.

References

Shawn Michael Bullock, P., *The Challenge ofDigital Technologies to Educational Reform*. 2010.

Ranasinghe, A.I., The Benefit of Integrating Technology into the Classroom. *International Mathematical Forum*, 2009. 4, 2009, no. 40, 1955-1961.

Janson, A., *Integrating Digital Learning Objects in the Classroom: A Need for Educational Leadership*. 2008.

McGee, P., *Planning for the Digital Classroom and Distributed Learning Policies and Planning for Online Instructional Resources*. 2005.

Kemker, K., *The Digital Learning Environment: What the Research Tells Us*. 2005.

Knight, A., A Digital Classroom Application Framework. 2003.

Bates, A.W., *Effective Teaching with Technology in Higher Education*. First ed. 2003

http://www.businessworld.in/article/Coronavirus-Impact-Education-Sector-Shifting-To-Digital-Learning/18-03-2020-186530/

https://www.weforum.org/agenda/2020/04/coronavirus-education-global-covid19-online-digital-learning/

2

COVID-19: AN OPPORTUNITY TO INTROSPECT

12

COVID-19: AN OPPORTUNITY TO INTROSPECT

Rumita Arora (Dr.)

> *"When you think everything is someone else' fault, you will suffer a lot,*
> *When you realise that everything springs only from yourself,*
> *You will learn both peace and joy."* – Dalai Lama.

Introduction

Covid-19, declared an international public health emergency on 30 January 2020 by World Health Organisation, has made us rethink on our priorities leading us to realise how many of our precious thoughts and concerns were quite meaningless. It has affected every aspect of our life — our education system, our thought processes, our lifestyle and the list goes on. The webinars and online classes are the natural outcome of this.

Due to the rapidly expanding mass hysteria and panic regarding Covid-19, it may beget enduring psychological problems in public from all the socio-economic domains, which could potentially be even more detrimental in the long run than the virus itself. The Covid-19 outbreak has also given rise to stigmatising factors like fear of isolation, racism, discrimination and marginalisation with all its social and economic ramifications. Often a stigmatised community tends to seek medical care late and hide important medical history.

Psycho-socio Burden of Quarantine and Isolation

Covid-19 has required many countries across the globe to implement early quarantine measures. Imposed mass quarantine applied by nationwide lockdown programme has produced mass hysteria, anxiety and distress, due to factors like sense of getting concerned and loss of control. This can be satisfied if families need separation, by uncertainty of disease progression, insufficient supply of basic essentials, financial losses, increased perception of risk, which usually get intensified by vague information and improper communications through media in the phases of a pandemic. History reveals that psychological impact of quarantine can vary from immediate effects like irritability, fear of contracting infection, anger, confusion, frustration, loneliness, denial, anxiety, depression, despair to the other extreme including suicide.

An Opportunity to Introspect

For a couple of decades now, we have imagined ourselves as travellers in a world of choices. We have played with time, a double track of online and

---

Assistant Professor, DAV College of Education for Women, Amritsar offline time, in several places at once. In fact, everyone was heading to a more successful version of oneself, consuming experiences and sensations and keeping as many options open as the apps on mobile phones. Suddenly things have changed. We find ourselves joined together across the world, in waiting for Covid-19 to reveal our future. However, it is a perverse oracle, revealing only our pasts, the disparities and distances between us and within us. Time is smiling to itself, refusing to be planned, pushing us to ask ourselves not whether time is enough, but whether we are enough for the times. Everyone is liberated from the calendar. Things have taken a 360 degree turn and some basic needs to be redefined.

Here are some popular learning outcomes to help one choose a goal during such trying times:

- *Boost employability*
  The world of work is chaotic for many right now. With new technologies and processes being created at a fast pace, closing the skill gap can give a significant advantage in career. Whether it is learning a totally new skill or improving on an existing one, it is the kind of thing that can make one stand out from the crowd.
- *Expand horizons*
  There are all kinds of hard and soft skills that one can start thinking about. Even a small amount of study can support the existing knowledge and broaden horizons. From there, one can think about the type of areas that will be most beneficial or interesting.
- *Improve understanding of world issues*
  Many of us have been gripped by the coverage of current affairs related to Covid-19, with the feed of information almost constant. However, it can sometimes be difficult to focus on global issues aside from the headlines. There are plenty of topics worth exploring that can give a more detailed understanding of the world we live in. Studying the Environment, Human rights, Ethics, Religion, can all help to give context to the current affairs.
- *Build better relationships*
  Emotional intelligence is an invaluable skill that can positively impact all areas of one's life. Similarly, improving communication skills can help in personal and professional relationships. Taking the time to work on one's own wellbeing can bring significant improvements in everyday interactions with important people in life. At this time of uncertainty, it could be just the thing we need.
- *Learn for pleasure*
  Lifelong learning is something that can bring benefits to all areas of one's life. Sometimes it is good to study something purely for the joy of learning.

Effects on Different Sections of Society

As one introspects, one realises one major overloaded issue is the psychological impact of Covid-19. It has affected different sections across the society differently.

- *Children:* During a severe pandemic like Covid-19, community based mitigation programmes such as closing of schools, parks, playgrounds disrupt children's usual lifestyle and have potentially promoted distress and confusion. Both young and older children are likely to become more demanding, having to cope up with these changes and so exhibit impatience, annoyance and hostility which in turn cause them to suffer physical and mental violence by overly pressurised parents. Stressors such as monotony, disappointment, lack of face to face contact with classmates, friends and teachers, lack of enough personal space at home and family financial losses during lockdowns, all potentially trigger troublesome and even prolonged mental consequences in children.
- *Aged people:* The notion that older adults and people with serious co-morbidities are particularly vulnerable to worse outcomes from Covid-19 can create considerable fear amongst the elderly. The older adults with cognitive decline may become much more anxious, agitated and socially withdrawn, thus their specific needs demand specific attention.
- *Marginalised community — migrants, daily wagers, slum dwellers and prisoners:* Vast majority of the world's refugees and international migrant workers (IMW) are contained in those nations where public health infrastructure is already overstretched. These people generally have a high prevalence of common psychiatric disorders like depression and poor quality of life further jeopardised by quarantine condition and lost income during Covid-19. Slum dwellers also experience constant fear of en masse eviction during this pandemic. Arguably Covid-19 has made the largest lockdown happen in the history of civilisation affecting millions of migrant workers, daily wagers and slum dwellers worldwide.
- *General public:* The general public has been extremely worried about financial restraint during lockdown. Many have experienced depressive symptoms and find it difficult to adjust with this "new normal". Long term lockdown causes unavailability of community services and collapse of many industries, leading to a negative impact on local and national economic stabilities. Reports of increasing domestic violence and women abuse are being reported globally during this pandemic.
- *People with pre-existing psychiatric illness:* Mentally challenged patients are substantially more prone to develop infectious diseases and are at considerable risk of experiencing more negative physical as well as psychological outcomes during a potentially fatal epidemic like Covid-19. Cognitive decline, poor awareness levels, impaired risk perception and

reduced concern about personal hygiene increase the chances of acquiring infection in such individuals. Psychiatric patients are also prone to develop relapses or deterioration of the pre-existing signs and symptoms.

- *Social media and Covid-19:* Within days of onset of the Covid-19 outbreak in China, the "social media panic" characterised by relentless plethora of false information as well as negatively skewed misinformation metastasised faster than the Corona virus itself. As soon as Covid-19 emerged to become a trending online content, many bloggers, groups or personal users on YouTube, WhatsApp, Facebook, Instagram and twitter started the business of making a profit of Covid's popularity in many impulsive and unpredictable courses of action. Since sensationally charged and appalling contents draw the most attention and garner the most developments on social media, several users feigned Covid-19 symptoms to gain easy popularity and thus purposefully sowed mass confusion and panic. Health care seekers have been too perplexed, catastrophised and morbidly worried about Covid-19 symptoms that the normal running of healthcare systems may get disrupted to address the mass anxiety owing to massive disinformation. All these certify the raw potential of social media during a public health disaster.

Future Directions and Conclusions

Today's self-centred, busier than ever human race could potentially appreciate home-confinement during Covid-19 as a mere opportunity to promote healthier parent-child relationships by correct parental strategies and thereby strengthen family bonding by spending more quality time together with older parents/ dependent members residing in the same household. Besides Covid-19, the 21st century is also the era of emerging pandemic of mental illnesses, psychological and social preparedness of this pandemic carries global importance. Due care needs to be taken to erase the stigma associated with disease, racism, religious propaganda and psycho-social impact. This is a time to introspect — to know yourself and to know what matters to you. Social media should be used sparingly and in good sense, to educate people on transmission dynamics and symptoms of disease. This pandemic has clearly shown us what a "virus" can negatively impact even in the 21st century and simultaneously make us realise that the greatest assets of mankind are health, peace, love, solidarity, ingenuity and knowledge.

References

https://economictimes.indiatimes.com/news/politics-and-nation/is-the-covid-19-pandemic-a-perfect-opportunity-for-humans-to-introspect/article

https://en.unesco.org/events/skills-development-during-pandemic-and-preparing-recovery-covid-19-education-webinar-8

13

INTROSPECTION TO EXCELLENCE: AN OPPORTUNITY DURING COVID-19

Gurmanjit Kaur (Dr.)[1] *and Parwinderjit Kaur (Dr.)*[2]

Introduction

Since many years, teachers have shown concern for the development of concepts, methodology and tools to align the students with their day to day activities and ultimately leading to achievement. For effective transmission of knowledge from the teacher to the student, social orientation of the student is given due importance. There is a huge diversity in the type of classrooms in our country not just at the level of physical infrastructure but it also manifests itself in different predispositions of the student to the teacher and to the delivery of the conceptual information. In teaching profession, the teachers not only manage the classrooms but are forever balancing the rigorous demands of the curriculum with their individual notions of holistic education.

With the outbreak of the novel coronavirus, technology has revolutionised the modern system of education as digital platform has opened new avenues of learning and teaching from remote places. The global pandemic has taken a massive hit on all the sectors including the education system around the world. With disruptions everywhere, several concerned scholars, citizens, politicians, and bureaucrats support the need for reimagining and reinventing the education system. This transformed and sudden switch is not only limited to private schools rather a number of government schools have also started running online classes resulting into technologically advanced environment. Hundreds of digital education tools like Edmodo, Socrative, Project, Thinglink, TED-Ed, Ck-12, Classdojo, EduClipper, Storybird, Animoto and Kahoot have been created for teachers and learners. But in many countries, students and teachers have to make bigger adjustments as at some places well equipped technological tools are not available.

The Indian Government as well as all state governments are firm to facilitate e-learning and trying to provide solutions like alternative academic calendars to make up for the loss of school hours. The entire system is being forced to work differently and act through delivery channels. This situation has provided an opportunity to work collectively towards an education system which is more agile, flexible and resistant to such global crises.

In the past decade, the government in India has focused on ensuring access to hardware and promoting digital literacy through Rashtriya Madhyamik

1. Associate Professor, Khalsa College of Education, Ranjit Avenue, Amritsar

2. Assistant Professor, Khalsa College of Education, Ranjit Avenue, Amritsar

Shiksha Abhiyan (RMSA). As smartphones are not available with almost 20% of the population, the channels like radio, television, Interactive Voice Response (IVR) and SMS, are deployed to provide age-appropriate content and instructions. But as these efforts are not enough during this pandemic, recent initiatives like NROER and e-Pathshala, have actively been promoted in the use of media in learning. Almost all states and UTs in India are leveraging SMS and IVR to provide parents with daily activities for students. While governments and schools tread along this path of uncertainty, they are starting to rely increasingly on technology to navigate through this situation prevailing in a poor country with huge population.

Self-introspection

Self-introspection is access to understand oneself. Self-reflection is a process of introspection what one has learnt, and finding answers for further growth with what one has acted upon. In the current miserable period, introspection offers a dynamic and reliable means by which professional growth of teachers can take place through the process of critical reflection. It is beneficial only when the teachers look inward and analyse the true nature of the challenge. It is perhaps an opportune moment to reflect on our lives that involves thoughtfully considering one's own experiences in applying knowledge to practice. There is a need for teachers and administrators to understand that educating students during Covid-19 is certainly no child's play, rather it is a matter of introspection at every stage. It has been observed that almost all normal-operating instructional requirements are working in a number of schools (lesson planning and submission, delivery, grading, recording). Communication with students via STVM email or via Google Meet, Zoom class is running effectively. Teachers are available for students and parents during student-contact time. Begin posts and emails with a warm and friendly introduction like video greetings or flipped video lessons are in use. Teachers are posting the answers to queries of students to come true to the expectations.

Need of Self-introspection during Covid-19

The need to self-introspection is felt as the internal conscience is a watchdog of oneself. A teacher may try to escape the external supervision of the head of the institution and inspecting authorities by a number of ways, but cannot escape the supervision of his/her own conscience. So some queries can be considered for introspection, which will enhance the process of introspection.

1. *Digital Transformation of Education System*: In a move to not let the crisis hamper the curriculum, digital transformation has become a new norm with educational institutes across the country. Many are leveraging it as a chance to be more productive and efficient while developing innovative and

improved professional skills through online learning and assessment.. To minimise the impact of the lockdown on education, various e-learning portals and apps have been launched by the government and education bodies such as DIKSHA portal, e-Pathshala, Swayam, STEM based games, etc. So the teachers here need to introspect about the benefit, he/she has taken from these programmes, if not why and how to improve in future.

2. *Attitude to Accept Major Responsibilities*: Before Covid-19 teachers were expected to be an important and responsible member of the functional groups to share administration and other functions of the institutions, possess knowledge of consultancy services and participate in professional activities outside the institute, work in inter-disciplinary field and imbibe students for social justice. But now they need to come in forefront, to understand and contribute in the new duties like developing e-content, preparing teaching material, handling software and hard ware simultaneously during on-line class, attending webinars, taking Zoom classes, Google Meets, etc. The best way is to do a self-introspection after the class. There is need to bridge the gap between Pre Covid-19, during Covid-19 and post Covid-19 duties.

3. *Requisite Knowledge of the Subject*: Many teachers are satisfied with what they had learnt before Covid-19. They forget the fact that learning is a continuous process and demand of time during the pandemic is somewhat different. Teachers need to have mastery over content taken from different technological resources in addition to prescribed books or one or two supplementary or non-detailed contents. There is need to introspect that how much time he is spending in a day for enrichment of his knowledge and competencies during Covid-19. The availability of Global Internet including online books, journals, and magazines can help the teachers in more than one way. The teachers can introspect their own efforts in the light of these availabilities.

4. *Parental Involvement*: In the past, the role of parental involvement in student learning has been minimal. This pandemic has put the onus on parents to ensure that learning continues at home, for which parents may not be adequately equipped. With access to a smartphone and internet, they now have an opportunity to access free digital content offered by multiple platforms, and help children be engaged and use their time productively. Parents should not be placed in the role of teaching and it must be taken care that students are able to carry out the tasks independently. The teachers need to continue to offer a rigorous programme of learning and assessment by providing a high level of detail for all learning experiences; specifying formative and summative assessments submission procedures (practice only, no submission; submission to Google Classroom); continuing to assess via projects and exams.

5. *Making Proper Balance in Private and Professional Duties*: All teachers are the normal social beings, facing joys and sorrows, problems and responsibilities of life. During this pandemic time they may have suffered from some family problems, health problems or any other social problems and above

all the financial crises to meet their needs. This is the time when they are expected to make proper balance in private affairs and professional duties. Here the introspection can help them to know to what extent they had been able exhibit balance in private affairs and professional duties.

6. *Working not in Isolation*: The changing global scenario demands promotion of alliance with society in order to achieve the goals of education. During Covid-19, this is the proper time to develop relevant programs after consulting the professionals, joining different associations, maintaining good relations with stakeholders and taking their opinions to decide about the important aspects of educational process. It may help the teacher to reduce burden or tension, as the people working in different fields can provide help at different levels to solve problems speedily and amicably. So this is the time when teachers need to introspect that they are going join hand with others including parents and must take care of it that they are not working in isolation.

7. *Not becoming Professionally Obsolete*: For a long time we have been talking about modern technology to come up with best results. The teacher and the student, even the toddlers have been using laptops, tablets, computers and mobiles to enhance the teaching and learning strategies. Expansion of knowledge resulting into new theories, new methodologies, new devices and new models has created a lag in the knowledge and skills. Even the knowledge gained by teachers before entering into the job becomes obsolete after a few years in the service, therefore, this is the best time for them to introspect. How much they knew about new developments, techniques and knowledge evolved in a short period of time, and how much is actually useful for them, so that they are not obsolete with the professional knowledge.

8. *Possessing Required Knowledge of ICT*: There are typically two approaches towards ICT in education. Many teachers are technophobic, and being unaware about the use of modern technology, they are unable to integrate technology into their teaching and research activities. On the other hand, some are propagated as technology vendors and push everything towards technology. Now there is need for a teacher to introspect himself/herself to adopt a balanced approach between the two extremes and examine the areas where education faces challenges that can be suitably and effectively responded to by the ICT. The teachers need to introspect that during Covid-19, which techniques they have used to keep in touch with students like Zoom classes, Google classroom, creating web-based portals and educational blogs to exchange ideas, information and experiences. The teacher can know about his/her efficiency and effectiveness of teaching-learning process through self-introspection.

9. *Teacher's Attitude*: A teacher who has positive attitude towards his profession can only bring the desirable changes in the child. Teacher should change his attitude towards his class. The establishment of good relationship between instructor and class is vitally important and determines whether the

process of learning is going to be a cooperative effort, an uneasy alliance or a cold war. Teacher's attitude must be fair, firm and friendly.

10. *Leadership Behaviour*: Today education is seen as a series of teaching, thinking, learning experiences, which serves to change student's behaviour in a specified desired manner. From the earliest times, teachers have had a hazardous and onerous task to perform, to mould the body, mind and soul. Teachers are leaders and leaders are always life-long learners. While teaching online, it is essential to have patience and compassion in any on-line classroom setting. When the teacher is dealing with behaviour problems, his/her growing relationship will be the foundation for a stable learning environment. He/she needs to keep things positive, light, and engaging. As an online teacher, one may meet disruption problems, but the teacher has to solve problems, answer questions, analyse opinions, and have open discussions. During the process a teacher should try to keep distractions to a minimum. A teacher needs to introspect whether he/she has been able to manage and address the issue in a right way, has not embarrassed any child in front of the other students, and has been able minimise the disruptions.

Moreover, the teachers can plan activities in the light of online existing programmes that are as closely related to current class content or skills. For instance, DIKSHA provides free vernacular content, backed by low bandwidth capability and strong offline functionality, so a teacher can reinforce existing understanding or introduce new content that will be continued to be covered in class. A teacher needs to introspect that all children are able to complete the learning activities properly because this is going to impact their learning and assessment.

Conclusion

In this era of knowledgeable society, a teacher would not be able to prove his/her worth without accepting the challenges. Therefore, the teacher should engage himself in self-introspection and no doubt, after self-introspecting a teacher would develop qualities of a good online teacher, who is able to motivate, having concern for students, possessing moral courage to deal with any situation, committed to profession, freshness in knowledge, free from obsolescence and having qualities of a good leader. In some institutions, administrators and managements act as anchors. To avail chances of professional leadership and new learning in such institutions is in the hands of teachers themselves only. Loss of face-to-face contact for an extended period can be an issue for some students. No doubt, a number of online instructions are evolved, but the approaches varied widely and all teachers are not able to handle these properly. Some teachers lack high-speed internet connections, too. But with all these challenges they have to prove their worth. Post-Covid-19, public education systems must use technology to ensure equal access to learning and administrative efficiency.

Refrences

Croy, N. (2012). Introspective inquiry: Self-study and its relevance in teacher education. *Journal of Purdue Undergraduate Research, 2,* 79–80.

Cai, W. (2017). Introspection of teaching contribution to safeguarding the physiological mechanism of children. https://www.alliedacademies.org/articles/introspection-of-teaching-contribution-to-safeguarding-the-physiological-mechanism-of-children.html

Eyal, N. (2019). *Here are the 4 simple introspection steps that will boost self-awareness*. https://medium.com/behavior-design/here-are-the-4-simple-intro

Ghanti, P. S. & Jagadesh (2009).Attitude of Secondary School Teachers their Teaching Profession. *Edutracks, 9*(3), 30-32.

Nuhfer, E.B. (2008). *Module 1 – Development of introspective reflection. Boot camp: Educating in fractal patterns exercises in introspective reflection*. http:/profcamp.tripod.com/BC08indiv.htm

Prasad, J. (2005). *Education and the teacher*. New Delhi: Kanishka Publishers.

Sadananthan, M., & Beraceh, K.L. Sheeba.(2009). Leadership Behavior of Teachers. *Edutracks, 9(*2).

Siddiqui, M.A., Sharma, A.K., & Arora, G.L. (2009). *Teacher education - Reflections towards policy formulation*. New Delhi: National Council of Teacher Education.

Smith, K.H. (2019). *5 Benefits of encouraging teacher self-reflection*. https://blog.irisconnect.com/us/5-benefits-of-encouraging-teacher-self-reflection

14

SELF-RELIANCE DURING LOCKDOWN

Satinder Kaur (Dr.)

Introduction

The world is at war against the pandemic of Novel Corona virus, but this is not the first time that this is happening, previous one was plague, whose catastrophic consequences were immediate death, displacement, downwind eradication for hundreds of miles and what not. Fast forward to the current situation, the corona virus pandemic is way too obvious in its consequences: death, economic collapse and recession, and an unprecedented global health crisis. The reach of disastrous events is long and unpredictable, both for better and for the worse. The bubonic collapse, according to the historians, brought the Renaissance. So, it is not wrong to think that this pandemic will bring changes — possibly big ones — that probably we are not thinking about right now.

Assistant Professor, Dev Samaj College for Women, Chandigarh

Pandemic has taken us 200 years back, where everything was swadeshi, when people used to greet each other by saying Namaste with folded hands instead of hugging and kissing as this practice may have been be one of the main reasons behind the spread of this deadly virus. Now it is time to revive our mother nature. Humans should start respecting nature because this planet belongs to everyone.

Covid-19, a deadly virus has taught us great lessons which humans have forgot in astonishing world of technology. Nations worldwide are going through a major breakthrough in economy. In the era of globalisation, privatisation and liberalisation, where the whole world is one market, nations depend on each other for their growth and development. This globalisation has led to revolution and evolution in the whole world. With the entry of foreign collaborations, most Indian private companies retreated into technology imports or collaboration. But on the other side, it has taken the strength of self-reliance from us. The whole world suffers today, it is believed because of China, the one of the leading trade partners.

After the virus breakout, we still looked towards China for test kits, masks and other medical essentials. This reliance needs to be turned into self-reliance. India has moved to cut down its trade dependency on China. There is growing din in India for boycotting trade with China.

As a remedy to this deadly virus, nations declared lockdown. The time gained by country has been used more gainfully. During this phase one has become self-reliant rather than depending on others for their work or resources. The challenges and problems thrown at us have taught us the lesson of self-reliance and self-sufficiency. We should not look for help from other nations, instead we should gain strength, ability and belief to find solutions on our own and hence become self-sufficient.

This pandemic has thrown new challenges and problems which were never imagined. But it has also taught us a lesson with a strong message to become self-sufficient and self-reliant. This is the statement of Prime Minister Narendra Modi when he addressed India's gram panchayat heads on National Panchayati Raj through video conferencing (Varma and Anuja, 2020). Dictionary meaning of self-reliance is relying on one's own powers and resources rather than those of others. And in simple words, self-reliance is to do things and make decisions by ourselves. Self-reliance could be related in two different senses. One could be at an individual level and other could be the economy as a whole.

Prime Minister in his address on 12 May 2020 announced that self-reliance would be a central policy objective and the 'new normal' for India, as the country takes first step to its exit strategy from the ongoing battle against the Coronavirus. He called this campaign as Aatman Nirbhar Bharat Abhiyaan (Self- Reliant India Movement).

Difficulties also offer opportunities. The Covid-19 crisis is one such example. There are few instances when the country like India has stepped forward on the path of self-reliance. During lockdown, Indians used this time to spread awareness about the Corona virus. Government doubled its efforts to equip hospitals with ventilators, oxygen cylinders, masks, personal protective equipment (PPE) kits and beds. The government also ramped up testing. Not only medical sector, but many business houses have stepped forward in this period of hardships to be self-reliant. The government has identified 12 sectors (food processing, organic farming, iron, aluminium and copper, agro chemicals, electronics, industrial machinery, furniture, leather and shoes, auto parts, textiles, masks, sanitisers and ventilators), where focus would be given to make India self-reliant country and a global supplier (PTI, 2020).

On the other hand, at micro or individual level, we can see that people have become more conscious about being self-sufficient and self-reliant. They are finding solutions of the daily routine problems on their own. They are fulfilling their basic needs by managing their money and resources in the most productive manner. Lockdown has provided the opportunities to such people to enhance their inner qualities and skills which will, for sure, help them in future in some or the other ways.

Earlier, all those who were not into doing their own chores and were habitual of taking help of housemaids or servants, now they are also doing their work without anyone's help. Amidst lockdown, many birthdays and anniversaries were celebrated but this time cakes were not ordered but they were self-made at home and snacks were prepared at home. Also, the doubt for usage of preservatives and hygiene is clear. People are cleaning their homes themselves. This is a step towards making children responsible and self-reliant. Parents are helping their children to study, making them understand their concepts. Also, there is a slight shift of concern towards fitness. All those who are not able to go to gym are exercising at their home. Education is also the other department which is affected by this pandemic. Government is suggesting schools and universities to take online classes but in India, online study is not possible for many students. In many areas, students are facing network issues and some even do not know about the devices like laptops and smartphones fully due to lack of resources. Students who belong to rural areas are incapable of online education due to lack of facilities and awareness. Government has made arrangements by broadcasting educational TV channels through various platforms free of cost. The teachers, not aware about many of the online applications, are making efforts to cope with the situation and updating themselves with online teaching.

This is a God-sent opportunity for India with our demographics and abundance of talent. As the adage goes, necessity is the mother of invention. Self-reliance not only comes from industrialisation but also from localisation. Dalit women farmers in Telangana used to face hunger and deprivation. But today they are contributing food grains for pandemic relief. Farmers in Tamil Nadu-Karnataka border have been sending organic produce to Bengaluru even during lockdown (Kothari, 2020).

Over the last three months, the government has committed to the creation of 7200 new self-help groups for the urban poor where over 30 million masks and 1,20,000 litres of sanitisers were produced thus creating employment opportunities (Yadav, 2020).

India therefore has an all-new hash tag in the era of Covid: VocalForLocal, i.e. Go local, Trust local, Go for a self-sufficient and self-reliant India (Bijoor, 2020).

We have learnt a lesson that we have to be self-reliant and self-sufficient and should not look outside for our problems. We should not depend on others for fulfilling our needs. The public health emergency has validated this by reducing dependency on China for critical goods — from active pharmaceutical ingredients (APIs) to personal protection equipment (PPEs) for medical professionals (Singh, 2020).

The lessons which we can learn from this crisis are — working on our skills, working on our positive and unexplored side, working on our family relations, working on our hobbies, working on learning something new. Self-reliance is what we need to do. As we cannot go outside, we should focus on going inside. Lockdown is for everyone but happy will be those who take it in a positive way. Like cooking is something that everyone should know and one should try learning it during this period.

Adding to this why only self-reliance, there are various lessons which need to be learnt by our country. India is a developing country. There are certain things which we still lack such as proper education facilities that contain both online and offline teaching methods. There are facilities of online teaching and we need to focus on improving it further for future, so that education of students does not suffer. Also, as we can see everyone has been allotted work from home, internet facilities are still not up to mark in our country. The internet connectivity in some parts of our country is very weak and internet buffering is one of the major issues during this pandemic that definitely needs to be taken in consideration. Also, the medical sector, which literally crashed during second Covid wave, is still underdeveloped So proper medical facilities need to be provided and more hospitals need to be opened up.

India has started moving towards a self-reliant but what the government and the citizens of the nation have to keep in mind is to continue to follow this exercise even after the post-lockdown period. India is a country which is not only self-sufficient in its natural resources but in its human resources as well. So now it is the right time for India to manage its natural and human resources in the best possible way. We should now learn to do more with less in terms of efforts, technology, resources and time.

Being self-reliant does not mean that the country will completely eliminate foreign companies, but will develop several MSME. When pandemic started, India did not produce a single PPE kit, but due to urgency and slow rate of imports forced India to produce kits here and now lakhs of PPE kits are being produced on daily basis. India has been on the road to protect its self-reliant strategy. Notwithstanding the disastrous pandemic, we will ultimately win though with a change in lifestyle, new economic order, behaviour and social systems. This crisis should be taken as an opportunity to reform.

Conclusion

This pandemic is resultant of human exploitation of the nature. Now it is time to revive our mother nature. It not only comes with the message that homo sapiens need to define limits to how they treat The Mother Earth, but also that it is high time we work towards sustainable development through judicious use of resources. The world needs to come together to attain this goal but we should not forget that, the need to become self-sufficient remains intact. To be able to fight anything should be our potential. To be able to protect everyone is what we should seek.

References

Bijoor, H., 'Self-reliant India: The bounce of vocal for local', www.newindianexpress.com, May 26, 2020.

Kothari, A., 'What does self-reliance really mean? Amazing stories emerge from India's villages', www.thehindu.com, July 5, 2020.

Luthra, G., 'Driving self-reliance while combating a pandemic,' www.orfonline.org, May 19, 2020.

Mathur, S.K and Paul, A., 'India's trade depending on China is huge. Covid-19 and India's trade dependency on China: Should we continue our ties?', www.economictimes.com), June 13, 2020.

PTI, 'Aatmanirbhar Bharat! Twelve sector's in which India can become self-reliant, global supplier', www.financialexpress.com May 21, 2020.

Singh, A.K., 'Corona's biggest lesson is to be self-reliant, says PM Modi', www.timesofindia.com, April 25, 2020.

Varma and Anuja, 'Biggest lesson from Covid-19 is to be self-reliant, says PM Modi', www.livemint.com, April 24, 2020).

Yadav, B., 'The lockdown worked. It helped battle Covid-19, turn India self-reliant', www.hindustantimes.com), June 25, 2020.

3

MORAL RESPONSIBILITIES OF TEACHERS DURING PANDEMIC

15

RESPONSIBILITIES OF TEACHERS DURING PANDEMIC

Surinder Kaur (Dr.)

Introduction

The global emergency of the Covid-19 pandemic confronts us all with unpredictable, disruptive situations which have changed our daily life. Important changes have been made in terms of online teaching, admission and exam schedules. Just as the pandemic has changed the dynamics of learning for students, it has also impacted methods of teaching. Whether they are tech-savvy or not, teachers have been shaken up overnight and forced to upgrade their pedagogical and communication tools. Even in urban areas, internet connectivity can be patchy. Not all homes may have multiple internet connections or a laptop or phone to spare, which can be used exclusively, or even uninterruptedly, by a school-going child. The problem becomes magnified if there are several school-going children in a family. The teaching profession has no doubt, been at the forefront in adapting to this change. We have seen so many innovative means followed by the teachers to reach out to the students. These innovative means could not have been useful if the students would not have participated in this exercise. We have to appreciate our students and parents for their active participation. Teachers may be better than parents in addressing emotional and psychological challenges of students in deprived situations. So the moral responsibility of teachers during pandemic is to manage the educational consequences of this crisis.

Parents Need Help

Parents are already putting a lot of pressure on themselves regarding their children's education. They are asked to teach and facilitate learning at home, which can become a major source of stress. So in this crisis situation, teachers must therefore be especially attentive to parents and respond to their concerns.

Reducing Social Inequalities

Inequalities among students must be identified and addressed, both in terms of basic needs, such as food and security, and educational needs. During this situation students may suffer from the lack of social interaction provided by school, it is desirable to provide opportunities for them to connect with their classmates and teachers by forming virtual discussion groups or offering interactive learning platforms.

Professor, Khalsa College of Education, Ranjit Avenue, Amritsar

Providing Varied Resources

Digital resources can be an aid to learning, but also a barrier. Not all families necessarily have access to these technological tools like internet, computer, television, telephone. They also do not have the same level of knowledge and skills in the use of technology. This can lead to further inequalities among students. It is, therefore, necessary to ensure that all students have access to sufficient resources to maintain their learning. Teacher support is absolutely necessary to make all aims a reality. Government initiatives to maintain student learning cannot be effective without teachers.

Take Care of Each Other

Teachers are teaching through online mode which is a smart solution and much needed. Full equality may not be possible as technological conditions vary too much, but all possible efforts are made to promote equal treatment. So for this we need to start by supporting each other, our students, and their families. As we work together, we not only need to focus on student learning, but also on the overall well-being of our colleagues through empathy, honesty, and generosity.

To Cater Diversity

We know that every student is different. We also know that teaching a class with a variety of languages, cultures, abilities, and identities enriches the experience for all learners. In online classrooms, this is great challenge for teachers to recognise the unique strengths and needs of every student by providing both high challenge and support. This is the responsibility of teachers to recognise the need to collaborate across borders and boundaries, to share what works and what does not. As teachers pay attention to linguistic diversity in their classes, they can rely on the global education community to help provide options for students.

Translating Learning Expectations

In addition, teachers should set clear and realistic goals, which should come from education ministries, and tailor these for each child. This action by teachers is particularly important for the most vulnerable students and their parents, with whom it is important to communicate regularly and make frequent assessments of their situation.

Raise Awareness

In response to the Covid-19 pandemic, teachers have needed to abruptly transition their lessons from physical classrooms to distance learning platforms. For this teachers should raise awareness among students and parents for the use of online learning platform. Teachers should attach great importance to online teaching, actively guide students, organise students in this class to do online learning.

Build Trust in the Classroom

To build trust in the classroom, teacher should repeat some of the lessons taught in class especially for those students who are missing the classroom environment; this will probably help to activate their memory of being part of a community and remind them that they are still part of one.

Engage in Self-Care

Self-care of students is very important. Once they have achieved some balance by addressing their physical and emotional needs, then they will be able to face challenges with a degree of calm and confidence. By maintaining balance in the life, they can practice self-care activities during times of crisis. When students see our calm and well-being, they are likely to be better able to imagine doing these things themselves.

Encourage Innovation

This is moral responsibility of teachers to encourage the students to develop innovative and creative thinking abilities for student's autonomous learning. Choices are an important key to unlocking access for all students in a virtual classroom. Universal Design for Learning (UDL) is a framework that helps teachers to plan for multiple means of engagement, multiple modes of representations, and multiple ways for students to take action or express themselves.

Conclusion

The outbreak of Corona virus disease (Covid-19) has been declared a Public Health Emergency of International Concern (PHEIC) and the virus has now spread in many countries and territories. The protection of children and educational facilities is particularly important. Precautions are necessary to prevent the potential spread of Covid-19 in the community. Teachers have a unique insight into the challenges being faced by the students and some of them are being quite innovative and resourceful during this time. So the moral responsibility of the teachers is to know the needs of their students well and help them effectively.

References

Ahmad, T. *Social and Moral Responsibility of the Individuals, Governments, and the Protection of Human Rights in the Coronavirus Pandemic* (Covid-19). (2020, April 15). Available at https://ssrn.com/abstract=3576237.https://doi.org/10.2139/ssrn.3576237

Arvisais, O. Martineau, M.D., & Charland, P. (2020, April 28). A shout-out to teachers: Why their expertise matters in the coronavirus pandemic, and always. *The Conversation.*https://theconversation.com/a-shout-out-to-teachers-why-their-expertise-matters-in-the-coronavirus-pandemic-and-always-136575.

Dove, M.G., & Honigsfeld, A. (2018). *Co-teaching for English learners: A guide to collaborative planning, instruction, assessment, and reflection.* CA: Corwin Press.

Held, V. (2006). *The ethics of care.* Oxford University Press.

Laurillard, D. (2002). *Rethinking University Teaching.* Routledge.

Liu, Y., Gayle, A.A., Wilder-Smith, A., & Rocklöv, J. (2020). The reproductive number of Covid-19 is higher compared to SARS coronavirus. *Journal of Travel Medicine, 27* (2), 1-4. https://doi.org/10.1093/jtm/taaa021

Reich, J., Buttimer, C.J., Fang, A., Hillaire, G., Hirsch, K., Larke, L.R., ...Slama, R. (2020, April 2). Remote Learning Guidance From State Education Agencies During the Covid-19 Pandemic: A First Look. https://doi.org/10.35542/osf.io/437e2

Salmon, G. (2002). *E-tivities.* Routledge Falmer.

16

MORAL RESPONSIBILITIES OF TEACHERS DURING PANDEMIC

Vani Datt Sharma (Dr.)

> "If a country is to be corruption free and become a nation of beautiful minds I strongly feel, there are three key societal members who can make a difference, they are the father, the mother and the teacher."
>
> — APJ Abdul Kalam, former President of India.

Introduction

In March 2020, the news shook the world, especially the academicians, that educational institutions would remain shut down for an indefinite period. For students it might be a pleasant news as of holidays for them and lockdown was of no concern in any manner initially and it was taken as if educational institutions would reopen after short lockdown. The global emergency of the Covid-19 pandemic confronted us all with unpredictable, disruptive situations which have changed our daily lives, economies, political decisions

Assistant Professor, Department of Political Science, Guru Nanak National College for Women, Nakodar

and universities working. A lot has been discussed and is still under discussion through webinars, social media, and talks on the repercussions of Covid-19 has had on economy, social, political, environment, health and so on but being a teacher, I feel that it has adversely affected upon our students and moreover on our present educational system. The current impact of the pandemic on education has made them difficult to even assess the effects in the long run. So in this grim circumstance all the stakeholders of educational institutions must perform their responsibilities and face the challenges and identify and avail the opportunities. In this present scenario, a teacher has to perform his moral responsibility towards society, family, state, educational institutions, students, etc. impartially and boldly. A teacher's job is to provide quality education to all students because they have a daily influence on the lives of children as the teachers are often held to high standards. In the midst of all of their responsibilities, they are required to serve as strong role models and demonstrate ethical behaviours when they interact with students, colleagues, parents and others.

The role of a teacher is much more than a tutor in the educational institution and in classrooms and it has changed to act as a moral guide as well. A student has a life beyond the classroom too. A teacher is a moulder and sculptor who with his skill and talent gives shape to the sculpture, plays a vital role as moral guide and paves the direction to the student's dreams and aspirations.

Education is a process of all round development of an individual — physical, intellectual, emotional, social, moral and spiritual. The teacher is expected to function not only as facilitator for acquisition of knowledge but also as inculcator of values and transformer of inner being. Ancient Indian Education was value based. Vivekananda has asserted:

"Education is not the amount of information put into your brain and runs riot there, undigested all your life. We must have life building, man making, and character making assimilation of ideas. The ideal, therefore, is that we must have the whole education of our country spiritual and secular, in our own hands and it must be on national methods as far as practical."

Education plays the greatest part in a democracy. Teachers have to train and mould the minds of our young people so as to make them worthy citizens of our democratic state. Whatever training they give them will change the society. That change will make for a better and healthier world. A tremendous responsibility rests upon the teachers.

A teacher can be a friend, a philosopher and a mentor who maintains the moral fabric of the society, nurtures the voice of sanity, empathy and peace and plays an important role in infusing sense of moral responsibility in the future makers of the society. Children begin the first perception of their life by their parents and teachers. Thus, teachers occupy an important space and time in the whole life of a student and undoubtedly he is a student's greatest concern and encouragement. A student learns or gains knowledge of academic, basic and valuable life lessons from his mentor. As a role model, a teacher must follow professional code of ethics which ensures to inculcate the values as fairness, honesty, truthfulness, and uncompromising education among the students itself. At the heart of education is a teacher who believes society is their responsibility. Their commitment to a student's future is the greatest gift of God in educational field and he can make the world a better place and brighten the future mission and vision of all the students.

As we are aware that Covid-19 pandemic has made us all to face toughest and challenging time and to the government affecting almost all spheres of life. During this alarming situation, we are facing multiple challenges of life, curtailed liberty, economy, trade, basic needs, employment, health, etc. in which education is the most affected factor because the pandemic has seriously affected the life and the teaching-learning process of several millions of students and academicians globally. Today we are imparting online education to our students at all levels to ensure their learning standards. Online learning is not to be confined to the delivery of course content by faculty to students rather it is a preferred medium of communication among students and must be opened up to our digital citizens as well. Colleges and universities along with other civic organisations are laboratories for what we want to become as a progressive society. Beyond the electronic connection we as teachers need to connect morally and emotionally during stress, anxiety and uncertainty. Character building and self-reliance are becoming important part of academic education.

Technology has opened a new window and path of new learning avenues and change the course of education. Online teaching is a smart solution and is much needed. Smart learning, e-learning, e-books, and e-library, innovative teaching methods have taken over the old college classrooms' culture besides changing student-teacher relationship. Many universities have developed creative solutions at short notice, but complaints about educational inequality, especially in developing countries, are increasing. Whatever India will be in the next generation will depend upon what teachers do to their students today in the e-classrooms. Today's children in school will start working and shouldering their responsibilities in the beginning of the next century. Teachers have to inculcate the sense of loyalty and responsibility and must help to remove from their minds whatever is negative and weakening in them. Our past history gives us some good and some bad; we have to eliminate what is bad and strengthen what is good.

Teaching and learning is a two way process. So both students and teachers are two sides of the same coin and both have their own strength and capabilities to overcome the situation at all levels. The moral development of students does not depend on the explicit character of educational efforts but on the maturity and ethical capacities of the adults with whom they interact especially parents, teachers and other community adults. Teacher-students' relationship shapes students' moral development through their influence on their emotional development. Teachers have to educate students on the need to recognise the equality of men and women in our democracy, to discard all caste discriminations and pride, untouchability, and communal distinctions and antagonisms, and to strengthen 'the dignity of the individual and the unity of the nation', as per spirit of our constitution.

A teacher helps students learn the academic basics; teach valuable life lessons by performing as their role model. The main responsibility is to train their students and define their role in students' lives. He must demonstrate integrity, impartiality and ethical behaviour in the e-classes and in their conduct with elders. Teachers have responsibility of building strong character traits such as perseverance, honesty, respect, lawfulness, patience, fairness, responsibility and unity. Today at present situation, it is the prime duty of a teacher to ensure that their teaching methods are up-to-date, fresh, relevant and comprehensive and must engage in educational research to continuously upgrade their teaching strategies. There must be a positive attitude, team centric mindset for the healthy relationship with the students during these present circumstances.

Students must recognise the difference between safe and being comfortable. They must feel safe but discomfort will help them learn and grow. During present condition of pandemic, modern India has ushered into the age of digital studentship. Under these circumstances, we can no longer treat our classrooms for imparting of information. We must transform our classrooms as chat rooms and twitter feed into theatre of engaged democracy.

Few steps must be adopted by a teacher towards their students such as: to shift the schedule according to new situation as we know change is a part of life; continue to provide moral support to our students; repeat lessons that has already been taught in class especially for those who are missing classroom environment — this will help activate their interest and memory; behaviour must be cordial, patience, optimistic, hopeful, cooperation etc.; must create student groups for interaction and discussion; discuss about Covid-19 and address their fears, misconceptions and misunderstandings about present circumstances of pandemic situation.

Students have missed their classes and academics so a teacher must create an environment to encourage them to learn about their non-academic lines — hobbies, sports, mental aptitude, and general awareness to come out of their stress and fear in this uncertain situation. A teacher must make their students realise that their teacher can also be a guide for them and if they need any help and support they can reach them at any time. This adverse situation has affected all at every levels so now we have to play the role of warriors to lend any kind of support and cooperation to our students and their families. It is the teacher who has long-lasting impact on students in their whole life and can help mould student's ideals and define for them a moral framework for the rest of their lives. By this manner they can nurture the future generations of youngsters. For teachers, students matter the most rewarding commitment to their profession. Teachers must wholeheartedly commit to their noble profession. It is our responsibility, rather moral responsibility, as teachers to design lesson plans, test plans, create learning environment that appeals to wide range of students and to make them continue learning according to academic requirements, cater to their needs and career developments. We must emphasise on research, new teaching methodology/techniques, up-to-date recent technical advancements, and digital knowledge for the students ensuring them with best relevant and comprehensive learning. Teacher education has downplayed the teacher's role as a transmitter of social and personal values and emphasised other areas such as teaching techniques, strategies, models and skills. Thus, the mission and vision of education and future prospects of learning rely upon the teachers who are the real makers, moulders, role models of the society so they have to fulfil all the needs and requirements of the students in this present scenario facing at global level. Teachers have to train and mould the minds of our young people so as to make them worthy citizens of our democratic state. Whatever training they give them will change the society. That change will make for a better and healthier society. This is our world, we belong to it; we are responsible for its development and welfare, and we are going to convert our work into dedicated service to our fellow citizens. To prepare better citizens is essential. Moral strength is much stronger than mental, physical strength. Despite all this, at the heart of education is a teacher who believes that society is their responsibility. The role of a teacher as a moral guide is pivotal and deserves nothing less than immense gratitude. Let us again be proud of being in this noble profession.

References

https://ethics.harvard.edu/files/center-for-ethics/files/17educationalethics.pdf

https://www.universityworldnews.com/post.php?story=20200410080845845

https://www.oecd.org/education/Supporting-the-continuation-of-teaching-and-learning-during-the-COVID-

https://www.search-institute.org/social-responsibility/

https://hundred.org/en/collections/quality-education-for-all-during-coronavirus

https://www.justiceinschools.org/event/educational-ethics-during-global-pandemic-discussion-group-research-

https://www.education.gov.gy/web/index.php/teachers/tips-for-teaching/item/2738-professional-code-of-e

17

TEACHERS AND MORAL RESPONSIBILITIES: COVID-19 PANDEMIC PERIOD

Jyotsna Sharma

Introduction

With worldwide crisis of the Covid-19, significant changes have been made regarding online education and admission and exam schedules, and have mixed conversations about what post-corona virus college/university scene may resemble. In the midst of all the vulnerability and stun, colleges are obliged to adhere to their essential qualities and moral duties, which provide scholastics a feeling of guidance and believability. Corona virus lead disease (Covid-19) pandemic has not only made us all face the toughest time in the last 80 years but also to the governments affecting almost all other spheres of life. During these troublesome times, we have different difficulties of life, freedom, business, commerce, trade, food, education, and it is normal to fall into state of mood swings, depression, nervousness, fear, anxiety and at times even self-destruction.

Education is the one of the most hit sectors because of the Covid-19 pandemic. It has seriously affected the teaching-learning process of several million students and faculty globally. As per UNICEF monitoring, 153 nations are presently executing across the nation terminations and 29 are actualising nearby terminations, affecting about 98.5 per cent of the world's understudy population. Eight nations' schools are right now open (UNICEF, 2020). It is a crucial time for education sector as all the institutions are closed and this closure is disrupting the education of more than 285 million young learners in India (Choudhary, 2020).

In times of crisis, schools provide children with a sense of stability and normalcy and ensure children have a routine and are emotionally supported to cope with a transforming situation. Schools also provide important aspects for children and their families to know about hygiene, proper hand washing techniques, and adjusting with situations that will break routines. Without access to schools, this prime responsibility falls on parents, guardians, and care-givers. When schools are closed, government agencies should step in to provide clear and accurate public health information through appropriate media. Current school terminations have added to the time that most understudies as of now spend at home throughout the mid-year months without

---

Assistant Professor, Khalsa College of Education, G.T. Road, Amritsar

face-to-face instructions and guidance from teachers. Meanwhile, teachers are scrambling to adapt content for an online platform and parents are juggling work responsibilities (if not joblessness) with caring for and educating their own children. Students themselves are faced with isolation, anxiety about the deadly virus, and uncertainty about the future.

Without access to education, as shocks are experienced – including loss of life, health impacts and loss of livelihoods – children are more vulnerable and unprotected. As household finances are being strained and needs increase, out-of-school children are more likely to be exposed to risks like family violence, child labour, forced marriage, trafficking and exploitation, including by responders. For the most vulnerable children, education is lifesaving. Not only does it provide safety and protection, importantly, it also instils hope for a brighter future (ECW, 2020). So proceeding with education through alternative learning pathways, at the earliest opportunity, should likewise be the main concern at the present time, to guarantee the interruption to education is as constrained as could be expected under the circumstances. We urgently need to support teachers, guardians/parental figures, innovators, communication experts and each one of the individuals who are positioned to give education, regardless of whether through radio projects, home schooling, internet learning and other inventive methodologies.

Away from their school, day-cares, or routine outings, children are feeling helpless and discomfort for they do not have an idea when this mayhem will be over and when they can return to normal days. Without playgrounds and friends, they are in a state of frustration. For older kids it is quite easy because they have the maturity level to understand and level their anxieties. When children are stressed, their bodies respond in a different way like by screaming, hiding, becoming sad, etc. (Saxena & Saxena, 2020). To help them cope with these responses, it is the responsibility of teacher to acknowledge their feelings and should do the following activities:

1. *Preparing the Children to deal with Pandemic*: When the children are stressed, their bodies respond in a different way like screaming, hiding, becoming sad, etc. To assist them with adapting to these responses, it is imperative to recognise their emotions and include them in various exercises like — reading books, engaging in art and craft, helping parents in daily chores, exercise and yoga to remain fit, meditation and spiritual talks to remain emotionally balanced, practising mindfulness, gardening to remain close to nature, searching online learning options, writing stories and poems, playing indoor games with family members, listening stories from parents and grandparents, etc. We need to teach our children that we have to tackle the situation by our positive approach, so that our children should strengthen themselves.

2. *Behavioural Management of Children*: As per the information circulating through the media, the risk of exposure to Covid-19 is low in children as compared to adults. Immature children with less understanding of the situation are more susceptible to behavioural changes that disrupt their daily lives. Therefore, supporting them and protecting their behaviour is necessary by people close to them not only during pandemic but also post-pandemic. Children watch and interpret on their own and are easily carried away by the reactions of their parents, peers, teachers and other community members, so we have to learn to guard our behaviour first in order to prevent turbulence in budding minds.
3. *Take Care of Each Other*: Above all else, we should recognise this new ordinary is not typical. As individuals we appear to be more defenceless than any other time in recent memory. As educators, this time we truly do not have all the appropriate responses. What we do have, be that as it may, is one another. Physical distancing cannot and should not mean professional isolation. Just the opposite: we need to start by supporting each other, our students, and their families. As we work together, we not only need to focus on student learning, but also on the overall well-being of our colleagues through empathy, honesty, and generosity. As we collaborate with colleagues, we can offer social-emotional support and lead honest conversations about what works and what does not in this new learning environment. We can share everything: teacher-created materials, freely available resources, course content, successes, challenges, and even total fails.
4. *Update the knowledge of the students with facts about Pandemic*: It is the responsibility of the teachers to keep their students updated with the facts and attend to their queries in a calm and polite way. The fears and anxieties of the children can be reduced by providing scientific facts and sharing accurate information about Covid-19. It is not an easy task to make children understand the acuteness of the pandemic so easily. They can learn best when correct sequence of knowledge is imparted to them. Based on reliable sources such as UNICEF and the World Health Organization, the preschool children should be engaged in some activities to make them understand the protocols of their safety during any pandemic, like hand washing, social distancing, avoiding handshakes, using handkerchief during cough and sneeze, etc. The secondary school children can be asked to form their own groups and portals to increase the awareness among their peers, families, and other community members through posters, public demonstrations, discussions to encourage them to express and communicate their feelings.
5. *Dealing with stress and depression in children during pandemic*: The countries as well as the global institutions need to put their hands

together to help each other for securing world peace and prosperity (UNESCO, 2020). To deal with the stress among children, various programmes need to be organised with the involvement of youth to understand their perspective and behavioural aspect to deal and confront future pandemics. We have to remember that together we can and will come out of any adverse situation.

6. *Ensuring mental well-being*: Activities like meditation, group prayers, reading spiritual and motivational stories, and singing spiritual or motivational songs can help out to release stress of an individual. The novel aspect of technology such as television, the Internet, and smartphone can also play an important role in delivering face-to-face support and training required during critical situations.
7. *Translate learning expectations*: Teachers need to set clear and realistic goals for educating the children during this pandemic. For teachers, this action is particularly important for the most vulnerable students and their parents, with whom it is important to communicate regularly and make frequent assessments of their situation. Teachers also need to strategically reduce their expectations for all students and identify a few specific areas they want students to focus on, while ensuring that expectations are clear on both sides. It is also possible to plan various tasks and activities to allow students to work at their own pace, on their own initiative or according to their areas of interests.
8. *Reduce social inequalities*: Inequalities among students must be identified and addressed, both in terms of basic needs, such as food and security, and educational needs. Again, the involvement of teachers is essential to ensure that social inequalities are reduced. Researches have shown that almost all students, and even more so vulnerable students, experience a drop in school performance or a delay in learning when they are out of school for long periods of time. Therefore, it is very crucial for the teachers to follow up with their students and identify their specific needs to maintain appropriate learning. Since students may suffer from the lack of social interaction provided by school, it is desirable to provide opportunities for them to connect with their classmates and their teacher by organising virtual discussion groups or offering interactive learning platforms.
9. *Provide various resources for learning*: Digital resources basically act as an aid to learning, but also act as a barrier. Not all families necessarily have the same access to the technological tools like internet, computer, television, telephone, etc. They also do not have the same level of knowledge and skills in the use of technology. This can lead to further inequalities among students. It is therefore necessary to ensure that all students have access to sufficient resources to

maintain their learning. The idea is not to set aside all digital learning platforms, but there is a need for various solutions that are stable and less vulnerable to breakdowns and technical difficulties. These might include mailing, talking on the phone and educational radio or TV. Teacher support is absolutely necessary to make these aims a reality. Government initiatives to maintain student learning cannot be effective without the use of an invaluable educational resource: the expertise of teachers.

10. *Co-relate lessons, resources, and communication*: Most teachers are in the process of building an entirely new online learning ecosystem, or, in the best-case scenario, repurposing an online platform that used to complement face-to-face teaching before the novel Corona virus related school closures. Since there are so many resources available, teachers often utilise a combination of multiple apps, media, websites, and teacher-created content. This can get overwhelming fast. In order to avoid fragmentation or confusion, teachers can build connections across resources, activities, and lessons.

As, basically, cognizant instructors, educators comprehend the social truth of their understudies comparative with the world and hence together can help change it, for the improvement of understudies' lives as well as for the nature of their families, and the communities they serve. This basic viewpoint possibly changes an instructor from the conventional role model to social change agent. All of our theoretical goals for preparing teachers to work as a social justice conscientious educators are being tested by the pandemic environment. In this environment, the responsibility of the teacher is to cater to the needs of their students morally, emotionally, intellectually, socially, etc.

Conclusion

Teachers are catapulted into dealing directly to serve students through process, expected to integrate the creation of values and constantly use diligent and skilful use of reasoning in all aspects of teaching. As educators explore their lead on moral and social needs, learning as a regular process, must focus on the significance of personal decision-making, conduct, and belief. Since most schools are currently functioning online in order to practice *social distancing, for the health and safety* of students, teachers face new realities dealing directly with students in their efforts designing protocols for teaching and learning. During Covid-19, children with mental trauma should be dealt in a very effective way to strengthen them emotionally and morally. Teachers have to ensure our children that they have to evolve as fighters in any disaster and come out as winners.

References

Choudhary, R. (2020). *Covid-19 blessing in disguise for Indian education sector.* Retrieved on 25 July 2020 from https://eduvoice.in/covid-19-blessing-in-disguise-for-indian-education-sector/

ECW. (2020). *Covid-19 and education in emergencies.* Retrieved on 25 July 2020 from https://www.educationcannotwait.org/covid-19/

Fisher, D., Wilder-Smith, A. (2020). *The global community needs to swiftly ramp up the response to contain Covid-19.* Lancet. Retrieved on 25 July 2020 from https://doi.org/10.1016/S0140-6736(20)30679-6

Honigsfeld, A., & Nordmeyer, J. (2020). Teacher collaboration during a global pandemic. *Educational Leadership*, *77*(10), 47-50.

Saxena, R., & Saxena, S.K. (2020). Preparing Children for Pandemics. In *Coronavirus Disease 2019 (Covid-19)* (pp. 187-198). Springer, Singapore.

United Nations Education Scientific and Cultural Organization (2020). Covid-19 Educational Disruption and Response. Retrieved on 20 May 2020 from https://en.unesco.org/covid19/educationresponse

United Nations Education Scientific and Cultural Organization (2020). Amidst global school closures UNESCO's Futures of Education initiative receives strong support. https://en.unesco.org/news/amidst-global-school-closures-unescos-futures-education-initiative-receives-strong-support. Retrieved on 26 July 2020

4

SOCIAL DISTANCING V/S WELLNESS AND MENTAL HEALTH OF YOUTH

18

MINDING THE MIND TO COMBAT WITH COVID-19

Bindu Sharma (Dr.)

Introduction

Covid-19, Corona virus, Pandemic, and lockdown — these are all that everyone is talking about these days. In a hyper connected world where news gets relayed in real time, the information overload flooding our sensory pathways is unavoidable and we have all felt that silver of cold steel twists into us — fear. While everyone is talking about physical aspects of the global health crisis and steps to protect themselves from the virus, few seem to be talking about the elephant in the room — anxiety.

An evolutionary tool meant to serve the preservation of life, modern civilisation has seen anxiety being branded as a sign of lack of mental strength. The false paradigms of mental strength and weakness have done great disservice to human beings, stigmatising mental disorders, inter alia. The contrived pressure to be strong has stigmatised the most basic of human emotions — distress. And if there ever was any right time to break these molds of social artifice, it is now.

The times that we are living in, the way the world has been for the last few months are not ordinary by any stretch of imagination. We are all, perhaps, living the most realistic portrayal of a dystopian fiction we may have seen or read. People have become more actually aware of their own mortality and that of their loved ones. Globalisation and increased domestic mobility have also resulted in families and loved ones being separated by geography, and the resultant feeling of isolation has been amplified by the self-imposed embargo on the movement of people that most countries have had to enter into in order to contain the spread of the virus.

Given the egregiousness of Covid-19, and its numerous direct and indirect fallouts, it is only natural to feel distressed, anxious, or even show signs of anxiety or depression disorders. The whole world is grieving for the loss of life all around us, and mostly, for the way we used to be because we all know that the world has changed forever. Hearing about the increasing number of patients and spread of virus has been definitely anxiety-evoking for many prone to anxiety. Other questions — How long will it last? Will there be enough ventilators and beds at the time of peak infection? If the government has improved health facilities or just given false reassurance amounting to zilch?

Moreover, the anxictics people will face when they return to work are:

- Continuing fear about an unseen foe which could infect them and their family members.

Assistant Professor, Khalsa Collegc of Education, G.T. Road, Amritsar

- Stress hormone rises in times of uncertainty, leading to unexpected anxiety, depression and fatigue.
- Neglect of self-care and ensuring worsening of existing illness, along with depression for those living alone.
- Absenteeism from work.
- Fear of losing job and an uncertain financial future.
- Worries about family members for those working away from home.

Many in quarantine have been reporting anxiety, low mood, and the feeling of insecurity which may persist for months. The feeling of testing positive and complete isolation can be daunting.

Coping with Stress and Anxiety

Following are some quick tips to cope up with stress:

- *Remain physically fit and active*: A sound mind lives in a sound body. Especially in the time of curfews and lockdowns when the whole world is passing through a phase of mental stress, it is very important to take care of our physical health. It will serve two purposes — one to develop immunity to fight against the virus and secondly to retain our mental health. Physical activity can be a good stress buster. Involve yourself in constructive activities like reading, cooking, cleaning, listening to music, etc.
- *Re-connect*: All the human beings are social beings. They cannot live in isolation. They feel comfortable in the company of others — family members, friends, relatives, colleagues, etc. Company of someone is a great moral support for all of us. During this pandemic when we all are confined to our homes, it is the right time to re-connect and communicate with old friends and relatives with whom we were not able to connect because of busy life. It will rejuvenate us and help us to cope up with stress and boredom.
- *Help others*: Helping people who are old and living alone gives a sense of satisfaction and solace to mind. Kindness, especially towards others less fortunate or in adverse position in the power hierarchy, may be just the one essential step in the redemption of society from the ravages of this multipronged pandemic. It will in turn help us to overcome adverse thoughts and feelings and help us to retain good mental health.
- *Exercise*: Exercise plays a vital role in enhancing immunity. So, in the present time, there is a great need to improve our immune system to fight against Covid-19. So, exercise well to boost your mood and immunity.
- *Be mindful*: In today's fast life, it is very common in our day-to-day life that we are doing one particular thing, while our mind is over-occupied with many other things also. But from the present situation of lockdown, we can learn to become mindful and enjoy each and every activity of our life. It will provide us peace and solace and help in improving our mental

health. Be fully involved in the activity we are doing. When we go for a walk, be mindful of things around you — trees, birds, air, sun, etc.

- *Maintain a routine*: Routine in life is very important. It makes our life organised and systematic, otherwise we may not be able to accomplish our set targets of the day. And this will lead to anxiety and stress. Especially in this crucial time of lockdown, there is a need to set daily routines to make our life comfortable and systematic. People who pray daily, exercise and do chores are able to keep off stress better.
- *Accept*: Good mental health includes acceptance — acceptance that everything is not under our control. At this point of time, survival is vital, perhaps the only thing that matters. It would be immensely useful to remember that anger, distress, grief, fear are natural human emotions. If we are distressed or anxious, we are not weak, we are just human. When we have negative thoughts, accept the situation and take five deep breaths. It will help us ease the tension.
- *Have a mantra ready*: For instance, "I choose to take one day at a time." "We are all in this together". Just focus on the present; forget about past and future.
- *Be resilient*: The persons who have the better ability to come out from the adverse are more adaptable. We have been through the Partition, wars, floods, etc. This too shall pass.
- *Sleep well*: Sleep is vital to stay healthy. Sleeping boosts immunity and reduces stress. So, in this time of lockdown, when you do not have any support to perform house chores and you are overburdened, it is very important for you to have enough sleep.
- *Be in touch with family and friends*: A good place to look for mental health is somewhere close to us — family, friends and loved ones. Expressing our feelings and emotions provide healthy cathartic relief and promote mental well-being. Keep your spirit up through frequent video calls. Platforms providing for more than four persons to connect are new rage. Stress hormones are kept at bay by having long chat with friends and family. Being able to see the faces while talking and the smiles can be therapeutic.
- *Enjoy nature*: In the lap of nature, you feel stress-free, calm and peaceful. Sit in your garden, enjoy watching birds, listening melodious voice of cuckoo and chirping of birds, it will definitely help you to release your stress.
- *Go for walk following all the precautions*: Return to walking with your masks, observing social distancing, to rejuvenate your body and soul.
- *Play games to stave off the boredom*: Badminton, carom board, snakes and ladders, card games are helping people stave off the boredom.
- *Go for meditation and deep breath sessions*: Meditation helps a lot in fighting with stress. Online meditation and deep breath sessions are the new normal. Meditate for ten minutes every day. It will definitely give you mental peace and calmness.

- *Simplify your life*: Simplify your life and prepare for an era of fewer needs. Once you do that, you realise that half of your stress and worries have vanished, and you will be a much happier and satisfied person. It will also help you unclutter and let go all the thoughts, feeling and actions from your life that are unnecessary.

Stress and anxiety are something many live with but do not reveal. Those who deal with these successfully can see the difference the lack of stress and anxiety brings. It brings quietude and the ability to focus on what is important. It allows one to appreciate little things in life and be thankful for them. So let us work on a plan for stress and learn to deal with it. It will allow us to live a much fuller and meaningful life. People work on their looks, their weight, on their high cholesterol, etc. We should work on our mental health also which is more important in this crucial time.

References

Simmi Waraich, (May 2020) "Minding the mind, article," *The Tribune*, p. 9

Shubhrata Prakash, (April 2020) "Survival matters more in times of corona virus," article, *The Tribune*, p. 7

https://www.frontierin.org

http://www.psychatrictimes.com

http://onlinelibrary.wiley.com

19

SOCIAL BEHAVIOUR CONTEXT OF COVID-19: LESSONS LEARNT FOR LIFE TIME

Mandeep Kaur Kochar (Dr.)[1] *and Jasdeep Kaur Sachdeva (Dr.)*[2]

Introduction

On 24 March 2020, the Government of India under Prime Minister Narendra Modi ordered a nationwide lockdown for 21 days, limiting movement of the entire 1.3 billion population of India as a preventive measure against the Covid-19 pandemic in India. It was ordered after a 14-hour voluntary public curfew on 22 March, followed by enforcement of a series of regulations in the country's Covid-19 affected regions. The lockdown was placed when the

1. Associate Professor & Vice Principal, Bombay Teachers Training College, Mumbai
2. Associate Professor, DAV College of Education for Women, Amritsar

number of confirmed positive coronavirus cases in India was approximately 500. Observers stated that the lockdown had slowed the growth rate of the pandemic by 6th April to a rate of doubling every six days, and by 18th April, to a rate of doubling every eight days. All the educational institutions were just on the verge of successful completion of their academic year. Schools and colleges had almost finished with their annual teaching of academic curriculum. Only the final evaluation and assessments were planned for April to May were remaining. The complete Indian education system became stand still. The second phase of lockdown and then the phases of unlocking kept on going, sometimes with more ease and sometimes with more restrictions. But how much attention has been paid to school and college education? In this paper, the researchers intend to answer the following questions.

1. Were we ready to face a complete lockdown in the country?
2. How has the education system changed due to Covid-19?
3. What are the challenges faced by administration, schoolteachers and students?
4. How are schools, parents and teachers adapting to this change?
5. How can we make the teaching-learning process joyful through online mode in the up-coming academic years?

The lockdown has affected all the sectors in India.

1. *Travel and Tourism* — The Covid-19 pandemic has had a substantial impact on tourism industry due to the resulting travel restrictions as well as decline in demand among travellers. The tourism industry has been massively affected by the spread of Corona virus, as many countries have introduced travel restrictions in an attempt to contain its spread. Indian industry followed the same.

2. *Entertainment Industry* — The film industry was vulnerable due to the pandemic as both the production and the consumption of its output required numerous people together in small spaces. The global entertainment industry includes various entertainment venues such as online video streaming, amusement parks, theatrical productions, sports, live events, and trade shows. The primary factors for the growth of the entertainment industry before the Covid-19 pandemic include the increased adoption of online video streaming especially Netflix, Amazon Prime, among others. The rise in the multiplex chain and their expansion in semi-urban areas along with the rising number of Chinese investors in Hollywood were also the growth-enhancing factors of the entertainment industry before the pandemic. However, the key factors that affect the entertainment industry after the Covid-19 pandemic include the shutdowns of the theatrical product, cinema theatres among others.

3. *Fine Dining Industry* — The Covid-19 pandemic affects the global food industry as governments close down restaurants and bars to slow the

spread of the virus. Across the world, restaurants' daily traffic dropped precipitously compared to the same period in 2019. Closures of restaurants caused a ripple effect among related industries such as food production, liquor, wine and beer production, food and beverage, shipping, fishing, and farming. The issues were particularly disruptive in industrialised areas where large proportions of entire categories of food are typically imported using just-in-time logistics. In June 2020, the United Nations warned that the world was facing the worst food crisis in half a century due to the recession caused by the pandemic.

4. *Sports and Fitness Industry* — Sport is a major contributor to economic and social development. Its role is well recognised by governments, including in the Political Declaration of the 2030 Agenda, which reflects on "the contribution of sports makes to the empowerment of women and of young people, individuals and communities, as well as to health, education and social inclusion objectives."

Since its onset, the Covid-19 pandemic has spread to almost all countries of the world. Social and physical distancing measures, lockdowns of businesses, schools and overall social life, which have become common place to curtail the spread of the disease, have also disrupted many regular aspects of life, including sport and physical activity. This policy brief highlights the challenges Covid-19 has posed to both the sporting world and to physical activity and well-being, including for marginalised or vulnerable groups. It further provides recommendations for governments and other stakeholders, as well as for the UN system, to support the safe reopening of sporting events, as well as to support physical activity during the pandemic and beyond. However, sports goods retailers such as Decathlon and marketplaces Flipkart, Amazon and Snapdeal have seen a surge in online sale of fitness equipment amid the Covid-19 lockdown. E-commerce has edged over physical stores in selling equipment such as dumbbell kits, yoga mats and push-up bars with closure of gyms and outdoor exercises pacing the consumers to set up home gyms since April.

5. *Manufacturing Industry* — The Covid-19 pandemic hit manufacturers in an unprecedented and unexpected way. It is the first time in contemporary manufacturing records that demand, supply, and workforce availability have been influenced by this pandemic globally at the same time. The ongoing lockdown has put a lot of pressure on the manufacturing industry to increase their sales, which contributes almost 20% of the GDP. Of this, 50% is contributed by the automotive industry. Thus, the automotive industry plays a vital role in the growth of the economy. But the Corona virus has shaken this auto industry very badly.

6. *Workforce Sector* — Much has been written about how Covid-19 is affecting people in rich countries but less has been reported on what was happening in poor countries. Paradoxically, the first images of Covid-19 that India associates

with are not ventilators or medical professionals in ICUs but of migrant labourers trudging back to their villages hundreds of miles away, lugging their belongings. With most of the economy shut down, the fragility of India's labour market was patent. It was estimated that in the first wave, almost 10 million people returned to their villages, half a million of them walking or bicycling. After the economic stoppage, the International Labor Organization has projected that 400 million people in India risk falling into poverty.

7. *Education Sector* — Human Rights Watch reported that more than 1.5 billion students are out of school already. Widespread job and income loss along with economic insecurity among families are likely to also increase child labour, sexual exploitation, teen pregnancies among other woes. While the entire world is currently in lockdown because of the Covid-19 pandemic, businesses have adapted (with varying levels of success) to work-from-home (WFH) policies. But what is the situation in the education sector? More than 91 per cent of the world's students are out of school, due to school closures in at least 188 countries.

School-going children are, naturally, the worst affected education sector stakeholders. For pupils, the lockdown does not just mean reduced cashflow or a professional setback: it represents an interruption to their learning journey. And in the case of dropouts, it was the final straw for at-risk children who struggled to get an education at the best of times.

The lockdown has aggravated deep-set class and social differences, especially between private and public-school systems. The Indian government spends 4.6 per cent of its GDP on education. This is lower than in sub-Saharan countries like Kenya, Togo, and Zimbabwe.

8. *Communication and Online Services* — As the global economy continues to reel from the shock and the lasting impact of the novel Corona virus (Covid-19) outbreak, "work from home" and "social distancing" have become the buzzwords in today's business landscape, with the telecom sector being the invisible hand driving this shift. Remote working, video conferencing, and telecommunications technology have quickly emerged as key enablers for business operations during this lockdown, and streaming services such as Netflix have become the go to source for entertainment, putting the telecom sector in the spotlight today.

Parental Anxiety

As reported by *Times* surveys in E-Journals

- 64% parents were not willing to send their children to Birthday Parties for the current calendar even social distancing norms are followed.
- 99% of the parents were not ready to go to crowded places like Malls, Movie Halls, Restaurants, etc.

- 45% were overthinking over analysing the situation which is causing a mental breakdown in the society.
- 35% parents were ready to send their children back to the playgrounds to play with friends

Student Anxiety

As reported by *Times* surveys in E-Journals

- 92% students were unwilling to go back to the school immediately.
- 79% students in graduation and post-graduation were worried about the future because of the ongoing recessions.

Teachers' Concerns, Confusion and Stress for Teachers

Researchers observed, Education sadly had been the last priority of government. Parents, students and teachers kept on waiting for the modified regulations in the Education System. Government had a lot of challenges for creating new setup for education system and maintaining and improving distance learning. The sudden demand for distance learning was skyrockets for parents with limited educational resources at home. Online education could lead to dicey behaviours, including increased influence of peer pressure of fancy digital devices. The gaps in childcare for working parents was another social challenge. Initially, no one could guess that it will prolong for that long. The sudden shift from face-to-face teaching to online teaching was a disastrous change for the whole system. First of all, the regulations and directions from the government for educational institutions came in very late; secondly, we were pushed over a period of time to prepare ourselves for new normal, without realising what exactly the new normal will look like. Researchers observed, education sector was least of the priority of government and most neglected in the whole process of pandemic. No right direction and guidance was given for the university examinations to be held well on time, no directions were given for the upcoming fees structure of schools and colleges and the admissions to be taken up for the next academic year, which ultimately kept students' parents and teachers under complete stress. Although Government of India had been taking all necessary steps to ensure that citizens are prepared well to face the challenge and threat posed by Covid-19 the Corona virus at medical and social distancing facets, but schools, colleges and universities remained unfocused. In fact, in many big cities and states, the physical infrastructure of schools and colleges was converted into containment and isolation zones which feared the parents more to send their children back to school even if zones were cleared up and sanitised well. With active support of the people of India and by procuring our toddlers and youth at home quarantined, we have been able to contain the spread of the virus in our country. The most important factor in preventing the spread of the virus locally was to keep schools shut, engage students online and empower the citizens with the right information and taking precautions as per the advisories being issued by Ministry of Health & Family Welfare.

Opportunities

1. Existing infrastructure like schools, railway coaches, hotels, offices, etc., were converted into isolation wards very quickly.
2. Rapid measures were undertaken such as imposing travel restrictions and lockdown that enabled India to balance its supply and demand.
3. All domestic/international travellers and offices are mandated to undergo a compulsory thermal screening check.
4. Transparent communication by the leadership led to compliance of requisite directions given to the masses to slow down the spread of Covid-19.
5. India is the largest producer and supplier of hydroxychloroquine, a prospective drug for treating Covid-19.

Challenges

- Lack of testing kits and relief materials like medical equipment, PPE kit, masks, and ventilators, during the first phase of Covid-19. And availability of Oxygen and vaccination in the second crucial phase of Covid-19.
- Challenge in manufacturing testing kits, oxygen and vaccines and other relief materials/medicines.
- Lack of awareness and carelessness among specific sections of the society.
- Psychological barrier relating to isolation: people fear the quarantine conditions.
- General Malnutrition and Poverty (poor Health Index).
- High level of orthodox and conservative belief systems — social and religious gatherings.
- High quarantine period for incubation ranging from 1 day to 14 days.
- Increase in Domestic Violence before and after Lockdown.
- Controlling prices and black-marketing of medicines and other relief materials.
- More hospitals and ICU beds with ventilators

Opportunities and Future Repercussions

Teachers took the backend lead, although not as forefront warriors to teach our youth that we must learn to live with the virus, and we need to change our habits and ways of living as per new social norms.

- Digital push was the impact of Covid-19 for education was the only obvious and visible pathway.
- Organised co-living and staying engaged to support the system resolved many crises on environment.
- Youth learnt to make use of start-ups, MSMEs and Indian labs for the productions of PPEs, testing kits, ventilators, oxygen cylinders etc.
- Development of necessary technical infrastructures to ensure smooth and flexible employee working arrangements to minimise job losses.

Online Learning Strategies for Teachers much Focused

- *Google Classroom* — It is a free web service developed by Google for schools that aims to simplify creating, distributing, and grading assignments. The primary purpose of Google Classroom is to streamline the process of sharing files between teachers and students.
- *YouTube* — It is an online video sharing platform that allows users to upload, view, rate, share, add to playlists, report, comment on videos, and subscribe to other users. It offers a wide variety of user-generated and corporate media videos. Available content includes video clips, TV show clips, music videos, short and documentary films, audio recordings, movie trailers, live streams, and other content such as video blogging, short original videos, and educational videos.
- *Coursera* — It is a worldwide online learning platform founded in 2012 by Stanford computer science professors Andrew Ng and Daphne Koller that offers massive open online courses, specialisations, degrees, professional and master track courses.
- *Edx* — edX is a massive open online course provider created by Harvard and MIT. It hosts online university-level courses in a wide range of disciplines to a worldwide student body, including some courses at no charge. It also conducts research into learning based on how people use its platform.

Post Lockdown Context (What is to be Restructured?)

Researchers suggest modification in Educational and Social Setup

- Classroom Modifications in Educational Setup
    - Administrations will have to have liberal times and days at work place,

  - Teachers will have to think about Classroom Modifications,
  - School Bag/ Homework/ Sharing of Resources will have to be zero down.
- Administration Outlook
  - Canteen Provisions are to be checked, children will have to bring home cooked food,
  - Examination Pattern Modifications are very essential to appreciate paper free system,
  - Transportation Modifications to keep up standards of social distancing till the vaccination is declared,
  - Online Assessment Strategies must become the part of Indian universities for all the times to come is the biggest lesson of learning of this pandemic.
- Lifestyle Changes and Mandatory Rules of New Normal
  - Shopping of goods, food and online Services will be made-up feature of life style,
  - Checking of temperature with infra-red thermometer or thermal scanner at schools and college campuses,
  - Multiple gate entries to prevent crowding should be prohibited,
  - Sanitisation of hands at the gate and compulsory wearing of face mask must be strictly observed,
  - No sharing of any stationary / tiffin foods be allowed,
  - Hand wash break as a part of the timetable must be imposed,
  - Well ventilated classrooms and regularly disinfected toilets for everyone's use,
  - Non-contacting sports must be developed, and mental well-being of children must be ensured by administrators, teachers and parents.

Researches' conclude, the Covid-19 pandemic had been a lifetime learning for each one of us. So, it is our responsibility to maintain the survival first and keep up our lifestyle as per the new normal norms.

References

https://www.bbc.com/news/business

https://www.unwto.org/tourism-covid-19

https://www.researchandmarkets.com/reports/5013572/the-impact-of-covid-19-on-the-entertainment-market

https://economictimes.indiatimes.com/industry/services/retail/covid-19-impact-e-commerce-gives-a-big-boost-to-home-fitness-accessories-as-gyms-remain-shuttered/articleshow/76574746.cms?from=mdr

https://www.hindustantimes.com/india-news/economic-impact-of-covid-19-pandemic-to-vary-in-sectors/story-DIWjwnBZoON7ZUvgSMSFOL.html

20

MENTAL WELLNESS AND PSYCHO-SOCIAL IMPACT OF COVID-19 ON STUDENTS

Satnam Kaur Johal (Dr.)[1] *and Pawanpreet Kaur*[2]

Introduction

Mental wellness is an integral part of overall health and wellbeing. It is more than the absence of mental disorders. How we think, feel, and act is all affected by our mental wellness. It also affects how we cope with stresses in life, relate to others, and take decisions in an emergency. People having a history of poor mental health or substance use disorders may be particularly vulnerable in an emergency. Depression, anxiety, bipolar disorder, or schizophrenia like mental health conditions affect a person's behaviour in a way that influences their ability to get along with others and day-to-day functioning. These conditions may be acute or chronic. Human race doubtlessly is passing through the most dangerous point in time of this millennium as its existence is being challenged by several severe acute respiratory syndrome corona virus (SARS-Cov-2) impinging on newer territories all over the world swiftly. The World Health Organization (WHO) has declared 2019 Corona Virus Disease (Covid-19) outbreak as an international public health emergency on January 30, 2020 as the disease. It was first reported from China in December 2019, continues to rush through the continents affecting almost all the countries from Europe, America and Asia severely. Due to nationwide lockdowns and home-confinement strategies implemented in the majority of the Covid-19-hit countries, a large section of world's population is primarily restricted to their homes to prevent further disease spread.

According to WHO, universal awareness, anxiety and distress are the natural psychological responses to the randomly changing conditions due to this unpredictable, fast spreading infectious disease. Adverse psychosomatic outcomes among children have increased significantly due to the pandemic itself and also due to constant flow of information and reinforced messaging through social media. Consequently, rapid expansion of mass hysteria and panic regarding Covid-19 have started enduring psychological problems among students from all the socioeconomic strata of society. Many previous studies explicated that mental wellbeing had been heavily affected in this kind of worldwide pandemic. Therefore, it is crucial to determine the various possible ways in which Covid-19 pandemic may impact the world's mental health. Many researchers have assessed that the mental health implications of

1. Assistant Professor, Khalsa College of Education, Ranjit Avenue, Amritsar
2. Assistant Professor, Khalsa College of Education, Ranjit Avenue, Amritsar

Covid-19 have a sharp prevalence of moderate-to-severe self-reported depression and anxiety symptoms among the general public (Wang, et al., 2020). Nevertheless, further researches are required to understand the individualised disruption of lives and its associated psychological impacts.

Impact on Students

People feel that there is not all good with our present education system as students heightened levels of psychological distress and downstream negative academic consequences are prevalent under normal circumstances. Owing to social and physical distancing measures implemented in response to Covid-19, our education institutions have shifted to an emergency online learning format. Researches vision the impact of academic distraction on students that they may experience like reduced motivation toward studies, increased pressures to independent learning, desertion of daily routines, and potentially higher rates of dropout. Therefore, by increasing academic stressors in a population with heightened pre-existing stress levels and a potentially reduced ability to rely upon typical coping strategies, the Covid-19 pandemic has placed an unprecedented mental health burden on students, which urgently requires further assessment and immediate intervention.

In a study on impact of Covid-19 on student's education and wellbeing (Cao et al. 2020), found approximately 25% experiencing anxiety symptoms, which were positively correlated with increased concerns about academic delays, economic effects of the pandemic. Many student surveys administered worldwide by Young Minds informed that 83% of young respondents agreed that the pandemic has worsened pre-existing mental health conditions and this is mainly due to school closures, hammering of routine, and constrained social connections (Young Minds, 2020).

"Corona Positive" — A Stigma

Another very important aspect regarding the pandemic Covid-19 is stigmatisation, a societal rejection regarding the quarantined barrier in forms of discrimination, suspicion and avoidance by neighborhood, insecurity regarding properties, workplace prejudice, and withdrawal from social events and mainly dehumanisation. Disgrace and dishonour associated with the disease among the sufferers makes it difficult to resume the natural day-to-day life routines. Children who are suspected to be or infected with Covid-19 and need isolation might require special attention to meet their fear, anxiety and other psychological effects. In the same way, it also gives rise to stigmatising factors like fear of isolation, racism, discrimination, and marginalisation with all its social and economic consequences among students. A stigmatised community tends to seek medical care late and hides important medical history, particularly of travel. This behaviour, in turn, increases the risk of community spread. The WHO has also issued specific psychosocial considerations for reducing the growing stigma of Covid. Health crime originated out of the fear of being Corona positive has also been reported at many places in our country also.

"Quarantine and Isolation" – Psychosocial Burden

India and many other countries across the globe implemented early quarantine measures as the fundamental disease control tool for Covid-19. Other than physical sufferings, the consequences of this quarantine on the mental wellness and well-being at personal and social levels are manifold. Forced quarantine may produce psychological diseases like mass hysteria, anxiety and distress. Psychological impact of quarantine may vary from immediate effects, like irritability, fear of contracting and spreading infection to family members, anger, confusion, frustration, loneliness, denial, anxiety, depression, insomnia, despair, to extremes of consequences, including suicide. Isolated cases may suffer from anxiety due to uncertainty about their health status and develop symptoms of obsessive-compulsive disorder. Post-traumatic stress disorder (PTSD) is also positively associated with the duration of quarantine. Post quarantine psychological effects may also include significant socioeconomic distress and psychological symptoms due to financial losses. Later all these may result in social disobedience, negligence behaviour, and low social discernment. Voluntary quarantine should be encouraged after proper clarification through mass communication to minimise distress and long-term complications of imposed quarantine.

"Social Media" – Exaggeration of Pandemic

New "info media ecosystems" of today's world, popularly termed as social media also have some disastrous effects on control and outcomes of an infectious disease or a pandemic. Within days of onset of the Covid-19 outbreak in China, the 'social media panic' characterised by relentless superfluity of fake information as well as negatively tilted propaganda faster than the Corona Virus itself. The director-general of WHO has referred this to "coronavirus infodemic" which is propagating fright and panic by laying out unchecked mind-boggling rumours, shocking news propaganda and sensationalism. Online popularity in many impulsive and unpredictable way invited a number of overwhelming mental burdens in the form of anxiety, phobia, panic spells, depression, obsession, irritability, delusions of having symptoms similar to Covid-19 and other paranoid ideas among youngsters too.

Psychology – Covid-19

Researches in developmental psychology largely found that learnt experiences through environmental factors during early childhood bring about the fundamentals for lifetime behaviour and success as it is a crucial phase for emotional, cognitive and psychosocial skill development. During pandemics community-based improvement programmes, like closing of schools, parks, and playgrounds will disrupt children's natural lifestyle and can potentially promote distress and confusion among them. In these situations, children are likely to become more demanding, having to cope up with these changes, and may exhibit impatience, annoyance and hostility, which may result to cause them suffering from physical and mental violence by excessively pressurised parents. Stressors, such as monotony, disappointment, lack of face-to-face contact with classmates, friends and teachers, lack of enough personal space at home, and family financial losses during lockdowns, all can potentially trigger troublesome and even prolonged adverse mental consequences in children. The interface between their day-to-day routine changes, home detention, and fear of infection could further exaggerate these undesirable mental reactions resulting in a vicious phase.

Conclusion

Besides Covid-19, the 21st century is also the era of emerging pandemic of mental illnesses. Therefore, psychological and social vigilance of this pandemic has global importance. The government and stakeholders in education must appreciate the psychosocial morbidities of this pandemic and assess the burden, fatalities and associated consequences. While online classes and assignments have been the only effective way for continuing education at this situation, the specific psychological and social needs, healthy and hygienic lifestyles, and good parenting counseling can be addressed through the same online platform.

There is a need for regular discussion with trained and specialist health care personnel. Setting up of mental health organisations specific for future pandemics at both personal and community levels is desperately needed. Structured websites and toll-free helpline numbers may be launched by educational institutions for alleviating psychological distress among the general public regarding this ongoing pandemic. Social media is to be used in good sense, to educate people about the disease and time when exact medical consultations are needed. To protect social media from depreciations, strict government laws and legislation regarding fake news, rumours, and misinformation are to be implemented. The Covid-19 pandemic has clearly shown the mankind that how a "virus" can negatively impact the lives of human being even in the 21st century and at the same time made us realise that the greatest assets of mankind are health, peace, love, solidarity, ingenuity, knowledge and sustainability of mother nature.

Refrences

Bao, Y., Sun, Y., Meng, S., Shi, J., Lu, L. (2019). nCoV epidemic: address mental health care to empower society. Lancet. 2020 Feb 22; 395(10224):e37-e38. doi: 10.1016/S0140-6736(20)30309-3. Epub 2020 Feb 7.

Cao, W., Fang, Z., Hou, G., Han, M., Xu, X., Dong, J., & Zheng, J. (2020). The psychological impact of the Covid-19 epidemic on college students in China. *Psychiatry Res*. 287:112934.

Hysenbegasi, A., Hass, S.L., & Rowland, C.R. (2005). The impact of depression on the academic productivity of university students. *J Ment Health Policy Econ*, Sep; 8(3):145-51.

Jones, D.S. (2020). History in a crisis - lessons for Covid-19. *N Eng. J Med*., Mar 12 doi: 10.1056/NEJMp2004361.

Lai, C.C., Shih, T.P., Ko, W.C., Tang, H.J., Hsueh, P.R. (2020). Severe acute respiratory syndrome coronavirus 2 (SARS-CoV-2) and coronavirus disease-2019 (Covid-19): the epidemic and the challenges. *Int J Antimicrob Agents*, 55:105924.

Wang, C., Pan, R., Wan, X., Tan, Y., Xu, L., Ho, C.S. (2020). Immediate psychological responses and associated factors during the initial stage of the 2019 coronavirus disease (Covid-19) epidemic among the general population in China. *Int J Environ Res Publ Health*, 17:1729.

Wang, G., Zhang, Y., Zhao, J., Zhang, J., Jiang, F. (2020). *Mitigate the effects of home confinement on children during the Covid-19 outbreak*. Lancet, 395:945–947.

WHO, OHCHR IOM, UNHCR and WHO joint press release: the rights and health of refugees, migrants and stateless must be protected in Covid-19 response. 2020. (Accessed on 1st April, 2020)

Wang, Y., Di, Y., Ye, J., Wei, W. (2020). Study on the public psychological states and its related factors during the outbreak of coronavirus disease 2019 (Covid-19) in some regions of China. *Psycho Health Med*. 30:1–10.

https://www.unicef-irc.org/covid-children-library?tag=impact

https://www.thelancet.com/journals/lanchi/article/PIIS2352-4642(20)30109-7/fulltext

https://www.collabovid.org/paper/10.23736/S0026-4946.20.05887-9

https://ichgcp.net/fi/clinical-trials-registry/NCT04365361https://ichgcp.net/fi/clinical-trials-registry/NCT04365361

https://twitter.com/kashishdhawan09?lang=bg

https://www.cdc.gov/mentalhealth/learn/index.htm#:~:text=Mental%20health%20includes%20our%20emotional,others%2C%20and%20make%20

https://www.kmtmed.com/En/blog/page/8299/Mental-Health-and-Coping-with-Stress-During-COVID-19-Outbreak

https://www.athenasoftware.net/blog/covid-mental-health/ https://www.trinityhealthofne.org/about-us/blog/managing-stress-and-anxiety-during-a-pandemic https://www.ncbi.nlm.nih.gov/pmc/articles/PMC7255207/

https://journals.sagepub.com/doi/full/10.1177/0020764020925108

https://europepmc.org/article/med/32526627

https://www.ncbi.nlm.nih.gov/pmc/articles/PMC7255207/ https://www.coursehero.com/file/p1qruu1/Community-based-mitigation-programs-to-combat-Covid-19-will-disruptchildrens/

https://euro-sd.com/2020/07/articles/18179/the-challenges-of-covid-19-quarantine/ http://www.journaljme.org/article.asp?issn=WKMP-

0202;year=2020;volume=1;issue=1;spage=51;epage=53;aulast=Balabantaray https://play.google.com/store/apps/details?id=au.gov.nsw.service

21

COVID-19 AND MENTAL HEALTH OF COLLEGE YOUTH

Paramjit Singh

Introduction

Though the world has dealt with other pandemics in the past, Covid-19 spread fast. Furthermore, the virus is quite contagious and can pass through people before there are symptoms. The virus is unknown, highly infectious and easily transmitted from person to person.

The Covid-19 epidemic has resulted not only in the risk of life from infection but also intolerable psychological stress. It induces tremendous fear, worry and concern among the general population and some groups in particular, such as senior citizens, care providers and people with underlying health conditions. In the context of the Covid-19 pandemic, anxiety and depression, the use of drugs, isolation and household abuse will undoubtedly increase substantially; and with schools closed, there is also a possibility of child abuse during an epidemic. This has a negative effect on our physical and mental health especially among college youth. University and college students have specific challenges that lead to poor mental wellbeing due to the outbreak of Covid-19 (Zhai & Du, 2020). Before the pandemic started, one in five college students experienced one or more diagnosable mental disorders worldwide (Auerbach et al, 2016).

During this phase mental health of the students is the topic of debate throughout the world. The whole academic as well as non-academic performance of the students rely on their mental health. Disturbances in the mental health not only have negative impact on the particular student but also have serious negative impacts on the community, as today's student is the future of the country contributing to its development by serving various roles like teacher, engineers, doctors, nurses, etc. Hence, the mental health of the students has to be given utmost importance (Goothy et al., 2020). The fact that the Covid-19 pandemic has diversely affected the mental health of college youth underscores the urgent need to understand these challenges and concerns in order to decide the future courses of action and public health messaging that can better support college students in this crisis (Zhai & Du, 2020).

All the educational institutes were locked down all of a sudden to break Covid-19 cycle and further spreading of virus. The students were in different phases of their academic year like some are about to complete the academic year, some are about to write their entrance examinations and some are writing their examinations. It is well known that the students experience

---

Assistant Professor, Khalsa College of Education, Ranjit Avenue, Amritsar

lots of stress especially before and during the examinations (Singh, Goyal, Tiwari, Ghildiyal, Nattu, & Das, 2012). Many universities decided to suspend in-person classes and evacuate students responding to the intensifying concerns surrounding Covid-19. This action can lead to negative psychological consequences among college students., along with stress, fear of examination procedures, loneliness, anxiety.

Impacts of Covid-19 on the Mental Health

Following are some of the severe impacts of Covid-19 on the mental health that the college youth is facing:

1. *Career of college students*: The examinations were postponed due to the lockdown effect and schedule of examination remains undecided. In this context, many students were undergoing mental stress and there is a strong need to consider their mental health status (Suresh, 2020). The students were preparing the examinations especially for the entrance examinations for years. For example, in India, NEET is the common entrance examination to enter into the professional colleges. As there is no announcement of the date of examination, there is quiet uncertainty about their future. To this, parents may add up more stress on their children as they are equally undergoing stress regarding the career of their kids. Though many of the educational institutes have launched online classes, adaptation of the student to the sudden transition from routine teaching method is stressful. This is true especially in case of the slow learners. Furthermore, the fear of corona virus is increasing their stress and tension.
2. *Negative emotions*: College students often experience compounded negative emotions during the closure of their educational institutions (Vanbortel, 2016). Some college students, who find the campus homelike and welcoming, harbour intense feelings such as frustration, anxiety, and betrayal. Some may struggle with loneliness and isolation while sheltering in place because of disconnections from friends and partners. For those who receive counselling services on campus, they can no longer access counselling services, which exacerbates their psychological symptoms and increase some students' risk for suicide and substance abuse.
3. *Disruption of projects and internships*: College students experience distress contributed by the uncertainty and abrupt disruption of the semester in addition to the anxiety caused by school closure. Many students have to cease their research projects and internships when universities evacuated them from campus. Moreover, disruptions of their research projects and internships jeopardise their programme of study,

delay their graduation, and undermine their competitiveness on the job market, which in turn fuels anxiety among college students. They may also struggle with the cost of returning home and managing belongings.

4. *Loss of on-campus jobs leads to financial hardship*: Many college students have lost their on-campus jobs due to the evacuation, and the pending settlement of room and board fees can aggravate their financial hardship and mental health outcomes. They also have concerns and fears of infection and transmission of Covid-19 to their family members when they return home. Given that youth can be asymptomatic carriers (Pan et al, 2020), students may be worried about putting their elder family members at increased risk for infection with severe complications from Covid-19.
5. *Missing friends*: Students may be upset because the need for physical distancing prevents them from hanging out with their friends the way they always do. Building and maintaining relationships is one of the hallmarks of being a teenager. It is their key developmental task, and now we are telling them to distance themselves physically from their friends. This can create some anxiety but more likely frustration, anger and resentment (Maes, 2020).
6. *Loneliness*: Loneliness is a widespread and significant problem impacting the mental health and success of college students. According to recent surveys, 79% of youth (18-22) are lonely. Recent survey results indicate dramatic rises in college students experiencing mild to extreme depression, attempting suicide, to leaving school because of mental health issues relative to previous years' statistics. The need to resolve the dynamic and acute social alienation and deprivation experienced by the young people has been triggered by the social distancing during the Covid-19 epidemic.
7. *Psychological stress*: Common causes of psychological stress during pandemics include fear of falling ill and dying, avoiding health care due to fear of being infected while in care, fear of losing work and livelihoods, fear of social exclusion, fear of being in quarantine, the feeling of impotence to protect oneself and others who are loved, fear of separation from others, loved ones and caregivers, refusal to care for vulnerable individuals due to fear of infection, feelings of helplessness, boredom, loneliness and depression due to being isolated and fear of re-living the experience of a previous pandemic.

Strategies to Cope with Mental Health Issues

One of the most powerful ways to cope with stress and anxiety, if other things feel unpredictable or out of hand, is by concentrating on the behaviour that are under our control. Here are some ways that college students can take voluntary steps to look after their physical, emotional and mental wellbeing during this challenging time (University of Melbourne, 2020):

1. *Learn how to protect yourself and others from Covid-19*: The recommended important actions we can all take to protect against infection and prevent the virus from spreading include practising good hygiene, self-isolation, and social (physical) distancing.
2. *Acknowledge your feelings*: Whatever you are feeling right now, know that it is okay to feel that way. Take the time to consider what you feel and express it. This could be through journaling, talking with others, or channelling your emotions into something creative, e.g., drawing, painting, poetry, music. Mindfulness meditation exercises can help us stay grounded in the midst of an emotional storm. You can learn how, without getting overwhelmed, to witness and let thoughts and feelings flow.
3. *Maintain your day-to-day activities and a routine as much as possible*: Having a healthy routine can have a positive impact on your thoughts and feelings. Go back to basics: healthy foods, exercise (for example, walking, stretching, running, cycling), sleeping and doing things you like. Even if you are in self-quarantine, there are many ways to develop new routines and stay healthy.
4. *Focus on different activities*: During this time of change, it is natural for our minds to think of all the usual activities we may not be able to do at the moment. Make a conscious shift to focus on the activities we are still able to do, or those that we may have more opportunity to do if we are at home more often. Some ideas could be to:
   - Keep learning and maintaining your study
   - Read a book
   - Listen to a podcast
   - Try out a new hobby or skill like cook a new recipe, play an instrument, learn a language, learn how to sew, gardening.
5. *Stay connected*: Receiving support and care from others has a powerful effect on helping college students to cope up with challenges. Spending time with friends and family can bring comfort and stability. Talking through our concerns, thoughts, and feelings with others can also help us find helpful ways of thinking about or dealing with a stressful situation.
6. *Remember that physical distancing does not need to mean social disconnection*: There are many ways we can use technology to stay connected, and both give and receive support (remotely). You could:
   - Call, text or video-chat with friends and family
   - Share quick and easy recipes

- Start a virtual book or movie club
- Schedule a workout together over video chat
- Join an online group or peer forum.

7. *Contribute*: Showing care towards friends, family, or vulnerable people in our community can be all the more important during times like this. It can encourage a sense of hope, purpose and significance.
   - Send someone you care about a message of encouragement or affirmation
   - Cook, pack and send meals to someone near you.
   - Donate to a cause.
8. *Seek accurate information*: It is important to find credible sources you can trust in order to avoid the fear and panic that can be caused by misinformation. Follow sources like the government instructions and Department of Health, or University Department of Education, Skills, and Employment for up-to-date fact sheets, including advice and support specifically for international students.
9. *Set limits around news and social media*: It is understandable to want to keep informed and prepared. Also, at the same time, watching, constantly reading or listening to upsetting media coverage can unnecessarily intensify worry and agitation. When you get the urge to check updates, see if you can pause, notice the urge, delay acting on the urge, and let it pass without judgement. Schedule a specific time to check in with the news instead. It is also recommended to take breaks from conversations with others about Covid-19 and suggest talking about other topics.
10. *Stay up to date with university advice and support*: Check the University's student support website for important information, including course-specific updates and other advice for affected students.

Conclusion

Covid-19 and its accompanying effects will continue impacting the mental health of college students and wellbeing profoundly; meanwhile, mental health serves a crucial role in combating the pandemic. It is thus imperative for universities to build awareness of students' mental health needs and concerns, and to empower their students to seek help and support during this biological disaster. College students should tailor coping strategies to meet their specific needs and promote their psychological resilience. Considerable efforts made by universities should be dedicated to helping students thrive in this crisis. With the experience attained supporting students in this pandemic, universities will be well positioned to help college students stay well in mind, body, and spirit during other challenging times.

References

Agnew, M., Poole, H., & Khan, A. (2019). Fall break fallout: Exploring student perceptions of the impact of an autumn break on stress. *Student Success*, *10*(3), 45-54.

Auerbach, R.P., Alonso, J., Axinn, W.G., Cuijpers, P., Ebert, D.D., Green, J.G., ... & Nock, M. K. (2016). Mental disorders among college students in the World Health Organization world mental health surveys. *Psychological medicine*, *46*(14), 2955-2970.

Cao, W., Fang, Z., Hou, G., Han, M., Xu, X., Dong, J., & Zheng, J. (2020). The psychological impact of the Covid-19 epidemic on college students in China. *Psychiatry Research*, 287. 112934.

Goothy, S.S.K., Goothy, S., Choudhary, A., Potey, G.G., Purohit, M., Chakraborty, H., Pathak, A., & Mahadik, V.K. (2020). Covid-19 lockdown impact on the mental health of students: need to start a mental health cell. *MOJ Anatomy and Physiology*. *7*(2):51–52.

Maes, N. (2020). *How covid-19 impact teens' mental health*. Retrieved July 13, 2020 from https://chicagohealthonline.com/how-covid-19-impacts-teens-mental-health/

Pan, X., Chen, D., Xia, Y., Wu, X., Li, T., Ou, X., Zhou, L., & Liu, J. (2020). Asymptomatic cases in a family cluster with SARS-CoV-2 infection. *The Lancet Infectious Diseases*, *20*(4), 410-411.

Singh, R., Goyal, M., Tiwari, S., Ghildiyal, A., Nattu, S. M., & Das, S. (2012). Effect of examination stress on mood, performance and cortisol levels in medical students. *Indian J PhysiolPharmacol*, *56*(1), 48-55.

Suresh, M.A. (2020). The Psychological Impact of Lockdown. *Studies in Indian Place Names*, *40*(74), 961-981.

UNESCO. (2020). Covid-19: Impact on Education. Retrieved 13 July, 2020 from https://en.unesco.org/covid19/educationresponse

University of Melbourne. (2020). *Coronavirus (Covid-19): Managing Stress and Anxiety*. Retrieved on July 13, 2020 from https://services.unimelb.edu.au/counsel/resources/wellbeing/coronavirus-covid-19-managing-stress-and-anxiety

VanBortel, T., Basnayake, A., Wurie, F., Jambai, M., Koroma, A.S., Muana, A.T., Hann, K., Eaton, J., Martin, S., & Nellums, L.B. (2016). Psychosocial effects of an Ebola outbreak at individual, community and international levels. *Bulletin of the World Health Organization*, *94*(3), 210.

WHO. (2020). *Mental health and Covid-19*. Retrieved on July 13, 2020 from http://www.euro.who.int/en/health-topics/health-emergencies/coronavirus-covid-19/novel-coronavirus-2019-ncov-technical-guidance-OLD/coronavirus-disease-covid-19-outbreak-technical-guidance-europe-OLD/mental-health-and-covid-19

Zhai, Y., & Du, X. (2020). Addressing collegiate mental health amid Covid-19 pandemic. *Psychiatry Research*, 113003.

5

FUTURE OF EDUCATION AFTER LOCKDOWN

22

FUTURE OF EDUCATION: THE POST COVID

Jyotpreet Kaur (Dr.)

Introduction

11 March 2020 will be marked as a black day in the world history for times immemorial. WHO declared Novel Corona virus Disease (Covid-19) outbreak as a pandemic and reckoned the call for countries to take immediate actions and scale up response to detect, treat and reduce transmission to save people's lives. In a video-conference held on 15 April 2020, MOHFW and WHO deliberated on further strengthening the partnership and additional measures that can be taken to step up the response to Covid-19 in the country. In his address, Dr Harsh Vardhan, the then Union Minister for Health and Family Welfare said, "WHO is an important partner in our fight against the Covid-19. I really value guidance and contributions made by the WHO in containing spread of Covid-19 across the country."

WHO country office in India has been working closely with MOHFW on preparedness and response measures for Covid-19, including surveillance and contact tracing, laboratory diagnosis, risk communications and community engagement, hospital preparedness, infection prevention and control, and implementation of containment plan.

India is now in a decisive phase of the response. As in the case of polio, in combating Covid-19 too, surveillance is playing a central role. Accordingly, at the request of the government, WHO has further stepped up the support in strengthening ongoing surveillance and responses at state, district and block levels, cluster containment activities, strengthening real-time data collection activities, and accelerated implementation of the national integrated health information platform. Our entire field presence, including the National Public Health Surveillance Project, has been fully re-proposed to support the government to overcome this challenge," says Dr. Henk Bekedam, WHO representative to India.

The Covid-19 pandemic has affected educational systems worldwide, leading to the near total closures of schools, colleges and universities. Most governments around the world have temporarily closed educational institutions in an attempt to contain the spread of Covid-19.

On 23 March 2020, Cambridge International Examinations (CIE) released a statement announcing the cancellation of Cambridge IGCSE, Cambridge O Level, Cambridge International AS & A Level, Cambridge AICE Diploma, and Cambridge Pre-uni examinations for May/June 2020 series across all countries. International Baccalaureate exams also cancelled.

Assistant Professor, Khalsa College of Education, G.T. Road, Amritsar

In addition, Advanced Placement Exams, SAT administrations have been moved online and cancelled. School closures impact not only students, teachers and families but have far-reaching economic and societal consequences.

School closures in response to the pandemic have shed light on various social and economic issues, including student debt, digital learning, food insecurity, and homelessness as well as access to childcare, healthcare, housing, internet and disability services. The impact was more severe for disadvantaged children and their families, causing interrupted learning, compromised nutrition, childcare problems and consequent economic cost to families who could not work.

The objective of the study was to survey positive and negative impact of Covid on education. In the present study, a self-constructed questionnaire was used to study the impact of Covid on education. The questionnaire was used to conduct survey from students in the locality of Amritsar. Percentage analysis showed that urban locality individuals gave feedback for positive impact of Covid on Education and rural locality individuals gave feedback for negative impact of Covid on Education.

Table 22.1

		Positive Impact of COVID on Education					
		Low		*Moderate*		*High*	
Locality	*N*	*N*	*%age*	*N*	*%age*	*N*	*%age*
Urban	10	1	10%	8	80%	1	10%
Rural	10	2	20%	6	60%	2	20%

The data of the given study clearly depicts that the percentage analysis on the urban individuals on the moderate group is 80% as compared to the rural group that comes out to be 20% when analysed on the group showing positive impact of Covid on education.

According to the data of the study 96% of the individuals showed positive impact of Covid on education while 4% showed negative impact of Covid on education.

According to UNESCO studies the negative impacts of Covid-19 that can result in future shock:

1. Sluggish cross border movement of students.
2. Passive learning by students.
3. Unprepared teachers for online education.
4. Interrupted learning due to weak internet connections or no internet connection.
5. Poor nutrition for students who are fully dependent on mid-day meal scheme.
6. Parents unprepared for distance and home schooling.
7. Challenges of creating, maintaining and improving distance learning
8. Confusion and stress for teachers who are using online resources for the first time.

9. Leading to confusion among the learners who are not well equipped with the online learning.
10. High economic costs.
11. Unintended strain on health care systems.
12. Increased pressure on schools and school systems that remain open.
13. Rise in dropout rates.
14. Increased exposure to violence and exploitation.
15. Social isolation.
16. Challenges measuring and validating learning.

Many new learnings, new perspectives, new trends will emerge as we head into The Great Unknown War against Covid-19:

1. Fewer kids will go back to school when schools re-open.
2. Fewer kids will go out of town, far from home, to study.
3. Fewer kids will go overseas to study.
4. Social distancing, little or no sports.
5. Two shifts or three shifts schools may emerge.
6. Social distance may lead to some getting socially distant.
7. Teaching versus learning will need figuring.
8. Teaching will go high tech which may lead to difficulty in understanding among masses.
9. Technology in education alone will not be the enabler.
10. Technology will be about the content not the container so it will lack the psychological development of learner and inhumane learning based on machines.
12. A lighter school bag may become a reality.
13. FOBO (Full Of Being Offline) and Bulldozer parents will intensify.
15. Distance learning courses may not be considered inferior.
16. Blended learning and personalised education can be torch bearing.
17. Learning outcomes will be effected.
19. Reskilling and upskilling will gain momentum.
20. Artificial Intelligence (AI) will personalise learning.
21. Artificial Intelligence and Cloud computing will enable MOOC.
22. Examination and grading will undergo a change.
23. Chatbots will provide personalised help and guidance.
24. Executive education will witness a sea-change.
25. AI will make visualisation, annotation and storytelling better.

Solutions/Answers

- Skill-based education
- Neighbourhood school
- More digital networks by government
- Antiviral plantations
- Sanitised surroundings

A child so enthusiastic to learn;
After this Covid educational wheel will surely yearn,
Have a heart, keep on moving;
Your aspirations, so genuine will be hovering.
Turning the fright and fear into ambitious expectations,
Soon time will be back for celebrations and jubilations.

References

Aggarwal, J.C. (2013). *Essentials of Educational Psychology* (2nd Ed). New Delhi: Vikas Publishing House.

Bhutia, Y. (2014). Attitude towards Sex Education. *Edutracks, 13*(11),P-43-46.

Das, D. (2014). Adolescent education: A challenge for teachers and teacher educators. *Edutracks,13*(12). P10-13.

Ediger, Marlow(2007):The school and students in society. *Experiments in Education,* 35(9), 17-20.

Mohan, A. (2006): *Psychological Foundation of Education.* Hyderabad: Neelkamal Publications Pvt.Ltd.

Shubhangini, A.J.(2018): *Nutrition and dietetic,* Tata McGraw Hill Education Pvt. Ltd. New Delhi. P 49.

www.economictimes

www.who.int

23

CHALLENGES AND OPPORTUNITIES IN EDUCATION IN FACE OF COVID-19 PANDEMIC

Sanjam Upadhyay (Dr.)[1] *and Davinder Singh Chhina (Dr.)*[2]

Introduction

Dr. APJ Abdul Kalam trusts that education is a pillar of developed and a powerful country. Education is the most important element for the growth and prosperity of a nation. He trusts that education is the most important area of the service sector and it provides the required knowledge and skill to do any work.

According to UNESCO, over 32 crore students are hit by Covid-19 as schools and colleges are shut in India. There are countries in the world that have an entire population less than this country. Considering the number given by UNESCO, it is a very big total to deal with. While some anticipated

1. Assistant Professor, Khalsa College of Education, G.T. Road, Amritsar
2. PES-1, Principal, Education Department, Punjab

that the situation would get under control in the near future and awaited the pandemic to end. Most of the schools and institutions decided to not halt the system for long and moved their classes to feasible medium like online learning and distance education. However, unfortunately, we still do not have a tech-savvy infrastructure in most parts of the country, hence the struggle.

Now, certainly, the time is harsh for the entire world, but, alternatively, it has also opened doors for the opportunities that we had in our minds for long but could not execute. We still had our traditional way of physical education as the primary medium.

Education is a dynamic, social, psychological, philosophical, rational, continuous and lifelong process; so several changes in the socio-economic, political arrangement should be adjusted in the education system. Knowledge explosion, on one side, has increased the use of information and communication technology, LPG (Liberalisation, Privatisation, and Globalisation) in education, etc. that have changed the role of teachers completely, on the other side, the Covid-19 pandemic attack has left the whole education system changed. Teacher-students' relationship has changed. Students have access to a universal source of knowledge at a single click on the Internet. Today, the needs and requirements of education have completely changed. New discoveries, inventions, and researches have changed the product and processes of education.

Opportunities and Challenges

The Covid-19 pandemic is an unprecedented challenge with immediate impacts on public and economic health. It has radically changed relationships across the globe. Our personal relationships have been radically altered as we have learned to socially distance ourselves, wear face masks when walking out or shopping, smile more with our eyes and nod or wave our greetings. We are holding zoom meetings and classes and forming exclusive social "pods" of quarantine buddies and sharing meals virtually.

Our relationship with food is changing too. It has brought about a change in behaviour. The current surge in home cooking spells a long-term reversal in the overall decline home cooking that stretches back to 1965.

Driven by the increased uncertainty about the food supply, home gardening is on the rise at rates not seen since the Great Recession of 2008. The food system policy director at the John Hopkins Centre for a Livable Future, Bob Martin, suggests that this virus is a warning shot, and it provides us with an opportunity to change our food system in ways that are less susceptible to destruction.

The Covid-19 pandemic and associated physical isolation practices are likely to result in a range of mental health and psychological challenges. These complications will be further magnified when considering their potential effect on cardiovascular disease and its management.

The structure of schooling and learning, including teaching and assessment methodologies, was the first to be affected by the closures. Only a handful of private schools could adopt online teaching methods. Their low-income private and government school counterparts, on the other hand, have completely shut down for not having access to e-learning solutions. The students, in addition to the missed opportunities for learning, no longer have access to healthy meals and are subject to economic and social stress during this pandemic time.

The pandemic has significantly disrupted the higher education sector as well, which is a critical determinant of a country's economic future. School and University closures will not only have a short-term impact on the continuity of learning for more than 285 million young learners in India but it will also endanger far-reaching economic and societal consequences. A large number of Indian students — second only to China — enroll in universities abroad. Many such students have now been barred from leaving these countries. If the situation persists, in the long run, a decline in the demand for international higher education is expected.

The bigger concern, however, is the effect of the disease on the employment rate. Many graduates in India are fearing the withdrawal of job offers from corporates. The Center for Monitoring Indian Economy's estimates on unemployment shot up from 8.4% in mid-march to 23% in early April 2020 and the urban unemployment rate to 30.9%.

Needless to say, the pandemic has transformed the centuries-old, chalk-talk teaching model to one driven by technology. This disruption in the delivery of education is pushing policymakers to figure out how to drive engagement at scale while ensuring inclusive e-learning solutions and tackling the digital divide. A multi-pronged strategy, having following characteristics, is necessary to manage the crisis and build a resilient Indian education system in the long term:

i) Immediate measures are essential to ensure continuity of learning in Government schools and universities. Open-source digital learning solutions and Learning Management Software should be adopted so that teachers can conduct online teaching. For example, the Diksha platform, with reach across all states in India, can be further strengthened to ensure accessibility of learning to the students.
ii) Inclusive learning solutions, especially for the most vulnerable and marginalised, need to be developed. With the rapid increase of mobile internet users in India, which is expected to reach 85% households by 2024, technology is enabling ubiquitous access and personalisation of education even in the remotest parts of the country. This can change the schooling system and increase the effectiveness of learning and teaching, giving students and teachers multiple options to choose from.

Many aspirational districts have initiated innovative, mobile-based learning models for effective delivery of education, which can be adopted by others.

iii) Strategies are required to prepare the higher education sector for the evolving demand-supply trends across the globe. Particularly those related to the global mobility of students and faculty and improving the quality of and demand for higher studies in India. Further, immediate measures are required to mitigate the effects of the pandemic on job offers, internship programmes, and research projects.

iv) It is also important to reconsider the current delivery and pedagogical methods in school and higher education by seamlessly integrating classroom learning with e-learning modes to build a unified learning system. The major challenge is EdTech reforms at the national level is the seamless integration of technology in the present Indian education system, which is the most diverse and largest in the world with more than 15 lakh schools and 50,000 higher education institutions.

It is also important to establish a quality assurance mechanism and quality benchmark for online learning developed and offered by India HEIs as well as e-learning platforms. Many e-learning players offer multiple courses on the same subjects with different levels of certifications, methodology, and assessment parameters. So, the quality of courses may differ across different e-learning platforms.

v) Indian traditional knowledge is well known across the globe for its scientific innovations, values, and benefits to develop sustainable technologies and medicines. The courses on Indian traditional knowledge systems in the fields of yoga, Indian medicine, architecture, hydraulics, ethno botany, metallurgy, and agriculture should be integrated with the present-day mainstream university education to serve the larger cause of humanity.

Scope for Online Learning

Required transformation in the field of education cannot be done overnight and it may take a lot of push in embracing and executing the desired result. But this pandemic has taught the industry that the scope of online education is extensive and it has to run in tandem with traditional learning. As per data of internet users, a large population in our country is already digitally sound, at least with the basics of it. So, making them learn about online tech stack such as Google Classroom, Blackboard, Zoom, and Microsoft Teams will not be as challenging. There are several Ed-tech start-ups in India that have already floated the knowledge about e-courses, e-books, e-classes, etc.

In the coming decade, the number of students in India is expected to rise by 50% which will eventually push the demand for educational needs. Online Education has a huge scope considering it was a library for learning. It is not just Physics, Chemistry and Mathematics. Students can apply for a lot of other courses that have a huge scope in the market place. Tomorrow, it will no longer be about the percentage scored in the board exam. There is an entire change in the education system with online education in the picture and this has been the only silver lining in the pandemic.

The quick turn-around from traditional to online sources in the education industry during the lockdown proves that we are ready to learn the unlearn. What is holding us is the mechanism that is required to streamline the process. Here is where the heed from the government comes into the picture. The government needs to help educators with the infrastructure and policies to install things in order.

Besides all the opportunities and there is also a lot of embog. A large section of our society lives in remote locations and do not have enough infrastructure to be a part of mainstream education. However, with the current situation, the government has to double the pace of their projects and introduce required mediums like better telecom networks and faster internet speed to the remote areas. This will enable the online education providers to get far and maximise the reach to every corner of the country.

Expectations from the New Education Policy

"Technology can become the 'wings' that will allow for the educational world to fly farther and faster than ever before — if we will allow it"

— Jenny Arledge

The days are obsolete when education was confined to textbooks learning, teachers using the blackboard to students, writing notes in their notebooks. Today, digital education has paved its way into the education system of India and is replacing the traditional classroom training. Also, the developments which have appeared in the field of educational technology like, EdTech are empowering educators to produce remarkable learning experiences for modern young minds. It can revolutionise the learning methods while enabling new grades of standardisation and democratised access. The present scenario is compelling policymakers to improve drive engagement at scale and combating the digital divide while ensuring comprehensive e-learning solutions.

In this time of crisis, a well-rounded and effective educational practice is what is needed for the capacity-building of young minds. It will develop skills that will drive their employability, productivity, health, and wellbeing in the decades to come, and ensure the overall progress of India.

References

Neil, A., Nicholls, S., & Redfem, J. (2020*). Challenges and Opportunities Created by the Covid-19 Pandemic*. Elsevier Public Health Emergency Collection, 52(7), 669–670.

Chandra, S.S., Shukla, P., & Sharma, A. (2018). A to Z Expectations from the New Policy on Education Sharma, *Edutracks* 17(6).

Chandra, S.S., & Sharma, A (Jan.2007), Thinker on Education — Swami Sivananda revisited, *Edutracks*, 6(5)

Chandra, S.S., and Sharma, R.K. (1986), Philosophy of Education, Atlantic Publishers and Distributers, New Delhi.

Chandra, S.S., & Sharma, A., Kumar, S. (Nov. 2008) "Thinker on Education: Dr. Shanker Dayal Sharma" — *Edutracks,* 8(3)

Winthrop R. ETGovernment.com (2020). Impact of Covid-19 on Higher Education-Challenges & opportunities. Retrieved from *http://jgu.edu.in/blog/2020/06/29/impact-of-covid-19-on-higher-education-challenges-opportunities/*

How Technology is Changing Education: From Whiteboard to Keyboard. Retrieved from *https://www.apogaeis.com/blog/how-technology-is-changing-education-the-journey-from-whiteboard-to-keyboard/*

24

CHALLENGES FOR E-LEARNING IN PUBLIC AND PRIVATE SCHOOLS: INFRASTRUCTURAL SET-UP, TEACHERS' EMPOWERMENT, PARENTAL INVOLVEMENT AND CHILDREN'S HEALTH

Manjinder Kaur (Dr.)

Introduction

Many countries have imposed emergency or lockdowns including India, to control the spread of Covid-19. These lockdowns have adversely affected the education. The teaching of school-going children from Standard I to XII seems to be profoundly affected as these children are not skilled enough in acquiring online education (Lange, 2020). During this period, the schools have no choice except imparting e-learning to children. Therefore, the Indian education system is witnessing a paradigm shift by adopting new methods of e-learning (Dhawan, 2020) which is going to be part and parcel of teaching and learning not only during an ongoing pandemic but even beyond that, which could encompass the blend of traditional education, e-learning and flipped learning in real or virtual set-up.

Assistant Professor, Sri Guru Teg Bahadur College of Education, Khankot, Amritsar and Former ICSSR Postdoctoral Fellow

Now, the question to consider is the quality of education provided through e-learning platforms in terms of the infrastructure, methods of teaching, resource appropriateness, and the child's ability to adjust with e-learning. The factors that would affect the quality include but are not limited to the locality (urban or rural), socio-economic status and participation of parents in e-learning. Based on the above background, herein, the challenges and opportunities brought by Covid-19 in the school education in India are discussed and measures to be taken to face these challenges are also considered.

Objectives

- To highlight the challenge of infrastructural set-up for providing e-learning to school-going children in different areas (urban, semi-urban and rural).
- To shed light on challenges for the empowerment of teachers for online teaching.
- To highlight the role and challenges faced by parents for imparting education to children via e-learning.
- To highlight the challenges posed by e-learning towards health (physical, mental, intellectual and social) of children.

Methodology

A large extent of work published at various platforms, including journals, newspapers, and blogs has been consulted. School teachers providing online classes to children and parents of children have been contacted to gather information via open-ended interviews..

Participants

School teachers (N = 20) from private (N = 10) and government schools (N = 10) from district Amritsar, Punjab have participated in this work. Similarly, parents (N =20) of school-going children (private schools and urban area, N = 10 and public schools and rural, N = 10) have participated in the study.

Results and Discussion

Infrastructural challenges: The availability of adequate infrastructure is the precondition to launch any academic programme (Rihai, 2015). The hardware (computer, laptop, writing pad or smartphone, etc.), software (Google meet, Google classroom, and Zoom, etc.), a secure internet connection with electricity is the first need both for teachers as well as students for proper and efficient e-learning. It has been observed that many of the schools are providing software and appropriate training to teachers for online teaching. However, hardware has to be arranged by the teachers. The teachers of small private and public schools were found having difficulty in immediate purchase of a laptop or i-pad, etc., and thus are struggling with smartphones for online teaching. Smartphones are easy to use for sharing soft study material (notes, voice message, small videos or YouTube links). However, it is impractical to impart efficient online teaching via smartphones. Some of the public schools are employing Google classroom as a virtual classroom for providing online classes to students on a routine basis; however, not much effort is being taken in public schools. The availability of economical internet connection and the speed of the internet are other concerns. The well-to-do parents, who could afford e-learning tools for their children complained about the slow internet speed especially in semi-urban or rural areas and the disruption of internet connection takes on the patience as well as education of their wards.

Empowerment of teachers: It has been observed that most of the teachers were not used to teach in virtual teaching-learning environment. Teachers of some well-established private schools are found to be tech-savvy and have previous experience of using ICT to impart education to pupils. A shift from the usage of ICT in physical environment towards e-learning is not challenging for them. Such schools have provided platforms to train their teachers for efficient use of various e-learning applications. On the other hand, teachers from public and small private schools are finding it very difficult to teach the pupils due to lack of experience as well as digital infrastructure and expertise to devise the study material. Such teachers are struggling to learn the various modes of online teaching.

Another concern is the proper utilisation of online resources along with physical ones as there are thousands of resources present online along with the knowledge of various online methods of assessment. All of the teachers have admitted to knowing about the open-book examination. But they were not aware of the responsibilities of the teacher for conducting and evaluating such exams. The teachers have acknowledged that what they can teach to students in physical set-up is not possible in virtual set-up. For example, a teacher is not readily available to help the children in practising writing skills in virtual set-up. In this regard, during the last couple of months, around 1.5 lakh teachers have been trained for digital teaching by CBSE (CBSE, 2020). However, for public sector schools and small private schools, it is up to the teachers to empower themselves without any external assistance.

Challenges for the parents: The use of technology for e-learning is now transforming the school education as a tri-centric one as the direct participation of parents in online education of their wards has increased. Their participation is related to the procurement of hardware, establishing the e-learning platforms, continuous monitoring of children and help the children in understanding the online teaching. The socio-economic divide and nature of work of parents, especially between private and public schools, have widened the gap for e-learning for children. In the educational system, where the enrolment of children for class I has increased by 30% in public schools following the introduction of mid-day meal scheme (Singh & Gupta, 2013; Sofal, F.A., 2018), it is even painful to dream about the availability of e-learning facilities with such children. Poverty has been one of the reasons for dropout from formal schooling (Sateesh & Sekhar, 2014), and the pandemic has badly affected the migrant workers (1.4 million) (Mukhra, Krishan & Kanchan, 2020) and those working in the unorganised sector and shattered their economic condition. Many of the parents having bad financial situation have admitted that online teaching is adversely affecting the education of their wards. It has been found that few children in rural areas share the smartphones for learning.

It has been observed that the private school students (in wealthier families) have all the e-learning facilities. However, the parents have admitted that e-learning is a hectic process as parents have to help their children to set-up e-learning platforms and monitor their pupils while online. Parents agreed that they used to remain cautious for the contents which children watch on smartphones or laptops. On the other hand, a majority of students attending urban private schools see their education continue through standard digital platforms.

However, the problem does not end here. For very young children studying in standard-I or II, parents are the teachers as well as evaluators in many cases, where schools only manage the curriculum and provide online teaching. Another challenge is the timing of the online classes, especially where both the parents of children in class I–III are working. In another case where both the parents are working from home, parents are finding it difficult to manage between their work, household work, and children's online education.

Physical, Social and Emotional Challenges for Children: The transformation of formal schooling to a virtual e-learning is taking place. This transformation has reduced the teacher-child contact, although the student and teachers remain in virtual contact with each other in a case where online classes are going on. In some of the private and majority of public schools, most teachers only manage the transfer of classwork and homework to children. This further diminishes the teacher-child relation. A healthy teacher-child relation is a must for social, emotional and mental wellbeing of children (Garcia-Moya, Moreno & Brooks, 2019). In the absence of any physical contact, the role of a teacher as an intervener for the problematic and other associated behaviours of children goes away, and this could lead to social problems in future.

Most of the children have been found to miss their peers and classmates, which makes them socially deprived, especially in the case of a single child. Many parents have complained about the onset of disrupting behaviour in their child during the lockdown. It is very much challenging for the parents to enhance the socialisation of children. It has been observed that many of the children, especially in urban and semi-urban areas, watch video games and cartoons excessively. This has not only decreased children's physical activity but also could harm their eyesight. The question is that how to engage children in different activities? Some of the parents engage their children in indoor activities such as gymnastic, chess, and carrom, along with creative art and craft activities. Such engagement promotes the mental health of children and protects them against ill effects of TV; however, the routine, physical activity and socialisation of children remains a big concern.

Conclusions and Suggestions

From the study, it has been found that online teaching and learning process needs an overhaul. The digital drive by the government might have helped during this lockdown period. However, the establishment of necessary infrastructure for online teaching and learning in public sector schools is a must. Teachers from public sector must be empowered with the use of modern-day technology and encouraged to get them updated. Children from the high socio-economic status receive online education; however, still there is a question over the quality of understanding, in general.

On the other hand, it is not easy to provide e-learning to underprivileged children both from rural and urban areas due to poverty and lack of appropriate infrastructure. Online classes should be aired on Doordarshan after setting a uniform curriculum across the state, which will solve the issues of hardware and software along with the availability to all. The education is becoming tri-centric with increasing participation of parents. The nuclear families where both the parents work, online teaching is stressful and traumatic for such parents, especially when the children are below eight years of age. Parents have to participate actively in the study of such children, along with their daily working schedule. The physical, social and emotional well-being of children is at stake with complete online teaching. It is quite apparent that after a certain period when regular schooling will operate, the schools would work with reduced capacity considering the safety of staff and children. In such a scenario, the blended model of education (30:70 = offline : online) may be useful. The children should have the option to choose the subject for online learning. Accordingly, different parameters of quality education such as qualification of teacher with particular emphasis on ICT and e-learning platforms, curriculum, student-teacher ratio, and infrastructure needs to be modified.

References

Ali, I & Alharbi, O.M.L. (2019). Covid-19: Disease, Management, Treatment, and Social Impact. *Science of the Total Environment*, 728, 138861-138866.

CBSE (July 24, 2020). Training Wing. Retrieved from http://59.179.16.89/cbse/training/default.aspx.

Dhawan, S. (2020). Online Learning: A Panacea in the Time of Covid-19 Crisis. J. Edu. Technol. Sys. (In Press). Retrieved from https://journals.sagepub.com/doi/pdf/10.1177/0047239520934018.

Garcia-Moya, I., Moreno, C. & Brooks, F.M. (2019). The 'Balancing Acts' of Building Positive Relationships with Students: Secondary School Teachers' Perspectives in England and Spain. *Teaching and Teacher Education*, 86, 102883-102894.

Kapasia, N., Paul, P., Roy, A., Saha, J., Zaveri, A., Mallick, R., Barman, B., Das, P. & Chouhan, P. (2020). Impact of lockdown on learning status of undergraduate and postgraduate students during Covid-19 pandemic in West Bengal, India. *Children and Youth Services Review*, 116, 105194-105198.

Lange, C.de. (2020). How Kids are Coping with Lockdown. *New Scientist*, 247 (3291), 10-11.

Mukhra, R., Krishan, K. & Kanchan, T. (2020). Covid-19 Sets off Mass Migration in India. Archives of Medical Research (In Press). Retrieved from https://www.sciencedirect.com/science/article/pii/S0188440920309401.

Rihai, G. (2015). E-learning Systems Based on Cloud Computing: A Review. *Procedia Computer Science*, 62, 352-359.

Saha, J., Barman, B. & Chouhan, P. (2020). Lockdown for Covid-19 and its Impact on Community Mobility in India: An analysis of the Covid-19 Community Mobility Reports, 2020. *Children and Youth Services Review*, 116, 105160-105174.

Sateesh, G. M. & Sekher, T. V. (2014). Factors Leading to School Dropouts in India: An Analysis of National Family Health Survey-3 Data. *IOSR Journal of Research & Method in Education* (IOSR-JRME),4(6), 75-83.

Singh, S. & Gupta, N. (2013). Impact of Mid-day Meal on Enrollment, Attendance and Retention of Primary School Children. *International Journal of Science and Research* (IJSR), 4(2), 1203-1205.

Sofal, F.A. (2018). Impact of the Mid-day Meal Scheme on the Enrollment Status of Secondary School Students in district Anantnag. *International Journal of Academic Research and Development*, 3(1), 100-104.

Tikam, M. (2013). Impact of ICT on Education. *International Journal of Information Communication Technologies and Human Development*, 5 (4), 1-9.

Worldometer (2020, July 27). Reported Cases and Deaths by Country, Territory, or Conveyance. Retrieved from https://www.worldometers.info/coronavirus/?utm_campaign=homeAdvegas1?.

6

CORONAVIRUS AND ECOLOGICAL LEARNING

25

IMPACT OF COVID-19 CRISIS ON ENVIRONMENT

Sandeep Sharma (Dr.)

Introduction

As per the Centers for Disease Control and Prevention (CDC), Corona Virus is an "Enveloped Virus" as it is surrounded by a fat layer, so, on dissolving this layer virus inside gets killed. It is called CORONA because it has crown like structure. Covid-19 has so many positive as well as negative effects on the environment. Some of them have dreaded while some may have mild influence on the human beings, plants and animals. However, more or less but environment is definitely going to be affected by this contagious/infectious disease.

Favourable and Positive Effects on Environment

Due to the spread of Covid-19, all the species have been affected whether to the more or lesser extent. Change is the law of nature. Nature always adjusts the environment in her own way. Now, in this lockdown period of Covid-19 the environment has been affected in many favourable ways. Here are some supporting factors given below:

1. Decrease in the Global Warming

Up to 8-12 km from the surface of earth it is called Troposphere, in which layer Carbon Dioxide (CO_2) is present; this is the main greenhouse gas along with Methane (CH_4) and water vapours, etc. These gasses collectively cause global warming in the earth's atmosphere. Now, due to Covid-19 automobiles are restricted, chimney smoke from the factories is lowered in almost the whole world hence production of greenhouse gasses is decreased due to which global warming has decreased, e.g., according to UK based journal; "National Climate Change", it has shown that emission of carbon dioxide is decreased by 17%.

2. Favourable Effect on Ozone Layer

Due to fuel combustion in engines of automobiles and factories etc. Freons (CCl_2F_2) i.e., Chlorofluorocarbons are produced which react with ozone (O_3) layer and it changes into Oxygen gas (O_2):

$$O_3 + Cl^* \rightarrow O_2 + OCl^*$$

Where this Cl^* *is the free radical produced from* CCl_2F_2

Assistant Professor, Postgraduate Deptt. of Chemistry, SMDRSD College, Pathankot

When the ozone layer gets changed into Oxygen gas, this is called depletion of ozone layer and hence ozone holes are formed. However, these days chlorofluorocarbons (CFCs) are being produced to very lesser extent due to which ozone layer is safely sustained. In this Covid-19 tenure quality of ozone layer has been improved. It will be now very helpful in controlling the harmful Ultraviolet Rays coming from the Sun to the Earth.

For example, according to a "Journal of Geophysical Research Letters", it has been found that Nitrogen dioxide pollution over northern China, Western Europe and US has decreased by 60% as compared to last year.

3. Depression in the Extent of Pollution

As maximum activities of human beings are restricted and reduced, all are staying home to control the spread of Covid-19, so the maximum ways of spreading of pollution are automatically decreased. Due to the stoppage of construction works, automobiles, factories and industries, the extent of pollution has decreased. Marriage functions, parties, gathering in hotels and restaurants, etc. are banned or reduced hence wastage of food, sound pollution, useless expenditures, etc. are decreased. In a nutshell, pollution is created by the human activities and as all these activities are under control these days, the level of pollution is also lowered. For example, according to Center for Science and Environment (CSE), pollution in Delhi and NCR has come down by 79% during the initial phase of lockdown.

4. Better Quality of Water – A Ventilator for Rivers

The quality of water has been improved. As pollution has been controlled, so Oxides of carbon (CO, CO_2, etc.), Oxides of nitrogen (NO, NO_2, NO_3, N_2O_5, etc.), Oxides of Sulphur (SO_2, SO_3, etc.) are being produced to very lesser extent hence the acids like sulphuric acid (H_2SO_4), nitric acid (HNO_3), carbonic acid (H_2CO_3) are present in the acid rain to very lesser extent due to which quality of water has been improved. Moreover, due to stoppage of chemical wastes of factories into rivers, the quality of river water has been markedly improved.

For example, according to Central Pollution Control Board (CPCB), out of 36 monitoring units placed in the river Ganga, water quality at 27 points was found suitable for bathing and propagation of wildlife and fisheries, etc. It is precisely said that "*Covid-19 is a gift to Ganga*".

5. Improved Quality of Soil

The quality of soil also depends more or less upon the acidity of the rain water. As the rain water itself is of better quality due to lesser extent of acids and other harmful chemicals in it, so this type of water is called soft water, which makes the quality of soil better.

For example, fertility of soil also depends upon its pH-value; pH value 6.5 to 7.5 is most suitable value to increase its fertility; at too high or too low pH values loss of microorganisms like fungi and bacteria will result in less healthy soil. In lockdown pollution is under control, so, suitable pH-value will enhance its fertility.

6. Air Quality Improved

It is very obvious that if automobiles are restricted, construction works are stopped, factories and industries are hindered, human beings are restricted to their homes only then level of air pollution will be controlled due to which quality of air will automatically be improved. For example, according to a study conducted by IIT Delhi the Air Quality Index (AQI) has dropped by 49% during lockdown.

Following is the Comparative study on vehicular pollution in Bengaluru during lockdown (8 February 2020 to 2 May 2020, Sudhir, A.).

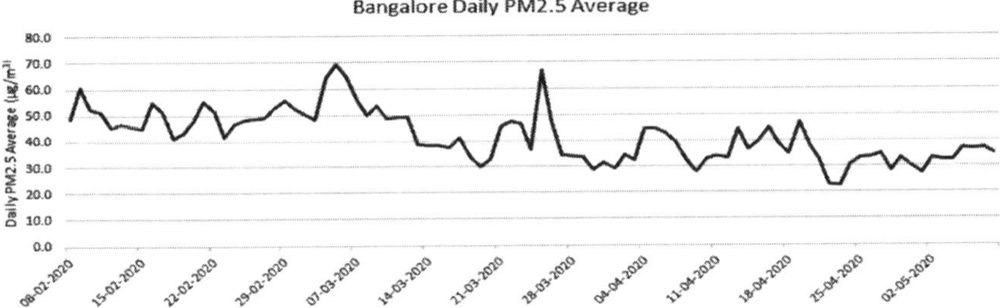

Comparative study on vehicular pollution in Bengaluru during lockdown

7. Lowering Sound Pollution

There is no or very less traffic on roads, loud-speakers and loud music is banned in marriage parties, functions and even other religious institutions, work in factories is going on in small scales. These are the reasons due to which sound pollution has decreased. Wildlife has been seen doing pleasures out of the forests, sparrows and other birds are seen around homes. It is due to decreased sound pollution in the environment.

8. Accidental Death Rate is Decreased

Due to very less traffic on roads the problem of overcrowding is reduced and hence chances of accidents are reduced to greater extent due to which casualties are very less and hence death rate is reduced remarkably. Moreover, people are now avoiding over speeding, doubling or tripling on two wheelers, etc. which also decreases chances of accidents and hence the death rate. For example, road accident death rate is decreased by almost 15%, patients with drug abuse, strokes and heart attack have been coming in fewer numbers.

9. Residential Areas and Colonies are More Clean and Green

People are now more or less free at their homes due to Covid-19. Some of them are doing work from home. So, in these circumstances most of the people are more concerned about the cleanliness of their homes and their surroundings. They are thus helping to make their areas more clean and green. Due to this lockdown, peoples are staying at their homes, police patrolling has been enhanced, security has been tightened, so, criminal cases have decreased remarkably.

10. Improved Quality of Plants, Vegetations, Wildlife and Aquatic Life

All of these are linked up with air pollution, sound pollution, water and soil pollution. Once different types of pollutions are under control then environment becomes the nice place to live in. Improved air quality index, reduced sound, water and soil pollution have remarkably enhanced the quality of plants, vegetations, wild and aquatic life.

11. Human beings are now more aware about their Fitness and Environment

This is also a very good impact of Covid-19 on the human beings that now people are giving priority to homemade food, they are more concerned about their immune systems and physical fitness. They are doing yoga and exercises to boost their immunity. If human beings are fit physically as well mentally, then automatically a healthy environment is created.

12. People at Home Spending Quality Time with their Families – A Healthy Atmosphere is Created Inside and Outside

It is pertinent to mention that due to lockdown in this Covid-19, most of the peoples are staying with their family members; a stronger bond between them is developing. This is also need of the hour. At homes peoples are spending quality time with family members, work from home culture is developed, e-learning has started, e-commerce has upgraded, e-governance has come into operation, all of us have understood the role of medical facilities in our lives. A healthy atmosphere at homes is required to maintain healthy atmosphere outside.

13. Pandemic of Civid-19 has Decreased the Danger of World War – III

Last but not the least, it is also a noteworthy point that according to the present situation of world, the terror of this Covid-19 on the countries is such that they are striving to control this Virus on top priority, all the other tasks are kept pending and hence there is no terror of a new world war in the near future. Super powers of the world are rather greatly affected by this Covid-19 and it is a great setback for them. They will require longer time to come out of this, so, the threat of war and conflicts are minimised now. A war between two countries during the present situation can lead to very dreaded circumstances. If nuclear war happens then long-lasting hazards to the human beings and environment would be imminent. However, this dreaded situation is now under control.

Negative or Unfavourable Effects on Environment

Along with the positive effects there are many negative or unfavourable effects of Covid-19 on the environment. They are mentioned below with all the supporting factors:

1. Natural Plantation on Hilly Areas has been affected
Natural plantation fulfills its need for nitrogen from the nitric acid (HNO_3) in rain water. Now, due to lockdown in Covid-19, production of oxides of nitrogen has decreased owing to which extent of nitric acid in rain water is decreased along with other essential minerals. If this lockdown continues then later or sooner the time will come when the circumstances will be perishable for natural plantation.

2. Skin and other Diseases in Living beings may Grow up
In acid rain with pH value 5-6 is called unpolluted acid rain or natural acid rain, it contains different acids and minerals which are naturally mixed to a very suitable proportion. They are very useful to prevent skin diseases in human beings and animals. Moreover, these minerals and acids are very much important for plants and other vegetations. Long-term lockdown will affect the environment badly. However, acid rain with pH value 3-4 is much polluted acid rain and it is very harmful for animals, plants, human beings and buildings, etc.

3. On Sudden Change in Environment People may not Adapt Themselves
Now pollution is very less, people are used to wear mask and gloves, and other protection gears, they are not going outside, staying at their homes, they have adapted this situation now but when this Covid-19 will be over, people may suddenly stop using such equipments. However, at that time pollution will be high due to restart of automobiles, factories and other construction works etc. So, this will be very harmful for the living beings i.e., plants, animals and human beings to readapt the old situation instantly. So, it is advisable to use masks, etc. even when the Covid-19 is over. Gradually we can get rid of it, not instantly.

4. Long Lockdown due to Covid-19 may Change Soil Fertility
In rain water numerous acids and minerals are dissolved. During this pandemic Oxides of Sulphur (SO_x), Oxides of nitrogen (NO_x), Oxides of carbon (CO_x) etc. are being produced very less, so, the rain water is devoid of

such minerals due to which fertility of land/soil will decrease if this lockdown period continues to be for longer time.

5. Excessive Use of Mobiles or other Electronic Appliances has Effected the Environment Badly

It is the Covid-19 responsible for the lockdown and for the home stay of all the peoples around the world. Owing to this home stay, people are more prone to internet through mobiles and other home appliances these days which in turn be harmful for their health and the environment.

For example, according to Natural Resources Defense Council (NRDC), Mercury (Hg) and Cadmium (Cd) found in Mobiles and other electronic devices release hazardous toxins into air or water when burnt or deposited in landfills improperly. Hence, they affect the environment very badly.

6. Overstaying at Homes may Increase Mental Unwellness

Our environment depends upon us and we depend upon our environment, it is a reciprocal relation. So, overstaying at home may disturb our mental wellness; this directly or indirectly will spoil our physical health too. Increased suicide rate due to depression or mental exertion is the cause of it. So, it is our utmost task to be safe at home, obey all necessary guidelines, so that this lockdown may not continue longer, otherwise it will be very hazardous for all of us.

7. Global Economic Downfall – A Threat to the Environment

Due to the global economic downfall, large number of fruitful tasks are kept pending. There will be no new projects, completion of old projects are difficult due to lack of funds and manpower, Moreover, every project related to environment or mankind is completed by funds and administrators/executors. All the administrations/governments are engrossed to curb this pandemic only. So, if both of these will not be available then whether it is mankind or environment, all of us are going to be affected. Global development will be retarded.

Reference

Sudhir, A. (2020) Air quality during lockdown. Retrieved from https://bengaluru.citizenmatters.in/bengaluru-air-pollution-pm-reduction-lockdown-study-47025

26

POSITIVE IMPACT OF COVID-19 CRISIS ON ENVIRONMENT

Surjit Kaur

Introduction

The coronavirus pandemic has caused a worldwide decrease in economic activity. Though this is significant reason for concern, yet the declining of human activity seems to have positively affected the earth. Industrial and transport emanations and effluents have decreased, and measurable information supports the freeing from poisons in the climate, soil and water. The long stretch of May, which typically records top carbon outflows because of the decomposition of leaves, has recorded what may be the most reduced degrees of poisons noticeable all around since the 2008 budgetary crisis. The overall disturbance brought about by the Covid-19 pandemic has brought about various effects on nature and the atmosphere. The extreme decrease in arranged travel has made numerous districts experience a drop in air pollution. In any case, the outbreak has likewise given spread to criminal activities, for example, deforestation of the Amazon rainforest and poaching in Africa, prevented environmental discretion endeavours and made financial fallout that is anticipated to slow investment in green energy technologies (Saigal, 2020).

Positive Impact of the Covid-19 Pandemic on the Environment

Air quality: Due to the corona virus outbreaks, effect on travel and industry numerous districts and the planet all in all accomplished a drop in air pollution. Reducing air pollution can lessen both environmental change and Covid-19 dangers yet till now it is not clear which kinds of air pollution are regular dangers to both environmental change and Covid-19. The Center for Research on Energy and Clean Air reported that techniques to contain the spread of corona virus for example, isolations and travel bans, brought about a 25% decrease of carbon emission in China. In the first month of lockdown, China created around 200 million very less amounts of carbon dioxide than a similar period in 2019, because of the decrease in air traffic, oil refining and coal utilisation. One Earth frameworks researcher assessed that this decrease may have spared at any rate 77,000 livcs. In any case, Sarah Ladislaw from the Center for Strategic and International Studies contended that decreases in emanations because of economic downturns ought not be viewed as useful,

---

Assistant Professor, MGN College of Education, Jalandhar

expressing that China's attempts to come back to previous rates of development in the midst of trade wars and flexibly chain interruptions in the energy market will exacerbate its ecological effect. Between 1 January and 11 March 2020, the European Space Agency observed a checked decrease in nitrous oxide emissions from vehicles, power plants and industrial facilities in the Po Valley region in northern Italy, coinciding with lockdowns in the region.

Water quality: In Venice, the water in the canals cleared and experienced more prominent water flow and visibility of fish. The Venice office explained that the expansion in water clearness was because of the settling of sediment that is upset by boat traffic and referenced the decline in air pollution along the waterways.

In India, The Uttarakhand Pollution Control Board, water from Har-Ki-Pauri in Haridwar was tested and the outcomes from the tests uncover that the water here has been delegated 'fit for drinking after chlorination', without precedent for decades. It is accepted that because of the lockdown, the drainage of industrial waste into the river water has halted and gotten a huge change in the water quality. (Goswami, 2020)

Effect on vegetation: Plants are developing better on the grounds that there is cleaner air and water and in light of the fact that once more there is no human interference. With everything at a stop, plants are permitted to flourish and develop and produce more coverage and oxygen. Less litter likewise implies lesser stopping up of waterway system, which is good over the long haul for the earth (NongrumEmail, 2020).

Wildlife: Demand of fish as well its price has gone down because of the pandemic and fishing fleets around the globe sit generally inactive. Rainer Faroese has said that the fish biomass will increase because of the sharp decrease in fishing and it is projected in European waters. For example, herring could double their biomass. As of April 2020, sign of sea-going recuperation remains generally recounted. As individuals remained at home because of lockdown and travel restrictions, some animals have been seen in urban areas. Ocean turtles were spotted laying eggs on seashores they once stayed away from, (for example, the shoreline of the Bay of Bengal), because of the lowered levels of human interference and light pollution.

Protectionists expect that African nations will experience a massive surge in shrubbery meat poaching. Matt Brown of the Nature Conservancy said that when individuals do not have some other option for money, poaching goes up for high-esteem items like rhino horn and ivory. On the other hand, Gabon decided to boycott the human utilisation of bats and pangolins, to stem the spread of zoom tic ailments, as the novel corona virus is thought to have transmitted itself to people through these animals.

Climate change: The emissions of carbon dioxide surely diminish because of the lockdown rules set by most nations. The absolute biggest producers of carbon dioxide are the trucks, cars and planes. While numerous trucks are as yet required, vehicle and air traffic has diminished impressively. For instance, reports show that air contamination from nitrogen oxide, another transportation polluter, has diminished fundamentally in China. Airborne particles in northern India are at a 20-year low because of diminished processing plant action just as decreased vehicle, transport, truck and plane traffic. A practically identical decrease in carbon dioxide emissions likewise should bring about India. Comparative decreases across other industrial nations should diminish carbon discharges worldwide and improve environmental change (Nassos, 2020).

Deforestation: The interruption from the pandemic gave spread to illegal deforestation activities. This was seen in Brazil, where satellite symbolism demonstrated deforestation of the Amazon rainforest flooding by more than 50% contrasted with gauge levels (n.d, 2020).

Reduction in waste recycling: Waste reusing has consistently been a significant ecological issue important to all nations. Reusing is a typical and successful approach to forestall pollution, save energy and monitor natural resources. Because of the pandemic, nations, for example, the USA have quit reusing programmes in a portion of their urban areas, as specialists have been worried about the danger of Covid-19 spreading in reusing focuses. In especially influenced European nations, waste management has been limited. For instance, Italy has denied contaminated occupants from arranging their waste. Additionally, the business has taken advantage of the chance to cancel expendable pack bans, despite the fact that solitary utilise plastic can in any case harbour infections and bacteria.

Reduction on environmental noise level: Environmental noise is defined as an unwanted sound that could be generated by anthropogenic activities (for instance, industrial or commercial activities), the transit of engine vehicles and melodies at high volume. Environmental noise is one of the main sources of discomfort for the population and the environment, causing health problems and altering the natural conditions of the ecosystems. The imposition of quarantine measures by most governments has caused people to stay at home. With this, the use of private and public transportation has decreased significantly. Also, commercial activities have stopped almost entirely. All these changes have caused the noise level to drop considerably in most cities in the world (Manuel A. Zambrano-Monserrate, 1-4).

Emissions from coal combustion are falling in China: Yet another effect on the environment as an outcome of corona virus is the marked drop in coal utilisation. This has contributed, in no little part, to the drop in air pollutants in places like China. In addition to the fact that this is improving air quality in the areas influenced, yet it is decreasing the quantity of airborne contaminations like carbon dioxide, carbon monoxide, and nitrous oxides. China is, at present, probably the greatest maker and purchasers of coal. It is evaluated that it devoured around 59% of it for its vitality needs in 2018. It helps runs quite a bit of its industry and is additionally utilised as a local fuel hotspot for a large number of its residents. China's significant coal-terminated force stations saw a 36% drop in utilisation during February and March this year, as indicated by CREA examination of WIND data.

Issues and Challenges

One significant issue to consider is whether these are simply short-lived changes or would it be able to prompt a more drawn out enduring fall in emissions.

- Behavioural Changes: Work From Home is one such positive change that can be relied upon to last even past the lockdown. Lesser number of private vehicles will guarantee less traffic-jams and less pollution.
- Industries and factories: Due to the lockdown the industrial waste generation has totally halted and this has played a significant role in the improvement of both air and water quality over the globe. Nonetheless, it is likely that the discharges may even outperform the previous levels, post-lockdown.
- Some nations may let their natural laws down to compensate for the economic loss endured during the lockdown.
- Poverty and Climate Change: Sustainable development objectives may endure a hit in the post corona world as a huge measure of poverty is going to return. The fight against climate changes will likewise endure as nations over the globe are relied upon to take automatic measures to fix the economic loss.

Conclusion

Declining human activities, during pandemic period, have positively affected the earth. Plants growth is better, there is cleaner air and water and more over there is no human interference. Corona-virus outbreaks effected on travel and industry which resulted in drop in air pollution. Reducing air pollution can lessen both environmental change and Covid-19 dangers yet it is not clear which kinds of air pollution are regular danger to both — environmental change and Covid-19.

References

Goswami, K. (2020, may 2). *Covid-19: 4 unbelievable environmental changes seen in India since lockdown*. Retrieved may 2020, from https://www.indiatoday.in/education.

Manuel A. Zambrano-Monserrate, M.A. (1-4). Indirect effects of Covid-19 on the environment. *Science of the Total Environment*, 2020.

n.d. (2020, May 25). *Impact of the Covid-19 pandemic on the environment.* Retrieved may 2020, from https://en.wikipedia.org/wiki/.

Nassos, G. (2020, May 19). *How coronavirus will affect 4 key environmental issues*. Retrieved July 2020, from https://www.greenbiz.com/.

NongrumEmail, D. (2020, june 3). *World Environment Day 2020: Positive Impact of Covid-19 Lockdown on Environment*. Retrieved July 21, 2020, from https://www.india.com/festivals-events/world-environment-day.

Saigal, K. (2020, April 6). *How is Covid-19 impacting the environment around us?* Retrieved May 25, from https://www.investindia.gov.in/team-india-blogs/how-covid-19-impacting-environment-around-us.

27

IMPACT OF COVID-19 LOCKDOWN ON ECOSYSTEM: COMMUNITY AND ENVIRONMENT

Rajbir Kaur[1] *and Satinder Kaur*[2]

Introduction

The new corona virus (SARS-CoV2) has generated an unprecedented impact in most countries of the world. The virus has affected almost every country on the planet (213 in total) and spread to more than two million people (WHO, 2020).

The term environment means the surrounding. It may be defined as "the whole complex of climatic, edaphic, physiological and biotic factors that act upon an organism or an ecological community and ultimately determine its form and survival". On the other hand, organisms react to differences or changes in their environment in several characteristic ways, either by trying to avoid harmful situations or by being able to adjust physiologically, within their genetic limits, to adverse factors (Singh and Kumar, 2006). In ecological studies, the total environment is said to be made of some non-living components as well as some biotic or living components, thus making the non-living environment and the living environment, respectively. The non-living environment includes the non-living factors, both physical and chemical, which influence the life of organisms. They are the temperature, light, energy, water,

1. Assistant Professor, PG Department of Zoology, Khalsa College, Amritsar, Punjab
2. Assistant Professor, PG Department of Zoology, Khalsa College, Amritsar, Punjab

atmosphere including atmospheric gases and air current, fire, gravity, topography, soil, pH, and nutrients, etc. The living environment includes the living or biotic factors, i.e., animals and plants. The term ecosystem was first proposed by A.G. Tansley in 1935. It may be defined as "a system formed by the community (assemblage of living/non-living component in a prescribed area) and the environment". The central theme of ecosystem concept is that the living organisms of a community not only interact among themselves but also have functional relationship with their non-living environment. This structural and functional system of communities and their environment is called an ecosystem (Singh and Kumar, 2006).

During past two decades, India has witnessed an expeditious industrial growth which has certainly improved the standard of living of its people and it is also evident from the rising vehicular fleet on roads. But we have paid a heavy price for this development in terms of poisoning the air we breathe. The Government of India ordered a nationwide lockdown on the 24th of March 2020 as India was on the list of countries affected with Covid-19 worldwide. Various restrictions posed by government and subsequent lockdown, anthropogenic activities like industrial projects, vehicular movement, construction projects, tourism, other common transportation activities witnessed a 'never before' stagnant phase. Screening tests and public policies of social distancing has been adopted by most countries to combat the spread of the virus. It is clear that the priority revolves around people's health (Zambrano-Monserrate et al., 2020). Social distancing policies adopted by most governments resulted in cleaning up of many beaches around the world as there was a major reduction in waste generated by tourists. Noise levels have also fallen lesser private and public transportation, as well as commercial activities.

Impact of Covid-19 on Ecosystem

The effect of Covid-19 on ecosystem can be studied in terms of effects on living as well as non-living components.

1. Effect on Non-living Components

Effect on Air Quality

Pollution is one of the major environmental problems these days. According to E.P. Odum (2005), pollution is an undesirable change in the physical, chemical or biological characteristics of our air, land and water that will harmfully affect the human life and the desirable species, or that may waste or deteriorate our raw material resources.

With the gradual rise in the number of motor vehicles and factories, air pollution in big cities and other industrial centres has now reached an alarming stage. But after the lockdown, clear atmosphere has been observed as cars, trains and flights were prohibited. Industries and factories were non-functional during this crisis. As a result of the lockdown and the disruption in human and industrial activities in numerous countries around the world, a significant reduction in air pollution, especially in the concentration of NO_2, has been noticed in China and several European and American countries (Tobías et al., 2020; Wang and Su, 2020; Zhang et al., 2020). Recent studies by Muhammad et al. (2020) and Dutheil et al. (2020) have reported a NO_2 reduction ranging between 20 and 30% in China, USA, Italy, Spain and France.

Effect on Water Quality

Water is one of the most important natural resources and a regular supply of clean water is very essential for the survival of all living organisms. Clear water has been observed and the fish could be seen with naked eye as there were no boats, for fishing and playing on the rivers were stopped. No doubt, because of the lesser human footfall even the oceans are recovering and marine life is thriving.

The Ganga water quality improved remarkably during the lockdown period. The 2,500-kilometre river has been an important part of India's history, identity, religious beliefs and economy for thousands of years. Many industries and offices are closed due to the lockdown and, therefore, the Yamuna is also looking cleaner these days. The stoppage of industrial pollutants and industrial waste has definitely had a positive effect on water quality.

2. Effect on Living Component

Effect on Humans

Corona virus is known to cause pneumonia like symptoms in human body. These symptoms include severe breathing problems, cough, high grade fever and cold. The most affected part of the body is lungs. After entrance into the body, virus multiplies and stimulate the lung cells to produce enough mucous which leads to clogging. This in turn creates breathing problems.

Apart from this effect, humans faced unemployment in India. Labour class was most affected during covid-19 lockdown. Economy rates were drastically reduced. Self-employed class also faced financial loss during lockdown period. In India, there is no recruitment in Government sector and fresh graduates are in pressure of fearing withdrawal of job offers from corporate sectors because of the pandemic situation. With increase of unemployment situation, the interest for education may gradually decrease as people struggle for food rather than education. Education department also suffered as the Indian education system was mostly based on the offline system and classes. Students across the education sector have been dramatically impacted by the spread of the corona virus. This has caused a lot of stress not only for students but also for faculties and authorities as they do not have basic internet access, laptops and smartphones to pursue online teaching. A rural and poor student cannot afford online teaching through these gadgets.

Effect on Wildlife

An opportunity has been given by nature itself to wildlife to venture beyond their usual territory as there was reduction in pollution levels, public spaces and human encounters. In most of the countries, animals were reported venturing into cities as people try to control the spread of Corona virus by confining themselves to their safe home. In such crisis, we must learn to co-exist and understand our relationship with nature if we want to survive and protect our ecosystem. Aquatic biomass has been increased as fishing practices were prohibited during lockdown period. Animals have been spotted in most of the countries. They are moving freely on the roads due to the lack of human interference. For example, sea turtles have been spotted in the areas where they are usually not found to lay their eggs. A massive Nilgai (Blue-bull) wandering outside a Mall in Noida, India, coyotes basking in the parks of San Francisco, cougars roaming the streets of Santiago, Chile, penguins waddling across Cape Town and even sea lions in Mar del Plata harbour in Argentina. The world has witnessed some rare wildlife sightings (Sandilya, 2020).

Effect on Vegetation

During and after lockdown period, flora has been blooming; plants are growing better as the air and water was cleaner, and this is all because of lack of human interference. Plants are allowed to thrive and grow by nature itself and produced more coverage and oxygen. Less litter also means lesser clogging of river systems, which is good in the long run for the environment.

Conclusion

The environment is an integral component of human and animal health. Covid-19 is a global health challenge in the twenty-first century. The only preventive step is to follow lockdown and social distancing. The environment and ecosystem of the world has started healing itself as there was restriction in human activities. Industries, transport, vehicles and flights all have stopped. This in turn led to reduction in carbon emissions and the quality of air has improved. Not only air but water quality has also improved like the rivers of India. Ganga, Yamuna, and Cauvery etc. have become clean and clear and aquatic life is visible. Most of the countries taking Covid-19 as a lesson for saving the environment and considering it as a recovery time of nature. Human activities were responsible for environmental degradation and it was not irreversible but Covid-19 gave some relief to environment. In a period of just 1–2 months, "recovery of nature" is being witnessed. This is the right time for us to understand and react. Government and policy makers should take necessary steps or actions like lockdown as an alternative measure for reduction in pollution. There is a need to restore ecosystem and environment at least in this present scenario of Covid-19 pandemic.

References

Chen, K., Wang, M., Huang, C., Kinney, P.L. and Paul, A.T. (2020). Air pollution reduction and mortality benefit during the Covid-19 outbreak in China. *MedRxiv*1-4. https://doi.org/10.1101/2020.03.23.20039842

Dutheil, F., Baker, J.S. and Navel, V. (2020). Covid-19 as a factor influencing air pollution?*Environmental Pollution* 263: 114466, 10.1016/j.envpol.2020.114466

Kanniah, K.D., Zaman, N.A.F.K., Kaskaoutis, D.G. and Latif, M.T. (2020). Covid-19's impact on the atmospheric environment in the Southeast Asia region. *Science of The Total Environment* 736: 139658.

Muhammad, S., Long, X. and Salman, M. (2020). Covid-19 pandemic and environmental pollution: a blessing in disguise? *Science of The Total Environment* 138820, 10.1016/j.scitotenv.2020.138820

Odum, E.P. (2005). *Fundamentals of Ecology*. Fifth Edition. Belmont, CA: Thomson Brooks/Cole.

Sandilya, A. (2020). How Covid-19 Pandemic Has Affected Wildlife. https://wildlifesos.org/chronological-news/how-covid-19-pandemic-has-affected-wildlife/

Shereen, M.A., Khan, S., Kazmi, A., Bashir, N. and Siddique, R. (2020). Covid-19 infection: origin, transmission, and characteristics of human coronaviruses. *Journal of Advanced Research* 24: 91–98.

Singh, H.R. and Kumar, N. (2006). *Ecology and Environmental Science*. Vishal Publishing Co., Jalandhar, India.

Tansley, A.G. (1935). The use and abuse of vegetational concepts and terms. Ecology 16: 284 307. In: *Progress in Physical Geography* 31(5): 517-522.

Tobías, A., Carnerero, C., Reche, C., Massagué, J., Via, M., Minguillón, M.C., Alastuey, A. and Querol, X. (2020). Changes in air quality during the lockdown in Barcelona (Spain) one month into the SARS-CoV-2 epidemic. *Science of The Total Environment* 726: 138540, 10.1016/j.scitotenv.2020.138540.

Wang, Q. and Su, M. (2020). A preliminary assessment of the impact of Covid-19 on environment–a case study of China. *Science of The Total Environment* 728: 138915, 10.1016/j.scitotenv.2020.138915

WHO. (2020). https://www.who.int/emergencies/diseases/novel-coronavirus-2019.

Zambrano-Monserrate, M.A., Ruano, M.A. and Sanchez-Alcalde, L. (2020). Indirect effects of Covid-19 on the environment. *Science of The Total Environment* 728: 138813.

Zhang, R., Zhang, Y., Lin, H., Feng, X., Fu, T.-M. and Wang, Y. (2020). NO_2 emission reduction and recovery during Covid-19 in east China. *Atmosphere* 11(4): 433, 10.3390/atmos11040433

28

IMPACT OF COVID-19 CRISIS ON ENVIRONMENT

Sandeep Kaur

Introduction

Coronavirus Disease 2019 (Covid-19) outbreak emerged in Wuhan, China, whose spreading dynamics is not yet fully understood, As the number of Coronavirus infections surged, governments, one after the other, put restrictive public health measures to beat off the pandemic. The most substantial measure taken was 'Stay home orders' which resulted in falling of pollution and greenhouse gas emission levels across the continents. Though clearer skies, water bodies, and better air quality speak of the effects of lockdown on the environment, yet more is to be digged into to get a better picture of the scenario.

The move for containing the virus spread led to some unexpected consequences. The air quality in major cities across the world improved dramatically during March, April and May 2020. As economic activities came to a halt, factory and road traffic emissions of Carbon Dioxide (CO_2), Nitrogen, and related Ozone(O_3) formation and particulate matter (PM) dropped significantly. Data from the Sentinel-5P satellite reveals that nitrogen dioxide levels have dipped in Europe since the pandemic. Besides, people are reporting seeing the Himalayas for the first time from their homes. While the pandemic has been devastating for thousands of migrant workers in India, Delhi witnessed a reduction of over 70% in PM2.5 and nitrogen oxide levels. The US witnessed a 33%, 22% and 19% drop in PM2.5 contractions in New York, Los Angeles, and Seattle respectively during March-April 2020. Also, ground station metrics from China, Italy and South Korea reported a downward trend in overall PM2.5 in places.

Negative Effects of Covid-19 Crisis to the Environment

Covid-19 crisis pandemic which restricts the daily mobility of people with increasing effect worldwide, caused the closure of factories, the stopping of education and training, the halt of social mobility and the reduction in greenhouse gas emission in industrial countries. Besides serious limitations in international travel, entertainment, sports, hospitality, tourism, transportation, manufacturing, many other sectors were also affected by the outbreak.

Assistant Professor, Mohan Lal Memorial Institute of Education, Mudhal, Amritsar

The global aviation industry expects that they suffered damage to the tune of $100 billion due to such restrictions. Such a wide crisis, of course, has environmentally destructive effects. One of these is medical waste resulting from the increased medical activity. It was stated that for the period when the outbreak peaked in Wuhan, an average of 240 tons of medical waste was produced daily in hospitals and this value was six times higher than the normal value. Also, plastic based medical masks used worldwide are an environmental problem. It is reported as good news that there is no evidence that the Covid-19 virus is transmitted through wastewater or the sewerage or water treatment workers.

Positive Effects of Covid-19 Crisis on the Environment

Environmentally, the Covid-19 crisis also had the constructive effects. Lesser mobility/travel of people will reduce carbon dioxide emissions as lesser vehicles would be in use. In addition, since the many events, meetings and political events started to be held in the form of a remote conference, environmental emission have decreased globally. A reduction of approximately 25% of carbon emission is reported that air pollution such as nitrogen dioxide and carbon dioxide emission is reduced in many regions. The greenhouse gas emission reduction is observed during the restrictions of the state, such as China and Italy. Therefore, atmospheric pollution is expected to decrease the Covid-19 crisis.

Those who are accustomed to the efficiency of teleconferencing and distance education are expected to increase the number of these activities after the crisis. Many countries in the world have switched to distance education..

On the other hand, a study revealed that the decrease in transportation and industrial activities in China is not enough to prevent air pollution cases when meteorology is unfavourable. Therefore, more efforts are required to achieve a serious reduction in air pollution. In another study, it was revealed that there was a decrease in air pollution, during the crises in Barcelona (Spain), but there were significant differences between the pollutants. It has been observed that most important reduction amount are on Black Carbon and NO_2, while a decrease occurs in the particulate matters with a diameter of less than 10. In contrast, an increase in O_3 level has been reported. One reason for the less decline in PM10 compared to other gasses pollutants like NO_2 is the effect of natural activities such as sea spray and desert powder, which strongly affected Spain, Italy, Greece and entire Mediterranean basin. It revealed that more in-depth analysis is required to see the reason for the decrease in PM10.

It is also revealed that individuals whose social activities were restricted during the Covid-19 crises were conscious of food waste, they tried to reduce waste, and displayed behaviours to prevent food wastage. Further, analysis revealed that the reason for avoiding food waste was negative socio-economic effects (food anxiety, limited movement, lack of income) of Covid-19 rather than environmental awareness. During this Covid-19 crisis, it will be beneficial to intensify educational and communication campaigns in order to increase environmental positive behaviours of people.

Conclusion

Worldwide, Covid-19 caused people to have limited social freedom. People who are isolated/strict at home are afraid of food wastage due to their sociological concerns. On the other hand, reductions in greenhouse gas emission were observed due to significantly reduced road transport, industrial, educational and other activities, but it was observed that this was not enough to curb air pollution for all pollutants. The crises caused very serious problems in the renewable energy sector, such as delays in the supply chain.

References

Ammar, F. (2020), Coronavirus at wind power plant in North Dakota shuts down production. Retrieve April 21, 2020, from https://www.cnbc.com/2020/04/20 Coronavirus-at-wind-power-plant-in-north-dakot-a-shuts-down-prodction.html

Contieini, E, Frediani, B., & Caro, D (2020), Con atmospheric pollution be considered a co-factor extremely high level of SARS-CoV-2 lethality in Northern Italy? Environmental Pollution https://doi.org/10.1016/j.envpol.2020.114565

Contini, D. & Costabile, F (2020). Does air pollution influences COVD-19 outbreaks? Atmosphere, 11(4), 377. https://doi.org/10.3390/atoms//040377

WHO. (2020a). Coronavirus disease (Covid-19) pandemic Retrieved April 20, 2020, from https://doi.org/10.1016/S0140-6736(20)30547-X

WHO. (2020b). Water, Sanitation, hygiene and waste management for the Covid-19 virus Geneva. World Health Organization.

7

IMPACT OF LOCKDOWN ON CREATIVITY AND READING HABITS

29

COVID-19: A TIME TO NURTURE CREATIVITY

Maninder Kaur (Dr.)

Introduction

Covid-19 has ravaged the world. India is no exception. The contagion has beaten all postulates of socio-economic growth. It has defeated science, technology, economics and even social systems. The common man is perplexed and shattered. And governments are struggling to find a way out of the present pandemic.

At this puzzling moment when everything is unsettled, our students are experiencing psychic stress and conventional bookish knowledge seems to have lost its relevance, what sort of therapeutic role can we play as teachers? Some would say that this question makes no sense because teachers are just employees, and their only responsibility is to engage with 'online teaching', complete the syllabus, and report to their bosses — principals and vice-chancellors. It would also be argued that teachers are 'professionals', they are not healers or gurus; and hence, their only task is to fill the minds of their students with packaged knowledge relating to history and biology, physics and civics or mathematics and sociology, they must see that time is not 'wasted', and students remain busy with assignments.

Possibly, as Ivan Illich would have said, in a schooled society we are led to believe that nothing can exist outside formal institutions, and education is essentially a process of graded learning with the reutilisation of teacher centric monologues, mastery of 'official' textbooks, and weekly, monthly, yearly examinations. Hence, as teachers, we too tend to think that even though people are dying, migrant workers are suffering, and financial anxieties are disturbing a significant section of our population, we need not bring out these issues while we appear on the screen and engage with our students; we would pretend that the business can go on as usual. Hence, as I was told by a parent, even a three-year-old child cannot be spared; a playschool wants the child to sit in front of the laptop, and learn drawing. Let the world outside suffer, but our children must close their eyes and only 'upload' all sorts of bookish assignments and useless projects.

What an ugly system of education we have created over the years! It confuses awakened intelligence with rote learning, inner flowering with grading, and life with bookish knowledge. Is it, therefore, surprising that even at this moment of the pandemic, when death is mere statistics and everything is

---

Assistant Professor, Khalsa College of Education, G.T. Road, Amritsar

upside down, the prevalent system cannot see beyond 'online teaching' and the ritualisation of examinations? It does not matter even if a girl from Kerala commits suicide, as she feels wounded because of her inability to attend online classes in this unequal society characterised by heightened digital divide. It does not matter if young students, their parents and the larger society are experiencing severe mental stress, and there is widespread fear. We are told that online classes must go on, the same age-old syllabus has to be covered and exams must be conducted.

All of us — parents, teachers, students and concerned citizens — who still cherish the idea of a more life-affirming and ethically meaningful education, must stand together and propose a new paradigm. It would be an act of betrayal, if even at this time of breakdown of the conventional notion of progress and development, we do not reimagine the way our children should grow up in the post-Covid world.

We must acquire the courage to speak a different language, activate our creative agency and see ourselves beyond loyal mediators between students and the official curriculum. We must assert that education is not merely about memorising texts like a parrot and writing the exams; it is about awakened intelligence and deep sensitivity to life. Education must prepare us to make sense of the times we live in, retain our sanity and acquire the psychic strength to cope with the new reality. Two points can be made in this context:

First, let us refer to the world of children and school students. Imagine what it means to them to remain deprived of parks, playgrounds, company of friends and the experience of the abundance. Image what it means to remain confined to a tiny apartment with other siblings and anxiety-ridden parents. They need conversations; they need warmth and intimacy; they need positive vibrations. At this moment, they are not required to be bombarded with, say, Chapter 7 of NCERT Class VI maths book; they need not be compelled to produce a chart mentioning the states that produce rice, wheat, bajra and other crops. Instead, they need to be listened to with great care; and teachers as friends and catalysts should try to open their eyes so that they feel encouraged to transform this moment of bewilderment into a life-affirming possibility. For instance, is it possible for a teacher to encourage a child to observe what she misses under 'normal' circumstances — for instance, how her mother works day and night to keep things in order? Is it possible for the teacher to encourage the child to further activate the power of observation by looking at the empty street, a barking dog, or a distant star in the evening? Is it possible to give an assignment of an altogether different kind writing a diary based on a conversation with the parents on the plight of the migrant workers? With these creatively nuanced pedagogical practices, children would learn the real lesson of life even if they miss a couple of routinised classes.

Second, think of college/university students. True, they are worried about their academic prospects and careers. But then, we should not forget that as they enter the post-Covid world, they would need a new sensitivity or a new politico-ethical consciousness. College/university teacher should not remain indifferent to it. A sociology lecturer tells me that she has to complete the syllabus, and asks her undergraduate students to write a paper on Rampura — the village where noted sociologist MN Srinivas studied. Does it make sense when one of her students located in a remote village in Bihar, because of poor Internet connectivity, misses the Zoom class? Imagine what would have happened had the teacher sent her a lovely mail, and, encouraged her to write a detailed monograph of his own village in Bihar: the way it refuses to give entry to a group of migrant workers who have walked thousands of kilometres from Surat, and then realised the trauma of yet another form of stigma, untouchability and homelessness.

Possibly, social anthropology would have acquired a new meaning at the time of the pandemic. Likewise, the students of science ought to be encouraged to see beyond the parameters of instrumental reasoning, and explore deeper issues relating to the meaning of existence at a time when death is statistics, fear is normal, human touch is a taboo. Imagine a bright professor of physics asking them to read Albert Camus, Leo Tolstoy and Gautam Buddha.

No harm would be done to the growth of knowledge, if at this time of the pandemic, schools or universities refuse to conduct the ritualisation of annual examinations, and declare the results on the basis of their performance in the papers they have already written. Our children would be free from chronic anxiety, and possibly find some meditative space which is needed to make sense of the issues relating to fear and death, science and uncertainty, and disease and stigma.

Sensitivity or a nuanced art of living — not a 'perfect' grade sheet from the academic bureaucracy is needed. As a matter of fact, we need to fight and strive for the kind of education that stresses more on the process of inner flowering, physical/mental and spiritual growth, art of relatedness with nature and the community, and everyday challenges that inspire young learners to relate theory and practice, book and life and science and ethics. If learning happens all the time, why should we be so neurotically obsessed with one examination.

Life has to be lived gracefully and meaningfully, and school/university examinations cannot be regarded as the soul of the learning experience. Hence, at this turning point, we all have to walk together, and reimagine a kind of education that radiates the spirit of love, care and integral learning which is needed in the post-Covid world. The spirit of life-affirming education has to be rescued from the alliance of academic bureaucrats and traders of 'knowledge'.

References

https://en.unesco.org/covid19/educationresponse

https://www-indiatoday-in.cdn.ampproject.org/v/s/www.indiatoday.in/amp/education-today/featurephilia/story/covid-19-impact-digital-education-conventional-education-divd-1661185-2020-03-30

https://www.educationinsider.net/detail_news.php?id=1326

https://www.education.ie/en/Schools-Colleges/Information/Information-CommunicationsTechnology-ICT-in-Schools/Digital-strategy-for-Schools/Building-Towards-a-Learning-Society-ANational-Digital-Strategy-for-Schools-Consultative-Paper.pdf

30

IMPACT OF LOCKDOWN ON READING HABITS: A PSYCHOLOGICAL PERSPECTIVE

Sharanjit Kaur (Dr.)

Introduction

The Corona Virus Disease – 2019 (Covid-19), being highly infective has universally caused a psychosocial impact, namely, psychological ill-effects, economic burden, financial losses, etc. The mass fear of this pandemic is termed as "Coronaphobia" which has spawned numerous psychological manifestations across the different spheres of the population (Dubey et al., 2020). Government strives to improve the awareness of the public about Covid-19 prevention and precautionary measures through different websites, mass media and social media. In order to get maximum information about the disease, people have started reading newspapers and various e-contents. Some have started reading books so that they can divert their mind from the prevailing uncertain situation. On the other hand, it has also been found that there are people who find it difficult to read during this pandemic because of the increase in their levels of stress and anxiety despite of the fact that they have more free time with them. In addition to this, a rise in the popularity of entertainment platforms, such as – Netflix and YouTube, is also making it hard for people to pick up a book and read.

Assistant Professor, PG Department of Psychology, Kanya Maha Vidyalaya, Jalandhar

Why is it difficult to read during this pandemic?

During the Corona lockdown time, there are many people complaining that they are unable to read despite the spare time on their hands. One of the reasons for this is that the "spare time" is actually a myth, given the increased amount of household chores and other responsibilities when there are no other social engagements. The other main and the utmost important reason for this is the "mental health" of an individual which acts as a hindrance in the ability and the desire to read. Stress at work or school, family conflicts, interpersonal problems and financial struggles can give birth to larger anxieties which can paralyse an individual's thought and ability to work efficiently (Kapur, 2020). The new life-style of working from home, managing home life and fretting that social contact can lead to infection has exacerbated the levels of anxiety and stress.

According to Bandura (1997), "Anxiety is a state of anticipatory apprehension over possible deleterious happenings". It includes worrying excessively over real or perceived threats in the environment of an individual. In a study conducted by Markham and Darke (1991), it was found that anxiety interferes with reading comprehension, making heavy demands on working memory. In another study conducted by Sellers (2000), it was found that the participants who experienced high anxiety were more likely to experience more off-task and interfering thoughts which messed up their reading comprehension. Therefore, a glance at various studies has clearly indicated the adverse effects of anxiety on the reading ability of an individual.

Stress is defined as a real or interpreted threat to the physiological or psychological integrity of an individual that results in the production of physiological and behavioural responses (McEwen, 2000). Kuang, Ashraf, Das and Biccheri (2020) conducted a study on a sample of people residing in Tamil Nadu and found that majority of them experienced increased stress due to financial troubles and lockdown. A number of studies have shown how stress has increased during this pandemic. It has also been found that the habit of reading is negatively associated with stress (Ross and Zhang, 2008). During this pandemic, as the ability to read becomes difficult, one is tempted to watch a movie or an online series for one's entertainment. In order to get relief from their stress and anxiety, people are more likely to spend time on the digital platform as one remains mentally passive unlike in reading where they have to mentally engage one's own mind. So, people are more inclined to watch TV because they are stressed.

On the contrary, this does not have to be this way. Reading can be a very effective stress-buster for all of us. It can prove to be a very effective and therapeutic aid that can help in coping with stress and provide creative ideas in the uncertain times of Covid-19.

Reading Habit Improves Mental Health Issues

Reading is one of those simple and daily activities which we often take for granted, but have we ever thought what actually reading does to our mind.

When we are reading, we are focusing our attention on the way the letters have been arranged on the page, how a letter has been spelled, how thought has been expressed through a sentence, thus enabling an individual to visualise what one is reading. Therefore, it altogether transports an individual to a different world where one can find peace and solace from the worries and cares of real life where there is an unending threat of this endemic. In the words of Dr. Shyam Bhat, a pioneer of holistic psychiatry in India, "Reading is a workout for the brain. Just as physical exercise decreases the risk of diabetes and heart disease, a regular habit of reading decreases the risk of various conditions, namely, dementia, and improves memory, concentration, and mood which are especially relevant in the times of Covid".

Therefore, it is highly advisable for those who are dealing with anxiety during these tough times that they should find the right book for them and it should be read for the sheer pursuit of pleasure and inner happiness. There can be times when you have started reading a book and later on, you realise that you are not enjoying it and it is not working for you. It is always okay to leave that book unread and find a book that works best for you. So, it is essential that in order to develop a habit of healthy reading, one should be aware of why they want to do it and only then, they will be able to find the right kind of book for themselves that will serve their purpose of reading. When one goes into the flow of reading, all the stresses and anxieties in one's life will be drained out and in the process, various novel ideas can generate in one's mind, thereby adding to the mental health of an individual.

Explaining the benefits of reading, Dr. Paul Byrne stated that, "Bibliotherapy, quite simply, is about books as therapy. It's not meant to take the place of medicine, but it can complement it." Numerous studies are in the same line of direction. In a study conducted by Clark and Teravainen-Goff (2018), it was found that reading is highly correlated with mental well-being. Children, who read more, had more positive attitudes and scored high on mental well-being. In addition, it was also found that individuals who read more and enjoyed reading, had higher mental well-being scores in comparison to those who did not enjoy reading and had negative attitudes towards reading. In another study conducted by Bahrami et al. (2011), it was found that there is a negative relationship between the habit of reading and depression. Therefore, *the tendency to read is considered to be one of the most important indices of human growth in terms of their abilities and potential to attain a mentally healthy and happy life.*

Reading Reinvented in Covid times

Since the time Covid lockdowns have been imposed, as people are staying at home, they have tried to reinvent things. Reading is one of those things which have also been reinvented. Rather than practising the traditional way of reading – opening the book and then sifting through the pages chapter by chapter – the modern generation has chosen to access books through listening to them. There are writers who have launched their books in the form of Audiobooks which have resulted in a spurt of interest in listening to the audio content of the books. When the bookstores and delivery of books ordered online were closed during the lockdown, audiobooks became the spotlight. Whether an individual is reading a physical book or listening to an audiobook, these are two different roads to the same destination, but both create different experiences for the reader. There are research evidences that reveal that either reading a story or listening to a story; both stimulate the brain in the same way. The same regions of the brain get activated with the same intensity when one reads or listens (Walter, 2019). According to Moyer (2012), listening to audiobooks fosters listening comprehension of an individual. So, it can be said that those who opt to download the audiobooks and listen to it instead of reading it are the Smart-readers of the present times.

Conclusion

For various life issues, a well-written and stimulating book can have an influential impact. Books can create an in-depth understanding of oneself and others. They also modify the way an individual perceives the world around him/ her resulting in developing insights that can help in handling various life situations. Likewise, the present situation of the pandemic can also be dealt with in a healthy way without panicking and excessively worrying about it through the habit of reading books. Studies have evidently shown that reading alleviates stress and anxiety. Thus, in the present times, in order to find relief from the uncertain Covid times, one can begin reading a book. It is rightly said that,

> *"A book is a garden, an orchard, a storehouse, a party, a company by the way, a counselor, a multitude of counselors."* – Charles Baudelaire

This quote clearly states the many benefits of reading books. It can provide us with a psyche which has the potential to be one's own counsellor, friend and source of entertainment which is one of the essential requirements in the times of Covid lockdown when 'Social Distancing' is of utmost importance.

References

Bandura, A. (1997). *Self-efficacy: The exercise of control.* New York: W.H. Freeman.

Clark, C. & Teravainen-Goff, A. (September, 2018). Mental well-being, reading and writing. National Literacy Trust Research Report, 1-37.

Dubey, S., Biswas, P., Ghosh, R., Chatterjee, S., Dubey, M.J. & Lavie, C.J. (2020). Psychosocial impact of Covid-19. *Diabetes and Metabolic Syndrome: Clinical Research and Reviews, 14*, 779-788.

Kapur, M. (July, 2020). Mental health: Why you could be finding it hard to read during Covid-19. Work Economic Forum. Retrieved from https://www.weforum.org/agenda/2020/07/reading-covid19-anxiety/

Kunag, J., Ashraf, S., Das, U. & Bicchieri, C. (2020). Awareness, risk perception, and stress during the Covid-19 pandemic in communities of Tamil Nadu, India. PsyArXiv. June 27, 2020. doi:10.31234/osf.io/qhgrd

Lai, C.C., Shih, T.P., Ko, W.C., Tang, H.J. & Huesh, P.R. (2020). Severe acute respiratory syndrome coronavirus 2 (SARS-CoV-2) and coronavirus disease-2019 (Covid-19): the epidemic and the challenges. *International Journal of Antimicrob Agents, 55(3),* 1-9.

Markham, R., & Darke, S. (1991). The effects of anxiety on verbal and spatial task performance. *Australian Journal of Psychology, 43*, 107-111.

McEwen, B. (2000). Stress, definition and concepts. In Fink, G. (Ed.), *Encyclopedia of Stress* (pp. 508–509). San Diego: Academic Press.

Moyer, J. E. (2012). Audiobooks and E-Books: A Literature Review. *Reference and User Services Quarterly, 51(4)*, 340-354.

Ross, C.E., & Zhang, W. (2008). Education and Psychological Distress among Older Chinese. *Journal of Aging and Health*, *20*(3), 273–289.

Sellers, V.D. (2000). Anxiety and reading comprehension in Spanish as a foreign language. *Foreign Language Annals, 33(5),* 512-521.

Walter, J. (August, 2019). Audiobooks or reading? To our brains, it doesn't matter. Discover. Retrieved from https://www.discovermagazine.com/mind/audiobooks-or-reading-to-our-brains-it-doesnt-matter

31

CHANGE IN READING HABITS DURING COVID-19 LOCKDOWN

Gurleen Kaur[1] and Mamta Rani[2]

Introduction

Countries all around the globe have been facing the spread of Covid-19 virus at very fast rate and locked the countries to get a hold on this spread. Prime Minister Mr. Narendra Modi announced a 21 days' lockdown in India on 24 March 2020 after a trial lockdown on 22 March 2020 called "Janata curfew". This was very important in a developing country like India due to its weak medical status to slow down the spread of this virus in order to gain some time to be ready to fight against it.

1. Research Scholar, Khalsa College of Education, G.T. Road, Amritsar
2. Research Scholar, Khalsa College of Education, G.T. Road, Amritsar

The lockdowns have changed the lives of people all around the globe in many ways. People, at home all the time during this lockdown, only went out to buy things like groceries, dairy products, medicines, etc. There was huge impact of this lockdown on economy of the countries because every kind of business, construction projects, schools, colleges, offices were closed except the things related to daily needs and medical help. International or local flights, trains, and every kind of public transport were abandoned. Apparently, there was no source of income for most of the people all over the world during this lockdown which was the biggest problem for all the developing countries. Students and teachers also faced difficulty in coping up with the sudden shift in teaching learning process from real face-to-face interaction to the digital mode.

Moreover, people were facing the sudden lifestyle change, they had to be careful about their and other's health whenever moving out, at the same time living at home all the time was also a big change in their lifestyle. They need to develop new ideas, new ways to keep themselves busy and happy to avoid the negative or bad thoughts of fear from this pandemic. Health and medical experts have given different advices to cope up with the anxiety during lockdown. One of those advices is reading books. Different age groups may like to read different genre of books but definitely it helps in coping up with anxiety and make them more positive and mindful. it has been found out in many surveys that just like many other things, reading habits of the people have also been influenced by these time-to-time lockdowns.

Impact of Lockdown on Reading Habits

Every aspect of life changed during this pandemic and we will be talking about the changes in lifestyle related to the media consumption of people during this crisis. So, our discussion relate to the transformation observed in the way individual or a group interact with various activities like media, reading books, magazines, etc. The reading habits are discussed broadly on three bases which are reading as leisure time activity, hobby and learning for educational purpose. The changes in these patterns of reading resulted in researches interested in this field of study which led to many researches in this field. The main questions that were focussed by these researchers included:

- How many individuals are reading during this pandemic?
- What is the reading frequency of people in lockdown?
- If there is a rise in buying of books, what types and kind of books are preferred by people?
- The most preferred genre of books?
- Is there a rise or fall in buying of books during Covid-19?

So, the media consumption of the people definitely increased during this pandemic and this could be attributed to the free time people had and this could be an easiest way to overcome the boredom that this crisis has created. Many people who were at home practising social distancing thought this could be a best way to get rid of stress and worry and this increase in reading habits is mostly considered as a way to escape the monotony that this lockdown has created. This lets us conclude that the reading frequency of people unquestionably saw a rise and the individuals were considering reading a part of their leisure time activity. According to a report by *The Economic Times*, it was concluded that the sales of E-books has been doubled in this pandemic and the readers are delighted to welcome this trend in reading. This change in reading has led to publishers interested in producing more E-books than before.

Now, talking about the types of books that the readers preferred, these included printed books or a hard copy, E-books or a soft copy, audio books and other reading materials like blogs, articles, and newspapers. According to a research, readers of age group 18-24 preferred using print books as compared to other age groups who were reading almost same amounts of these books. In the initial phases of lockdown as the bookshops, book deliveries and libraries were shut down, this brought about a major change in the approach of reading and the readers as well as students of schools, colleges and universities were shifting from traditional reading to E-books and audio books. The consequences of lockdown and reading were difficult for school going children and students as compared to other readers and higher education students. According to report by The Christian Science Monitor, the children missed reading in classes and teachers faced this challenge of bringing back the essence of classrooms and the interactions between students and teachers in these virtual classrooms. Methods of hearing (audio) books and reading aloud the books through a video call included as a way to cope up with such situation.

Not only educational books but children books like stories, poems presented through online platforms like YouTube, Spotify have also seen a tremendous rise. The hard copies were no longer available and teachers instead of presenting these print books through camera to their students shifted to use E-books and use methods like screen recording, circulating pdf versions of books among students. Also many apps help readers to listen to the content from screen by enabling screen reading. Video lessons is another approach used by many to circulate information, podcasts and so on. So, the lockdown without any doubt has changed the way we read.

Coming to how these readers discovered the books for reading a common answer one gets is by communicating with friends, family, etc. and the second is the social media applications and the search engines which classify books as bestsellers or highly rated by critiques, for educational books suggestions of fellow colleagues and professors. Many digital book clubs came into existence, webinars conducted, reading parties through virtual technology and practices like digital and online libraries gained momentum.

The genre that was most liked by the readers included fiction as well as non-fiction. The readers read many self-help books during this crisis to cope up with the problems of day-today-life, to gain better understanding about their lives and books that could generate positivity within the minds of people. Initially, the books about isolation and pandemics were gaining popularity but later the genre that made a lot of money includes subjects like romance, crime, mystery, inspirational and self-help books, science fictions and then horror. Coming to the education field, the practices like online books, E-books have been increasing rapidly and many educators, researchers, professors, teachers are working on making educational materials and books available to all.

Although during this time of pandemic, many publishing houses and bookshops faced a downfall but the sales definitely increased for E-books and audio books and many budding authors are choosing this platform for showcasing their work whether it is related to fiction or non-fiction and education related to life as well as school and higher education has underwent this transformation of becoming digital and has changed the way we read.

Conclusion

Covid-19 surely has an impact on our lives. Without any doubt, almost every profession felt some unique challenges, and technology is viewed as one of the tools to manage these difficult times. The ways of doing things have changed and coming to the reading habits it has certainly faced a transformation too. People have been reading but ways of reading has changed, the reading is no more traditional; it is digital now, the publishers and authors are choosing online platforms to showcase their work. This shift will be helpful if we keep in mind the advantages of using E-books, online books and audio books as this will ensure that the books can now reach everywhere and there are lesser restrictions. The reading frequency of people unquestionably increased and the lockdown without any doubt has changed the way people read.

References

Abigail Boucher Lecturer in English Literature, et al. "How Reading Habits Have Changed during the Covid-19 Lockdown." *The Conversation*, 5 Oct. 2020, theconversation.com/how-reading-habits-have-changed-during-the-covid-19-lockdown-146894.

Chettri, Kushmeeta. (2013). Reading Habits — An Overview. *IOSR Journal of Humanities and Social Science*. 14. 13-17. 10.9790/0837-01461317.

Covid-19: Lockdown across India, in line with WHO guidance. (2020, March 27). UN News. https://news.un.org/en/story/2020/03/1060132

Book Genres That Make the Most Money. (2018, November 20). Bookstr. https://bookstr.com/article/book-genres-that-make-the-most-money/

Online, E.T. (2020, March 25). *India will be under complete lockdown for 21 days: Narendra Modi. The Economic Times*. https://economictimes.indiatimes.com/news/politics-and-nation/india-will-be-under-complete-lockdown-starting-midnight-narendra-modi/articleshow/74796908.cms

Team, T.H.D. (2020, April 6). *Data | What is the effect of India's coronavirus lockdown on people's mobility? The Hindu*. https://www.thehindu.com/data/data-what-is-the-effect-of-indias-coronavirus-lockdown-on-peoples-mobility/article31265439.ece

Bhaskar, U. (2020, April 14). *India to remain closed till 3 May, economy to open up gradually in lockdown 2.0*. Mint. https://www.livemint.com/news/india/pm-modi-announces-extension-of-lockdown-till-3-may-11586839412073.html

COV-IND-19 Study Group. (2020, April 27). *Predictions and role of interventions for Covid-19 outbreak in India*. Medium. https://bhramarm.medium.com/predictions-and-role-of-interventions-for-covid-19-outbreak-in-india-52903e2544e6Sharma, N., Prabhu, S., & Ghosh, D. (2020, May 2). *Lockdown For 2 More Weeks. What Will Be Different Now: 10 Points*. NDTV.Com. https://www.ndtv.com/india-news/nationwide-lockdown-over-coronavirus-extended-for-two-weeks-beyond-may-4-2221782

Hirchberg, S. (2020, May 5). *The impact of Covid-19 on reading, part 2*. BookNet Canada. https://www.booknetcanada.ca/blog/2020/5/5/the-impact-of-covid-19-on-reading-part-2

P. (2020, May 8). *Dog-eared pages turn to digital bookmarks: Readers move to ebooks, publishers welcome change. The Economic Times*. https://economictimes.indiatimes.com/magazines/panache/dog-eared-pages-turn-to-digital-bookmarks-readers-move-to-ebooks-publishers-welcome-change/articleshow/75621981.cms?from=mdr

Lockdown Anxiety - 5 Tips To Cope With It! (2020, May 12). PharmEasy Blog. https://pharmeasy.in/blog/lockdown-anxiety-5-tips-to-cope-with-it/

India, T. (2020, May 18). *Centre extends nationwide lockdown till May 31, new guidelines issued*. Tribune India News Service. https://www.tribuneindia.com/news/nation/centre-extends-nationwide-lockdown-till-may-31-new-guidelines-issued-86042

Nayar, M. (2020, May 20). *Audiobooks: Reinventing reading in the time of Covid-19*. The Week. https://www.theweek.in/leisure/society/2020/05/19/audiobooks-reinventing-reading-in-the-time-covid19.html

The Monitor's Editorial Board. (2020, June 26). *The lockdown's lesson in reading books aloud*. The Christian Science Monitor. https://www.csmonitor.com/Commentary/the-monitors-view/2020/0622/The-lockdown-s-lesson-in-reading-books-aloud

32

IMPACT OF LOCKDOWN ON CREATIVITY

Indu Sudhir (Dr.)

The lockdown restriction and highly contagious virus have got the entire world to a standstill. If we look at positive side, people are now able to spend a reasonable amount of time with their families. The positive and homely environment has got a good change in human behaviour. People are relaxing, spending more time on their hobbies and interests and are having fun at home. The bonds have grown thicker. People are more enjoying 'Me-Time', listening to the birds chirping and breathing fresh air.

There are always two sides to a coin and this lockdown also has a negative impact on human behaviour. There has been an increase in domestic violence cases, suicides, people losing their jobs, lack of supply of basic needs, people getting stuck at the work locations, travel ban, closure of schools and loss of lives due to pandemic.

The Covid-19 has led to a psychological imbalance of people. The layoffs and salary cut increasing with each passing day led to people suffering from depression and fear of losing financial stability. The migrant workers lost their jobs, could not return to their homes and were devoid of necessities.

Social isolation led to an increase in domestic violence cases. The victim locked down with the abuser, nowhere to go, and nobody to help the victim, has given the complete control and power to the abuser to increase the intensity of violence.

Closure of schools have a considerable impact on the child's growth in the long run. There are no physical and other such activities that help in a child's development.

"Nothing is permanent in this temporary world," it is well known saying. Life will never be the same again. Everyone in this world is trying his/her best to be innovative and creative with the changing times. Lockdown has given us the chance to do interesting things, think inside and learn new skills to create rather than consume. It is one of the most valuable time to break the pain barrier, allow the flow of ideas to get over your boredom. Experiments are going on to handle the pandemic as 'necessity is the mother of invention'. It is very important to stay positive and inspired during the lockdown. Amid the ongoing corona crisis, people are forced to think more deeply, keeping their mind engaged in creative things in productive ways. To keep ourselves as well as others safe, it might have become challenging for few to cope up with this

Assistant Professor, Khalsa College of Education, G.T. Road, Amritsar

situation. A few tips for students to still remain productive in this crisis situation are mentioned below:

- One day at a time: Take one day at a time, plan for the day in the first hour. Write it down and keep unfinished work for tomorrow.
- Stay active: Follow a schedule. It is important that you do not sleep too much. Sleeping in the day disrupts routine. Irregular sleeping can make the mind vulnerable.
- Meditate: Plan your routine and make time for meditation, yoga, zumba or any other such physical activities. It could even be brisk-walking in your house, it can relieve the physical and the internal soul and thoughts..
- Manage Media Consumption: Limit the amount of screen time focused on Covid-19. Too much information can lead to unnecessary anxiety. Encourage your family engaged in other activities instead.
- Be prepared for what's coming next: It might be extended lockdown or you might get back to work, write these things on paper about what you will do. Planning well ahead reduces anxiety and stress.
- Practice "Me" time: When everyone is at home, getting space for yourself is tough. Go to the balcony or sit down on the stairs of your apartment and let the thoughts flow without any resistance for 10-15 minutes. This will help you feel relaxed.
- Gardening can be a great stress reliever for many reasons, including getting into the sunshine and fresh air, creating more beautiful surroundings to come home to each day and more.
- Explore: Photography may help to see things differently.
- Scrapbooking can be a great hobby. Typically, more of a female part time, scrapbooking offers many social opportunities to break stresses.
- Maintaining an Aquarium of beautiful fish can be considered a useful hobby because it requires regular attention.
- Puzzles can take one's focus off what's stressing and develop brain power at the same time.
- Drawing, Painting and Colouring are used as a way to process emotions, distract yourself and achieve other stress management benefits. Explore hobbies and plan out creative activities. One can choose according to his personality and potential, i.e., music, dance, craft making, cooking, drawing, writing and any other skill that gives pleasure.
- Physical activity or exercise can not only improve physical health, it can also relieve stress and improve mental well-being.
- Knitting provides with an opportunity to relieve stress. The repetitive motion can get into an experience of flow or can at least provide an outlet for nervous energy.

- Playing an instrument or music has many health and stress relief benefits. It can absorb the attention fully.
- Writing whether in a personal journal, as an amateur author or even as a professional is a hobby that can be cathartic and relaxing.
- Skill up new learnings by computer courses or online vocational programmes.
- One may charter out academic and non-academic researches or new projects.

Decades of research have demonstrated that in people with dementia and other progressive neurological diseases continue to have the ability to create art. Research has also shown that creating visual art can reduce stress and promote relaxation in people who are hospitalised or homebound due to illness.

So, positive thing about being at home is that one can finally spend time in reading, listening to music and audiobooks, teaching, watching, recipes online platforms, playing games, accepting fitness challenges online, finding new ways to help the vulnerable and many more ways to contribute during the outbreak. It is time to prepare for the future and the opportunity to do something different.

References

Gulati, S. (2017). *Art of Stress Management*. New Delhi: Rupa Publication.

Simonton, K.D. (2000) Creativity- Cognitive, personal and social aspects. *American Psychologist, 55*(1), 151–158. Retrieved from https://doi.org/10.1037/0003-066X.55.1.151.

8

COVID-19 AND ITS FUTURE REPERCUSSIONS

33

SELF-RELIANCE: A KEY TO POST-PANDEMIC RENAISSANCE

Sunita Gupta (Dr.)[1] *and Vani Gupta*[2]

> "Don't wish it were easier.
> Wish you were better."
>
> — Jim Rohn

Introduction

Let us imagine, just for a second, all the ways in which the world could end. It could be something from above or something from below or something that we did to ourselves. But one thing that consistently ranks as one of the most likely things to end the world is a global pandemic. 2020, a year of delight turns into a woe. History repeats itself; in year 1918 'Spanish flu' was a global disaster, now Covid-19 has taken over. The novel Corona virus is a new strain that has not been earlier identified in the human body. Public health has been affected to a great extent due to it. It has defeated science, technology, economics and even social systems. The common man is deranged and flummox and even governments are struggling to find a way out of this pandemic. Being a deadly virus, it has taught us great lessons that humans have forgotten in stupendous magic of technology. The devastation by pandemic is difficult to quantify. It has exposed many weaknesses of our lifestyle, administrative system and health system across the nations.

The challenges and problems thrown at us that we have never come across prior Covid-19 have taught us the lesson of self-reliance and self-sufficiency. During such misery, we should not look for help from other nations, instead we should gain strength, ability and belief to find solutions on our own and hence become self-sufficient. Ralph Waldo Emerson in his essay quoted — "Ne tequaesiveris extra." (Meaning — Do not seek anything outside you). This quotation vividly sums up the significance of self-reliance in post-pandemic renaissance.

Literature Review

Tisdell in his article outlined and discussed Mao's approach of self-reliance and its consequences. It further aimed to consider how China's market reforms have impacted on sub national economic self-reliance within China. It also assesses how China's open door policy reduced its national self-reliance.

1. Assistant Professor, Dev Samaj College for Women, Chandigarh
2. Student, Punjab Engineering College, Chandigarh

It concluded that China's economy became more interdependent as a result of market reforms. China has become more dependent on international trade for its economic welfare. He concluded that still Chinese endeavour to be masters of their own destiny.

Dey in his paper argues that the Indian citizens in general and policy makers in particular should immediately address three major issues which limit India's self-reliance and economic sustainability. These are:

i. Indian core industries are suffering from the 'Dutch Disease Syndrome' due to large scale virtual brain drain.
ii. There is a disconnect between the traditional knowledge system.
iii. Capitalism is passing through serious crisis.

Gughane in his article analyses the policy statement announced by the Prime Minister Modi that focuses on self-reliance of the country in the future. He has explained what exactly the term self-reliance includes and what are the areas in which India is dependent on other economies. He identified India's dependence on oil exporting economies, foreign exchange, defense equipment, electronics and pharmaceutical.

Midmore and Thomas in his paper describe the outcome of an investigation to identify the scope for innovation and improvement of local economic interdependence in Pembrokeshire through greater self-reliance. It outlines a strategic framework identifying collaboration between various stakeholders. The paper concludes with more generalised observations regarding the lessons to be learned for self reliance strategies in peripheral regions.

Kapoor and Yadav argued that the idea of self-reliance should come with caveat of key sector focus and not an economy wide spread. The latter would take us back to pre-1980 India. The final pillar of Modi's agenda for self-reliance, demand, also needs an amendment. They pointed out that the exact contours of self-reliance are unclear. They said that the idea of self-reliance should not be to build growth upon domestic demand alone. India will need to tap into the world markets as well if it aims to achieve sustained fast-paced growth.

Research Design, Need and Objectives

A descriptive and qualitative research has been done with the goal of describing the phenomenon and characteristics of self-reliance as a key to pandemic. To strengthen the results, exploratory research was undertaken.

The Corona virus outbreak has crippled the ecosystem first with human loss and then with economic loss. The economic package of 20 lakh crore under Atmanirbhar Bharat Abhiyan is a much needed one. Self-reliance is a key to sustainable development and its indispensability has been highlighted by the government ever since India gained independence. The present study not only highlights the historical background of pandemics but also endeavours to culminate the significance of self-reliance in this time of crisis.

Historical Background

A pandemic is a disease that escapes our control, sweeping across the world, killing millions and changing civilisations. In the 6th century, a pandemic killed half the world's population. The Black Death arrived in Europe around the 14th century. It was two distinct diseases, the Bubonic plague, which killed as many as 60% of the people who got it, and pneumonic plague, which killed almost everyone who got it. Then there was small pox, less deadly than the Black Death killing 30% of the people who got it, but it was more contagious. In the 20th century alone, it killed around 400 million people. Discussing the past century, experts believe the 1918 flu pandemic could have started when an infected bird and an infected human came in contact with the same pig at a small farm in Kansas. The two viruses could not affect each other but they could infect pigs, and in one pig cell, those two viruses combined, creating a new zoonotic virus, H1N1. It killed somewhere between 50 and 100 million people around the world. It was so contagious that it infected one out of every three people in the world. Then it killed almost 5% of the world's population. Other diseases such as HIV, tuberculosis, typhoid, polio, measles and cholera have also become pandemics. But eventually, we developed technology that could defend us from these diseases and made them less deadly, for example, vaccines, antibiotics etc. Then, in 2002 came the Severe Acute Respiratory Syndrome (SARS), it originated in China and killed almost 10% of the people it infected, however, it was quickly contained and no transmission occurred since 2004.

To avoid the spread of these deadly viruses one needs to be self-reliant and be responsible for one's own safety.

Self-reliance

Self-reliance term became popular when it was used by the American philosopher and essayist Ralph Waldo Emerson in 1841. He emphasised on the idea of individualism and said individuals should follow their unique paths rather than falling into conformity, to strive for greatness. The meaning of self-reliance in simple words is the ability to depend on yourself or your own abilities. Self-reliance could be understood in two different senses: one could be at an individual level and the other could be at the level of economy as a whole. If we talk about self-reliance in context of an economy, it has been the objective of several countries to be self-reliant. The concept is sometimes confused with self-sufficiency. Self-sufficiency simply means that a country produces all the goods and services it requires without depending on others. Self-reliance, on the other hand, implies that the country generates sufficient surplus to buy what it needs and therefore, it does not have to bank upon the loans and aids of outside countries for resources.

India, now the largest democracy of the world was ruled by Britain for over 200 years before it got independence. More than seven decades on, the country has experienced various forms of self-reliance — Swaadheenta! The Swadeshi Movement of self-sufficiency aimed to weaken the control of the British Empire on the Indian economy was a major step towards self-reliance. Self-sufficiency was at the heart of the campaigns Gandhiji led to achieve India's independence from Britain. For him it meant a focus on village life, farming and self-reliance, symbolised by the image of himself hand-spinning thread on a wooden wheel. India's first Prime Minister Jawaharlal Nehru transformed the concept into a national economic strategy. A key part of that strategy, which guided the country for decades after its founding in 1947 were extensive measures to stop or disadvantage imports in favour of domestic production.

The Corona virus pandemic has taught the country "to be self-reliant and self-sufficient" and not look for solutions abroad, Prime Minister Narendra Modi told grassroots leaders on 8 May 2020 as he stressed that every village, district and state should be able to provide for its basic needs. The whole country has to be self-reliant at its own level. A special economic package has been announced to the tune of rupees 20 lakh crore under the 'Aatmanirbhar Bharat Abhiyaan'. Economy, infrastructure, technology driven system, vibrant demography and demand are the five pillars to make India self-reliant.

As per the outline provided by the Prime Minister, mantra in these changed times is 'Vocal for Local'. An absolute lateral shift from global business to local manufacturing, local market and local supply chain is the guiding force. This implies that at all levels – rural, district and state – community-based efforts are required to sustain the economy. The country's manufacturing capabilities for Personal Protective Equipment skyrocketed from 47,000 annually to 200,000 daily. Time has, hence, re-instilled the values of crisis management. Greater role needs to be given to decentralisation to empower local regulatory bodies for ensuring a smooth road ahead. An extensive research needs to be done to identify economic ventures that can be carried forward without external help. Indigenous communities, local craftsmen and handlooms can be resurrected and reinforced during approaching times. It would build a base for durable local integration and partnership. This would also help in rural job creation, food security and poverty reduction in the long run. Additionally, we can potentially cease the 'brain drain' to the West if we are effective in utilising the local talent. Best utilisation of national resources can be made to combat budgetary constraints. 'Make in India' project can reach unprecedented heights which may also pave way for global competition by India in international market in the decade to come. Being self-reliant does not mean the country will completely eliminate foreign companies but will develop several MSME. In the words of Amitabh Kant, CEO NITI Aayog, "the Aatmanirbhar Bharat initiative is not about isolation and anti-globalisation. It is about getting the best from the world. It's about creating world class products. It's not about protectionism. It's about abilities of Indian companies to create world class products, capture the Indian market and then use the strength of the domestic market to penetrate the global market."

Conclusion

Corona virus pandemic hit the world in ways that no one was ready to combat. An invisible threat that has confined us to our homes would require reorienting our life and work relationship in post-pandemic environment. Extraordinary measures are necessary to foster the crashing world and Indian economy. Notwithstanding the disastrous pandemic, we will ultimately win but with a change in lifestyle, new economic order, behaviour and social systems. Covid-19 is in fact a new tryst with our destiny. It is going to remain unfinished for a long time. Now we may require new laws and new approach for economic growth and regularity systems in which more of core space is conceded to social and economic betterment and not nearly for economic market growth. This crisis is an opportunity to reform. Herodotus, a Greek philosopher said — "Adversity has an effect of drawing out strength and qualities of a man that would have lain dormant in its absence." The adversity of Covid-19 has also drawn out our idiosyncratic quality of self-reliance which is the key to post-pandemic renaissance.

References

Dey, Dipankar. (5 August 2016). Three Major Issues which Hinder Self-Reliance and Sustainability of the Indian Economy. www.ssrn.com

Gughane, Nitesh. What Self-reliant Economy Means? www.civilsdaily.com

Luthra, Girish. (19 May 2020). Driving Self-Reliance While Combating a Pandemic. ORF. www.orfonline-org.cdn.ampproject.org

Marwah, Nandini. (13 May 2020). Covid-19 Pandemic: Can India Be Self Reliant in the Middle of a Pandemic. Inventiva. www.inventiva.co.in

Midmore, Peter, & Thomas, Dennis. (1 November 2006). Regional Self-reliance and Economic Development: The Pembrokeshire Case. Local Economy. *The Journal of the Local Economy Policy Unit.* www.journals.sagepub.com

Ramachandran, Sushma. (10 June 2020), Self-reliance After Lockdown a Long-term Goal. The Tribune. www.tribuneindia.com

Sarabu, Kumar Vijay. (April 2020). Covid-19 –A Pandemic Crisis – Challenges: Lessons for Future. www.researhcgate.net

Sharma, Samrat. (2 June 2020). Modi's Five 'I's to Make India Self-Reliant Economy; Tells Industry to 'Trust Me', Govt. is Supporting You. Financial Express. https://m-economictimes-com.cdn.ampproject.org

Spindle, Bill, & Roy, Rajesh. (17 May 2020). India's Coronavirus Crisis Spurs a New Look at Self-reliance. *The Wall Street Journal*. www.wsj.com

Tisdell, Allan Clement. (September, 2013). Economic Self-reliance and China's Development: Changing Perspectives. *International Journal of Development Issues*. https://ideas.repec.org/

34

ISSUES, CHALLENGES AND OPPORTUNITIES FOR TEACHERS DURING AND POST COVID-19

Kiran Walia (Dr.)

Introduction

The world as we know has changed in a matter of moments. Schools shut for the time being, students were freed from schools (however limited to their homes) and guardians needed to wrestle with keeping children productive at home. In the pressure of lockdown, hand-washing and following the world-wide spread of the virus, nobody has paid regard to the unexpected stress. Teachers, who are threatened by technology presently, have to take the bull by its horns. For some, who are capable at planning and educating in the conventional study room are making arrangements for a web based learning. Learning how to utilise the different highlights effectively is significant. In any case, utilising a platform and its features to educate successfully and guarantee that all students are in fact learning is foremost. Be that as it may, more than anything, online study has raised the issues of classroom management. On the offline mode teachers thought that they experienced enough difficulty maintaining their classrooms control, seem to be nothing compared with the hardships of distant classrooms.

Types of Online Education

Online education is directed in two different ways:

1. The first is using recorded classes, which, when opened out to public are alluded to as Massive Open Online Courses (MOOCs).
2. The second one is through live online classes directed as online courses, webinars or zoom meetings. Colleges require fast speed internet and educational platforms or learning the management systems and teachers who are comfortable with teaching online. Students likewise need high-speed internet and PCs/mobiles to go to these meetings or watch pre-recorded classes.

Platforms Created to Enable Online Education in India

There are numerous platforms created to empower online education in India. These are supported by the Ministry of Education, NCERT and the branch of specialised education. There are also additional activities like e-PG Pathshala,

---

Assistant Professor, MGN College of Education, Jalandhar

SWAYAM and NEAT. These are used for course materials and classes, and running of online modules. There are also National Project for Technology Enhanced Learning (NPTEL), National Knowledge Network (NKN), and National Academic Depository (NAD), among others. Virtual classrooms and different online devices today permit us to make the commitment between the teacher and students as near a real — in classroom type understanding — as could reasonably be expected. Going ahead, these devices can likewise make PTM just as staff and the management meetings possible, and these are cost savings while at the same time giving the fundamental interactivity.

Teaching method in digital training is a significant connection between course content, educationists, innovation and course-takers. Democratisation of technology is presently a significant issue, involving web network, telecom infrastructure and affordability of online system, accessibility of PC/desktop, software, educational devices, online evaluation tools, and so forth. Yet, technology based education is progressively straightforward and does not make distinction between front versus back benchers, or girls and boys. A few of the activities are SWAYAM online courses for teachers, UG/PG MOOCs for non-innovation courses, e-PG Pathshala or e-content containing modules on sociology, expressions, expressive arts, regular and numerical science, CEC-UGC, YouTube channel, Vidwan – a database of specialists who give data to peers and forthcoming colleagues, NEAT – an activity by AICTE dependent on the PPP model to upgrade the employability expertise among channel, as a team with Education Technology Companies and National Digital Library (NDL), a repository of learning assets with single window office. Numerous essential activities have been taken up like Spoken Tutorial, Free and Open Source Software for Education (FOSSEE), e-Yantra, Google Classroom, etc. (Sharma, 2020).

Issues Before Teachers for Online Teaching

- Teachers who are not tech-conversant are discovering this new adaption incredibly challenging. In spite of being specialists in their own fields, teachers are troubled over the way that their value as teachers is being connected with a specialised expertise of an application or the web. Some are likewise too shy to even think about seeking help from the younger generation who are generally snappier to learn out how these applications and services work.
- Since educating is playing out, each class closes with a quick reaction from the understudies something that instructors long for. Without eye-to-eye connection and individual communication, the entire execution stands invalid and void through these applications.
- Parents are likewise confronting a few difficulties. Prominent among these is the issue of affordability. Numerous guardians feel awkward

that their children's education is hanging problematically on these smart phones without which their children would lag behind in the learning procedure.

- Being powerless to manage the web which is not free, the marginalised students feel denied from getting information. This has raised the issue of rejection and as there is fear that such issues of access and reasonableness may increase the gap between "those who are well off" and "have not's", despite the fact that education should be an equal right. (Sarkar, 2020)

Risks and Challenges for Teachers

- *Distance learning will strengthen teaching and learning approaches that we know do not work well*: Many nations are moving to distance learning approaches, regardless of whether through disseminating physical packets of materials for students or through utilising technology to encourage web-based learning. There are real risks in light of the fact that huge numbers of these methodologies can be exceptionally singular and instructional when you are simply asking students to sit and discreetly watch recordings, read archives on the web or navigate introductions — that are truly dull. The most noticeably awful type of learning is to sit inactively and listen and this might be the structure that most students will get during school closures. It serves nobody well, particularly the individuals who are the farthest behind.
- *Educators will be overwhelmed and unsupportive to do their jobs* well: Teachers had almost no notification about their schools shutting and moving to web-based learning. They have shared that they are overwhelmed with a wide range of materials and items. Simultaneously, teachers are much the same as all of us in that they are experiencing this strange new world as moms, fathers, aunties, uncles and grandparents are experiencing. They are attempting to manage their individual lives and deal with their children and find better approaches to ensure that learning proceeds.
- *School* ***closures*** *will enlarge the* ***equity gaps***: Over the most recent decade or somewhere in the vicinity, progress has been made in the number of students who approach devices and availability, making this move to internet learning possible. But many students are deprived of these devices because of unavailability of resources or facilities at home which will result into equality gap.
- *Poor* ***experiences*** *during the pandemic with ed-tech will make it harder to use in later for good utilisation of ed-tech*: We realise that a few students using ed-tech will have a poor experience since they are not

used to it. A few people will say, "During the virus we attempted the ed-tech-empowered learning draws near, it was horrible and take at my test scores." People's test will be affected. Individuals will become troubled in light of the fact that the emotional wellness impacts of being separated will be significant. We should be set up for that. Those helpless experiences are extremely imperative to learn what does and what does not work.

Opportunities to Leverage

1. Blended learning approaches will be **tested**, tried and progressively utilised.
2. Teachers and schools will get more regard, thankfulness and support for their significant role in the society.
3. Teachers' joint effort will develop and help improve learning.
4. This pandemic will help us come together across boundaries.

Conclusion

We likewise realise blended learning can draw on the best of the two universes and make a superior learning experience than one hundred per cent eye to eye learning. Virtual classrooms and different online tools today permit us to make the engagement between the teacher and students as near a genuine, in classroom type experience, as could reasonably be expected. Going ahead, these tools can likewise make the PTMs possible, just as of teaching institute's staff and the management gatherings in additional time and cost sparing.

References

Farooqui, S. (2020, May 01). *Education in the time of Covid-19: How institutions and students are coping*. Retrieved June 2020, from https://www.business-standard.com/.

Ramamoorthy, S. (2020, June 06). *Teaching in the time of Covid-19*. Retrieved June 2020, from https://www.thehindu.com.

Sarkar, T. (2020, May 30). *Disappearing classrooms: Teaching in a post-Covid world*. Retrieved June 2020, from https://www.downtoearth.org.in/.

Sharma, D.A. (2020, April 15). *Covid-19: Creating a paradigm shift in India's Education System*. Retrieved June 2020, from https://economictimes.indiatimes.com/.

Winthrop, R. (2020, April 10). *Top 10 risks and opportunities for education in the face of Covid-19*. Retrieved June 2020, from https://www.brookings.edu/.

35

COVID-19: USHERING A NEW WORLD

Surinder Kaur (Dr.)

Introduction

The Covid-19 pandemic has wreaked unprecedented havoc on mankind and across nations. The contagion is global and, perhaps, requires a coordinated worldwide response. It has blurred the distinction between the developed and under-developed worlds and seems to be pushing for a new socio-economic world order.

The devastation caused by the pandemic is debated and feared by everyone. Trade, business and industry have been impacted in equal measure, though agriculture seems to have shown some resilience to beat the ill-effects of the virus. Even the governments are at ease in distributing grains in the face of broken food supply chains because of sufficient buffer stocks. But the loss of producers of perishable commodities such as fruits and vegetables, dairy and poultry products could not be prevented owing to disruptions in transportation and demand contraction.

Likewise, loss of jobs, particularly those in unorganised sectors could not be avoided as production processes halted and the markets were closed. Even after unlocking the markets, there are not many buyers due to the declining income and liquidity crunch. The gradual opening of businesses has, however, created hope for many in the MSME sector. The revival of employment in agriculture has somehow shown more response than the other sectors of the economy.

Without undermining the losses thrust upon society and the economy, it has to be admitted that the pandemic has compelled the people for a change in behaviour that is otherwise difficult to achieve. Avoidance of non-essential travel and luxurious spending, maintenance of social distancing, hand hygiene, and the wearing of the mask or any such thing that keeps one's health assured or good and saves life are liked or at least not abhorred by the common man. Even those who preferred free loitering in groups are now maintaining social distancing.

At times, it was difficult to persuade people to take potable piped water connections, build toilets, avoid open defecation, ensure safe food quality and maintain sanitation in *galis* (lanes) and *mohallas* (localities). Today, the demand for such basic services has increased. The communities are compelled for making provisions of these essentials. They are even ensuring surveillance

---

Associate Professor, SR Govt. College for Women, Amritsar

on Covid-19 cases and travellers around their villages or habitations. Health consciousness has risen to a new high. Even the addicts are seeking treatment to return to normal living, much to the detriment of drug suppliers and peddlers.

The pandemic has propelled the use of digital technology. Fintech, proptech, edu-tech and agri-tech are now common in day-to-day conduct of business. Digital education, unknown to over 90 per cent of teachers, is now widely preferred. During the harvesting and sowing of crops, it is noted in Punjab that most of the farmers were eager to be a part of digital messaging through WhatsApp or other apps. They downloaded e-passes for the sale of their produces and used debit/credit cards more often than ever before. The disrupted food supply chains were also kicking, even in containment areas, due to the use of digital technology. Many e-commerce sites like Amazon and Zomato were able to reach more households despite restrictions.

Another satisfying change is the decline in avoidable lavish spending on social occasions such as marriages and other such celebrations that are identified as one of the major reasons for the rising indebtedness for many. The restrictions on social extravaganza, tried many times earlier, succeeded, though forcibly during the pandemic. No policy or programme could achieve this and hopefully, it will be maintained in the future.

The pandemic has unlocked hidden energy in governments. The lethargy and inertia in governance disappeared without any loss of time as the threat to life and livelihood for the common man was grave and hugely perilous. It led to prompt decision-making; rapid re-formulation of programmes and adjustment of public policies to minimise the devastation and provide immediate relief to the affected vulnerable populations. The quick proclamation of lockdown, rapid upgrade of health infrastructure, swift identification and resolution of unrealised problems such as migrant workers and fiscal stimulus are some of the outcomes of a new way of life and, of course, governance.

The pandemic has surely led to a new normal in our lives. It is different, but not so unusual. It may sometimes appear to be absurd and restrictive, but is not reprehensible or difficult. In many ways, it has taught us discipline, care for one another, use of technology, financial responsibility, and prudence in life. Covid-19 has made us realise the values and systems, some of which can be termed as traditional, concerning hygiene, health, education and even society and communities in which we live. 'Leave your shoes out'; 'Take off your shoes'; 'Spitting not allowed' or 'Wash your hands', though may appear to be the new normal, yet are not new or unfamiliar phrases for us. The pandemic has perhaps enforced conduct that requires the use of new techniques and technologies with the widespread adoption of old but otherwise normal systems and practices, which were lost in our pursuits to grow, perhaps unknowingly. The pandemic has driven us to a new world of work and living.

References

https://en.unesco.org/covid19/educationresponse

https://www-indiatoday-in.cdn.ampproject.org/v/s/www.indiatoday.in/amp/education-today/featurephilia/story/covid-19-impact-digital-education-conventional-education-divd-1661185-2020-03-30

https://www.educationinsider.net/detail_news.php?id=1326

https://www.education.ie/en/Schools-Colleges/Information/Information-CommunicationsTechnology-ICT-in-Schools/Digital-strategy-for-Schools/Building-Towards-a-Learning-Society-ANational-Digital-Strategy-for-Schools-Consultative-Paper.pdf

9

OTHER RELATED ISSUES

36

CORONA PANDEMIC AND ITS HEALTH IMPLICATIONS IN INDIAN POPULATION

Satinder Kaur (Dr.)[1] *and Rajbir Kaur*[2]

Introduction

Corona virus infection in humans was first identified back in mid of 1960s, and named due to crown like spikes on the surface of virus. Hence, the word Corona that shook the whole world is not new to the science. These viruses are further sub grouped into categories as alpha, beta, gamma and delta. Seven known human corona viruses are 229E (α coronavirus), NL63 (α coronavirus), OC43 (β coronavirus), HKU1 (β coronavirus), MERS-CoV (β coronavirus that causes Middle East Respiratory Syndrome, or MERS), SARS-CoV (β coronavirus that causes Severe Acute Respiratory Syndrome, or SARS) and SARS-CoV-2 (the novel corona virus that causes corona virus disease 2019, or Covid-19). According to different studies, humans in the past got infected mainly with corona viruses such as 229E, NL63, OC43, and HKU1 (Liu et al., 2020).

Difference between SARS-CoV, MERS-CoV and SARS-CoV-2

SARS-CoV, MERS-CoV and Covid-19 (SARS-CoV-2) viral infections are known to be zoonotic in nature as these are transmitted to humans from other vertebrate mammals such as birds, reptiles and mammals. The virus uses these animals as reservoir hosts for their amplification (Reed, 2018). Covid-19 is caused by SARS-CoV-2 (Severe Acute Respiratory Syndrome corona virus 2) which is the strain of coronavirus having genetic similarity to bat corona viruses, and causes respiratory illness in patients (Anonymous, 2020). This viral outbreak due to its mass mortality has been declared global health emergency by World Health Organisation on 30th January, 2020. The recent studies concluded that 2019-nCoV is more contagious than SARS-CoV and MERS-CoV having diverse characteristics. Covid-19 infected greater number of people in lesser time period when compared to SARS-CoV and MERS-CoV. Although the mortality rate of MERS-CoV was higher than SARS-CoV and 2019-nCoV (Meo et al., 2019).

The first case of Covid-19 was reported in Wuhan, a city of China in December 2019, though the world was totally unaware about its outbreak and even the word Corona. India reported its first case on 30 January 2020 in Kerala when a student returned home from Wuhan, China.

1. Assistant Professor, PG Department of Zoology, Khalsa College, Amritsar
2. Assistant Professor, PG Department of Zoology, Khalsa College, Amritsar

Table 36.1: Classification of 2019-nCoV

Realm	Riboviria
Kingdom	*Orthornavirae*
Phylum	*Pisuviricota*
Class	*Pisoniviricetes*
Order	*Nidovirales*
Family	*Coronaviridae*
Genus	*Betacoronavirus*
Species	*Severe acute respiratory syndrome-related coronavirus*
Strain	Severe acute respiratory syndrome coronavirus 2

Source: Wikipedia, dated 26.07.20.

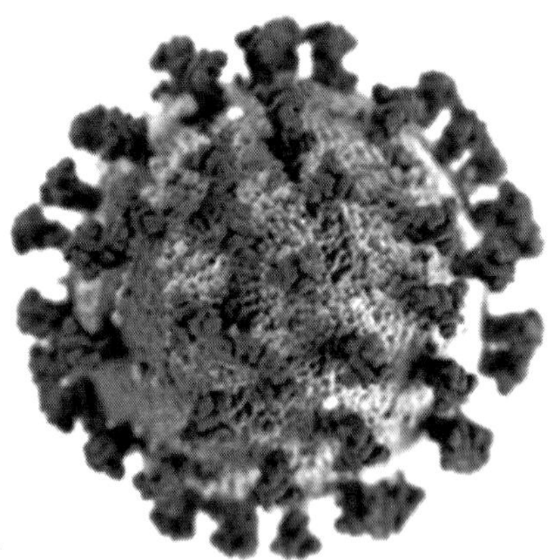

Figure 36.1: Illustration of a SARS-CoV-2 virionRed protrusions: spike proteins (S), Grey coating: the envelope, composed mainly of lipids, which can be destroyed with alcohol or soap, Yellow deposits: envelope proteins (E), Orange deposits: membrane proteins (M).

Source: Wikipedia, dated 26.07.20

As per the #IndiaFightsCorona app of Government of India, 1,62,91,331 total samples were tested up to 25 July 2020, out of which 8,85,576 cases cured and discharged from hospitals, 4,67,882 numbers of cases were still positive or active and 32,063 lost their lives due to this. Maharashtra reported maximum number of cases (3,66,368) while no case is reported from Daman and Diu and Lakshadweep. Punjab reported 291 deaths, active cases are 4,096 out of 12,684 cases, with 8,297 discharged negative cases.

Symptoms of SARS-CoV-19

The disease symptoms include fever, dry cough, body ache, tiredness, nasal congestion, headache, diarrhoea, loss of sense of taste and smell, dry skin, malaise, drowsy, confusion, dyspnoea, and pneumonia (Meo et al., 2019). The severe symptoms are shortness of breath, chest pain and even loss of speech and movement. These symptoms are not seen in all the patients as the severity of disease varies in different patients and so forth the symptoms. The disease manifest different symptoms in different individuals as older people, migrant workers, refugees, people living in camps and small residential areas and persons already suffering from other health issues are more prone to infection. Individuals suffering with high blood pressure, diabetes, cancer, and heart and lung disease have more chances to get infected due to weak immune system.

Transmission of SARS-CoV-19

The disease can be transmitted from infected person to a healthy person via direct, indirect and close contact. It happens via small viral droplets coming out of mouth and nose when infected person coughs, sneezes or breathes. This is the direct transmission as the viral particles directly enter into the healthy person while breathing in contaminated air. People can also get infected by touching surfaces or objects such as door handles or any contaminated thing and putting those hands in mouth, nose and eyes. This is called as indirect transmission of virus. "Respiratory droplets are >5-10 μm in diameter whereas droplets <5μm in diameter are referred to as droplet nuclei or aerosols". Airborne transmission of SARS-CoV-2 can occur during medical procedures that generate aerosols that is aerosol generating procedures. SARS-CoV-2 RNA has also been detected in other biological samples, including the urine and faeces of some patients. However, there have been no published data of transmission of SARS-CoV-2 through faeces or urine till date (WHO, 2020b).

The virus from the throat enters the lungs where it results in the production of large amounts of mucus, decreasing the alveolar function. The alveoli are known to exchange gases as CO_2 from the blood moves to lungs for its removal and O_2 from lungs moves to blood to enter in tissues for various body functions. Due to infection patients do not get enough O_2 as the alveolar surfaces of lung decrease leading to less O_2 transfer, resulting in shortness of breath in patients. Immediate medical attention must be sought in cases of serious symptoms. Mild symptoms should be observed by staying at home if otherwise the persons are healthy. The time varies from 5-6 days to 14 days for symptoms to appear in individuals after getting infected with the virus (WHO, 2020a).

Health Effects of SARS-CoV-2

The virus not only affects the diseased person but also creates stress element for all those who are in blood relation to the sufferer. When the Government of India ordered a nationwide lockdown on 24 March 2020, people were very emotional and fearful about the pandemic. They were forced to live in homes which affected every person financially adding to stress and anxiety among people who need to go outside so as to earn and feed their family. The social media including TV, mobile was flooded with news and information that exaggerated the situation of fear more. Many new words such as quarantine, confinement, home isolation, social distancing, and work from home are linked with the present pandemic situation. Garfin et al. (2020) in a recent study concluded that illustrations containing blood and other scary images must be scanned prior of publishing as these produce anxiety, fear and hopelessness in people reading such news or posts.

All the educational institutions in the country were completely shut down as per the directives of Government of India. Online teaching started as an alternative to classroom teaching both for schools and higher education. This creates a pressure on students to study online, staying for hours on mobile and computer systems. This mode of education is very harmful for the health of children as it affects their eyes, heart and other body functions. Even cases of student deaths while studying online are reported in the country. All these things affect each individual differently leading to deterioration of public health, not only of infected persons but also among healthy persons. One study reported that social distancing techniques, along with careful hygiene, cleaning, and use of quarantine, can reduce the spread of disease in schools (Melnick et al., 2020). Torales et al. (2020) summarised that viral outbreak not only affected the health of people but also leads to other problems such as stress, anxiety, depressive symptoms, insomnia, denial, anger and fear globally.

The situation is even worse for the health care departments as they are short of personal protective equipment (PPE) kits, and even very basic amenities such as N19 masks. This brings fear in their minds to work in corona isolation wards and their concern for their family if they got infected while dealing with corona positive cases. One study focused on the staff health, providing with proper equipment, by giving them some leisure time, helping them emotionally so that they can effectively perform their duty (Chen et al., 2020).

Precautions against SARS-CoV-2

Ministry of Health & Family Welfare issued strict instructions for Indian citizens so as to stop the chain of infection transmission. Proper knowledge about the pandemic, how the virus enters in the body, how it invades one's immune system, the appearance of symptoms and prevention measures is very important. Only dispersal of authentic information can be useful in fight against the virus. The measures such as the use of mask while working or going outdoors, by limiting the visits that are not needed, coughing into a flexed elbow, by maintaining the said physical distance of one metre from person who is coughing or sneezing, by restricting yourself from going in large gatherings, washing hands with soap at least for 20 seconds, avoiding touching the face, covering of mouth and nose while coughing and sneezing, staying home if not feeling well, refraining from smoking for healthy lungs, washing fruits and vegetables, use of sanitisers can restrict the transmission chain (WHO, 2020a). Government can fight against this situation only with the support of its citizens otherwise by ignoring these instructions; the situation can even become worse.

Treatment of SARS-CoV-2

Till date, no vaccine is available against the virus but many clinical trials are in progress to find a potential treatment against the virus. Medicines are given to patients so as to ease the symptoms of fever (paracetamol) and sore throat and cough (expectorants such as guaifenesin). Patients with severe acute respiratory infection, respiratory distress, hypoxaemia or shock require the administration of immediate oxygen therapy (Sohrabi et al., 2020). Plasma therapy proved to be very effective in many cases and patients responded to it well. Hence, plasma donations are also welcomed by hospitals from healthy individuals having protective Covid-19 antibodies. One such plasma donation campaign is being launched by AIIMS Delhi and provided to patients where their response to conventional treatment is less.

Conclusion

Every sphere of life is being impacted by the outbreak of Corona Virus Disease. The transmission of infection is a chained process leading to large numbers in population. The Government has implemented a range of health and social measures which includes partial closure of educational institutions, movement restrictions, international travel restrictions and 14 days of quarantine on movement, home isolation in case of mild symptoms. WHO directs the Governments to relax or tighten the restrictions as per the state of disease changes in their countries. Government has also issued the rules for protective measures to be taken on workplaces so as to reduce the public transmission of virus. These measures include physical distancing, frequent washing of hands, and thermal monitoring on workplace, sanitisation tunnels, and respiratory etiquettes. Public health measures must be taken to break the chain of transmission by identifying the potential infected persons, isolating them and taking proper testing procedures and clinical care of the cases. If the person after testing comes out to be positive, it is very important to locate or trace and quarantine all the contacts. It is the duty of each and every citizen of India to follow these instructions, helping government to slow down the infection transmission. Now everybody is looking to global health agencies for vaccine launch so as to fight against this pandemic locally as well as globally.

References

Anonymous (2020). Coronavirus Disease 2019 (Covid-19), Human coronavirus types, centers for disease control and prevention (CDC), 24/7, Saving lives, Protecting People, National Center for Immunization and Respiratory Diseases (NCIRD), Division of Viral Diseases, https://www.cdc.gov/coronavirus/types.html

Chen, Q., Liang, M., Li, Y., Guo, J., Fei, D., Wang, L., & Wang, J. (2020). Mental health care for medical staff in China during the Covid-19 outbreak. *The Lancet Psychiatry, 7*(4), e15-e16.

Garfin, D.R., Silver, R.C., & Holman, E.A. (2020). The novel coronavirus (Covid-2019) outbreak: Amplification of public health consequences by media exposure. *Health Psychology, 39*(5), 355-357. http://dx.doi.org/10.1037/hea0000875

https://www.mygov.in/Covid-19/

https://en.wikipedia.org/wiki/Severe_acute_respiratory_syndrome_coronavirus_2

Liu, Z., Xiao, X., Wei, X., Li, J., Yang, J., Tan, H., Zhu, J., Zhang, Q., Wu, J., & Liu, L. (2020). Composition and divergence of coronavirus spike proteins and host ACE2 receptors predict potential intermediate hosts of SARS-CoV-2. *Journal of Medical Virology*, *92*(6), 595-601.

Melnick, H., Darling-Hammond, L., Leung, M., Yun, C., Schachner, A., Plasencia, S., & Ondrasek, N. (2020). Reopening schools in the context of Covid-19: Health and safety guidelines from other countries. *Learning Policy Institute,* 1-13.

Meo, S.A., Alhowikan, A.M., Al-Khlaiwi, T., Meo, I.M., Halepoto, D.M., Iqbal, Usmani, A.M., Hajjar, W. and Ahmed, N. (2020). Novel coronavirus 2019-nCoV: prevalence, biological and clinical characteristics comparison with SARS-CoV and MERS-CoV. *European Review for Medical and Pharmacological Sciences*, *24*(4), 2012-2019. doi:10.26355/eurrev_202002_20379

Reed, K.D. (2018). Viral Zoonoses. *Reference Module in Biomedical Sciences,* 1-12.

WHO (2020a). Overview of public health and social measures in the context of Covid-19: Interim Guidance, World Health Organization, 1-8.

WHO (2020b). Transmission of SARS-CoV-2 – implications for infection prevention precautions: Scientific brief. World Health Organization, 1-10.

Sohrabi, C., Alsafi, Z., O'Neill, N., Khan, M., Kerwan, A., Al-Jabir, A., Losifidis, C., & Agha, R. (2020). World Health Organization declares global emergency: A review of the 2019 novel coronavirus (Covid-19). *International Journal of Surgery*, *76*: 71-76.

Torales, J., O'Higgins, M., Castaldelli-Maia, J.M., & Ventriglio, A. (2020). The outbreak of Covid-19 coronavirus and its impact on global mental health. *International Journal of Social Psychiatry*, *66*: 317-320.doi: 10.1177/0020764020915212.

37

IMPACT OF COVID-19 PANDEMIC ON CHILDREN

Baljit Kaur (Dr.)

Introduction

The Covid-19 pandemic is considered as the most crucial global health calamity of the century and the greatest challenge in front of the society. All of us are experiencing social, emotional and psychological problems which we have never experienced before. It is not that there were no pandemics earlier. Pandemics, particularly plague outbreaks have been known since times immemorial. People have faced many infectious diseases earlier like SARS but Covid-19 has shaken the whole world. As Covid-19 initially crept in and subsequently spread at a galloping pace, it has ravaged country after country. The pandemic has significant and variable psychological impacts in each country, depending on the stage of the pandemic. Many psychologists and researchers reported that widespread outbreak of infectious disease, as Covid-19, are associated with psychological distress and symptoms of mental illness (Bao et al., 2020). Psychiatrists across the world should be aware of these manifestations, their correlates, and strategies to manage them that encompass both the needs of specific populations (Yang et al., 2020). Dong & Bouey (2020) pointed out that the wide scope and spread of Covid-19 could lead to a true mental health crisis, especially in countries with high caseloads which would require both large-scale psychosocial crisis interventions, and the incorporation of mental health care in disaster management plans in the future.

Spectrum of Effects

The psychological impact of the pandemic are best understood in terms of psychiatric and psychological problems that were present before the pandemic and the pathoplastic effects of the pandemic on these problems. During lockdown people felt isolation. In India, the first and foremost responses to the pandemic has been fear and a sense of clear and imminent danger. Fears have ranged from those based on facts to unfounded fears based on information/misinformation circulating in the media, particularly social media. At a time when change is the only constant (concerning advisories and precautions, as we move through different stages), the What to do? What not to do? questions are near-universal and give rise to worry and fear. Each one of us responds differently to the barrage of information from global and local sources. This can lead to those who are the "worried

Khalsa College of Education, G.T. Road, Amritsar

well", those who develop distressful psychological symptoms and maladaptive coping with stress, and those who develop a mental disorder. The fears of contracting the illness are also frequent and range from misinterpreting every fever or cough as a Covid-19 infection, wanting a test done for reassurance even though there are strict guidelines for testing, to hoarding medications despite there not being indications for their generalised use. Apart from the advisories regarding hand washing, doubts about whether or not to use a mask, what type of mask, what distances to maintain, what surfaces need disinfection with what? There are also real worries of job losses and economic slowdown during and following the pandemic. The list is endless and leads to a cycle of concern, worry, and distress.

Impact of Covid-19 on Children

Parents are anxious and fearful about their kids because this disease can be easily transmitted to children specially when third wave of Covid-19 is feared. Children and adolescents have already been at home – with schools remain shut as consecutively second session could not be started in most parts of India. Their regular schedules have been disrupted, with no clear idea of when they will be restored. In this situation, without an opportunity for outdoor play and socialisation, they can become very easily bored, frustrated. So they may become increasingly engrossed in social media and online entertainment, which can make them even more socially isolated when they emerge out of this situation. Parents need to know means of keeping the children engaged, providing an opportunity to learn new skills at home, as well as encourage children to participate in activities, get them engaged in "edutainment" and hone their extra-curricular skills as well. Children with special needs may need innovative approaches to engage them and keep them active at home. For the elderly, they can feel further isolated and neglected, become more worried about their families, and increasingly worried about their health. They may not have the support systems to care for them, particularly in terms of their medical needs. This can aggravate into anxiety and depression. Pregnant mothers can have a host of concerns, from worries about whether or not to go for ante-natal examinations, worries about risks to the unborn child, worries about their contracting the infection and concerns about the future. Gender perspectives also need attention as times like this can amplify an abusive relationship and increase intimate partner violence.

Covid-19 and Education of Children

The Covid-19 has resulted in schools shut all across the world. Globally, over 1.2 billion children are out of the classroom. As a result, education has changed dramatically, with the distinctive rise of e-learning, whereby teaching is undertaken remotely and on digital platforms. Covid-19 forced millions of parents around the world to educate their children at home. At the start of the pandemic, nearly 80% of parents were educating their child at home. This came alongside a plethora of issues for parents, including lack of resources such as computers and poor internet connection and a feeling of being overwhelmed. The Covid-19 pandemic presented parents with new challenges on how best to prepare and support their children for a different school experience. Researchers found results that about 24% of parents indicated that their child was fearful or anxious and 30% of parents indicated their child was nervous, high strung, or tense and nearly 60% of parents who utilised free or reduced-cost breakfast or lunch programmes were no longer able to receive that resource. This problem suggests that many school-age children faced hunger due to Covid-19.

What Parents of Children Need to Do?

In this situation, this is the responsibility of parents to encourage their child to participate in different activities so that they learn new skills at home.

1. Involve children in household activities.
2. Answer children's queries but figure out a way of striking a balance. Too much information can cause panic and severe anxiety. Take your cues from the child.
3. Make sure that children are not excessively exposed to pandemic related information. Limit media exposure, especially if there is fear-mongering or exposure to alarming content. If the child hears or sees something upsetting, please put it in context for them. Avoid discussing the topic frequently in front of children.
4. Answer questions honestly. Do not dismiss their worries. Do not make false promises. For instance by saying, "what is there to worry?" or "nothing will happen". Talk about what the family will do should anyone fall ill.
5. Figure a new routine for the household and the child. This routine must include academic work, chores, play, interaction with peers and relatives over the phone or using other forms of technology as well as family time. Have a set time for meals and bedtime. It would be wonderful to also have some indoor exercise as part of this routine – for instance, yoga, stretches, skipping, etc. However, this routine need not be set in stone. The routine must be made collaboratively including changes over time.
6. Family time can include games that parents may not have had time to play thus far. This is a good opportunity to reconnect with the family playing board games, cards, carrom, *antakshari*, etc.
7. Model calmness to the extent possible. You are their anxicty barometer. Do not transfer your anxiety on to children. Seek help if you are suffering from emotional issues.
8. Watch out for repetitive reassurance-seeking – a sign of distress in children. If there is significant distress, consider an evaluation by a

mental health professional. Seek out the options available in your locality, or online.

9. If the child already has a mental illness, please reach out to your doctor via phone or email.
10. Use medicines sparingly and judiciously. However, continue any psychotropic medication the child is already prescribed at the prescribed dose unless otherwise recommended by your doctor. Please do not discontinue the medication abruptly.
11. Please find telemedicine resources, if possible, to start or continue psychotherapy or other therapies including speech therapy, special education.
12. Parents should keenly observe for any emotional or behavioural changes in their adolescent kids. Sometimes these changes can be subtle.
13. Parents can play a vital role in ensuring that their adolescents maintain their mental health by listening to them, acknowledging their difficulties, clarifying their doubts, reassuring them, generating hope and providing emotional support in resolving issues.
14. Excessive use of mobile and other devices can result in behavioural addiction. Parents have to negotiate with adolescents to ensure the limited use of gadgets and to discuss the inclusion of healthy non-gadget activities as a part of the daily routine.
15. Urgent professional help has to be sought if the behavioural and/or emotional changes last for more than two weeks, if the changes are severe, if there is a significant loss of sleep or appetite, if there is physical aggression towards others, if the adolescent expresses death wishes or suicidal ideas or hopelessness or attempts self-harm, and in case of any use of alcohol or other substances.

Conclusion

Covid-19 is too big a problem for a health professional or a parent to solve on their own. All school going children are at home with their parents or few with their grandparents, but many psychological problems are faced by them. For parents who are struggling with their daily needs, expecting them to structure their child's schedule may be impractical. This advice can be dispensed to parents by healthcare professionals. This is the responsibility of the parents to encourage their child in household work and responsibilities. This is a difficult time for all with no easy answers but some of these simple strategies may help.

References

Christie, D., Viner, R. (2005). Adolescent development. *British Medical Journal*, 330(7486):301-4.

Dalton, L., Rapa, E., Stein, A. (2020). Protecting the psychological health of children through effective communication about Covid-19. *The Lancet Child & Adolescent Health*.

Dong, L. Bouey, J. (2020). Public mental health crisis during Covid-19 pandemic, China *Emerg. Infect. Dis., 23 (26)*. Retrievedfrom10.3201/eid2607.200407

Rajkumar, R.P. (2020). Covid-19 and mental health: A review of the existing literature. *Asian Journal of Psychiatry.* Retrieved from https://doi.org/10.1016/j.ajp.2020.102066

Wang, G., Zhang, Y., Zhao, J., Zhang, J.J.F. (2020). Mitigate the effects of home confinement on children during the Covid-19 outbreak. *The Lancet*, 395(10228): 945-947.

Yang, Y., Li, W., Zhang, Q., Zhang, L. (2020). Mental health services for older adults in China during the Covid-19 outbreak. *Lancet Psychiatry*, 7 (4), 19.

Bao, Y., Sun, Y., Meng, S., Shi, J., Lu, L. (2019). CoV epidemic: address mental health care to empower society. *Lancet, 22 (395)*, 37- 38.

https://mhanational.org/blog/how-talk-your-anxious-child-or-teen-about-coronavirus

https://www.weforum.org/agenda/2020/09/covid19-home-child-education-depression-anxiety-hardware-education-tools/

https://www.escap.eu/index/coronavirus-and-mental-health

38

PREPARING CHILDREN FOR PANDEMIC

Ramanpreet Kaur (Dr.)

Introduction

The Covid-19 pandemic has resulted not only in the risk life from infection but has also caused intolerable psychological stress. This has a negative effect on our physical and mental health especially among college youth. University and college students have specific challenges that lead to poor mental well-being due to the outbreak of Covid-19. Before the pandemic started, one in five students experienced one or more diagnosable mental disorders worldwide. During this phase mental health of the students is the topic of discussion throughout the world. The whole academic as well as non-academic performances of the students rely on their mental health. Disturbances in the mental health not only have negative impact on the particular student but also have serious negative impacts on the community.

During crisis period, when social distancing and refrained outdoor activities have brought children into a knotty situation, it is necessary that we understand their fears and myths, try to resolve their concerns in a gentle way

---

Assistant Professor, Khalsa College of Education, G.T. Road, Amritsar

and strengthen their minds. Appropriate planning for preparing the children for pandemics has to be incorporated in our system, so that any future crisis can be dealt with in an easier way.

Preparing Children for Pandemic

Few steps must be adopted by a teacher towards their students such as:

- Take Care of Each Other: Physical distancing cannot and should not mean professional isolation. As we work together, we not only need to focus on student learning through online mode which is a smart solution but also on the overall wellbeing of our colleagues through empathy, honesty and generosity. So, for this we need to start by supporting each other, our students, and their families.
- Raise Awareness: The fears and anxieties of the children can be reduced by providing scientific facts and sharing accurate information about Covid-19. So it is the responsibility of the teachers to keep their students updated with the facts and attend to their problems in a very healthy manner.
- Engage students in Self-Care: Based on reliable sources as UNICEF and WHO, the preschool children should be engaged in some activities to make them understand the protocols of safety during any type of pandemic like social distancing, avoiding handshakes, and using napkin during sneeze and cough, washing hands, etc. So, self-care is very important, only then they will be able to face challenges with a degree of calm and confidence.
- Strengthen innovation: Opportunities are an important key to unlocking access for all students in a virtual classroom. Universal Design for Learning is a framework that helps teachers to plan for multiple means of engagement, multiple modes of representations, and multiple techniques for students to apply and express themselves. This basic viewpoint possibly changes conventional role model to social change agent and in turn an instructor to facilitator.
- Use of Varied Learning Resources: It is necessary to ensure that all students have access to sufficient resources to maintain their learning. Not all families necessarily have access to digital resources. They also even do not have efficient skills in the use of technology. Government initiatives to maintain student learning cannot be effective without the use of an invaluable educational resource, that is, the expertise of teacher. So, there is a need for various solutions that are stable and less vulnerable to breakdowns and technical difficulties.
- Diminish Social Disparities: Researches have shown that almost all students and even more so vulnerable students, experience a drop in school performance or a delay in learning when they are out of school for long periods of time. Disparities among students must be identified

in terms of basic needs, such as food and security, and educational needs. During this situation, students may suffer from the lack of social interaction provided by school. Also, it is desirable to provide opportunities for them to connect with their classmates and teachers by forming virtual discussion groups. Thus, involvement of teachers is essential to ensure that social disparities are reduced.

- Translate learning expectations: This is the foremost duty of teacher to set clear and realistic goals for educating the children during this pandemic. This action by teachers is particularly important for the students and their parents, with whom it is important to communicate regularly and make periodic assessment of their situation. Therefore, the teachers also need to strategically reduce their expectations for all students and identify a few specific areas they want students to focus on, while ensuring that expectations are clear on both sides.
- Coping with Depression and Stress: To cope up with stress and depression among children, various programmes need to be organised with the involvement of youth to understand their perspective and behavioural aspect to deal and confront future pandemics. Activities like meditation, group prayers, reading spiritual and motivational stories and singing motivational songs also help out to release stress of an individual. Also, it is imperative to recognise their emotions and include them in various exercises like reading books, engaging in art and craft, helping parent in daily chores, exercise and yoga to remain fit.

Conclusion

Right from the grassroot level involving homes, community, local bodies and national and international organisations all have to combat the pandemic jointly as well; all have only one future: our "children". We cannot afford to wait further for any adverse situation to formulate new guidelines. We have to ensure that the children have to evolve as fighters in any disaster, and come out as winners.

References

https://www.search-institute.org/social-responsibility/

https://www.oecd.org/education/Supporting-the-continuation-of teaching-and-learning-during-the-Covid-

Honigsfeld, A. & Nordmeyer, J. (2020). Teacher collaboration during a global pandemic. *Educational Leadership*, *77*(10),47-50.

Mohan, A. (2006): *Psychological foundation of Education*. Hyderabad: Neelkamal Publications Pvt. Ltd.

Saxena, R., & Saxena, S.K. (2020). "Preparing Children for Pandemics." In *Coronavirus Disease 2019* (Covid-19) (pp187-198). Springer, Singapore.

Shubhangini, A,J. (2018): Nutrition and dietetics-Tata McGraw Hill Education Pvt. Ltd. New Delhi. P 49.

39

ASSESSING STUDENT'S LEARNING DURING THE LOCKDOWN

Vijay Laxmi

As the corona-virus pandemic spreads all over the world, there has been an increasing move towards teaching online as schools and universities are shut. This situation is new for the teachers and students equally. It has presented many hurdles not only to teachers for teaching online and assessing students' learning but also to experienced educators and those who advocate the use of technology in classrooms.

Educational institutions have started making efforts for equipping the teachers for the effective use of the technology and ensuring that the students are learning what they need to learn. Many educational institutions have planned for webinars and online workshops in this context. Teachers are informed during these workshops about the ways in which knowledge can be acquired, disseminated by making use of technological tools at their disposal to facilitate teaching-learning process.

Initial directives to the teaching faculty during this period (lockdown) were to continue with the curriculum currently in place and to follow the academic calendar by sharing PDFs of printed material on WhatsApp group, sharing links of already prepared YouTube lessons, preparing own video lessons and sharing through YouTube, sharing audio clippings, teaching on-line using Zoom, Google apps and so on.

Teachers were assessing the learning of students by asking them to send the answers to open-text book assignments, asking students to summarise what they had learnt during the class, asking questions during online class and by asking students to attempt the online quiz. However, during interaction with teachers of different schools it is found that students' participation was lesser. Students either did not participate or left the online class reporting network issue. Students showed less interest for such assessment.

The teachers for assessing learning of the students can involve the students during assessment process. Teachers can assign the students the role of creating the quiz to the students. Teachers can divide the whole class into small groups of four to five students and assign the sub-topics for devising the quiz questions along with their expected answers. This would facilitate students' thinking and reasoning skills, and communication skills in the context of their subject learning. The progress made and skills developed during

Assistant Professor, SSSS College of Commerce for Women, Amritsar

planning and coordination will help the students for developing the life-skills. Such an assessment involving students is not entirely teacher-led and hence, students may perform better in assessments when their inputs are appreciated and involved in the process — a phenomenon known as the generation effect (Slamecka and Graf, 1978).

Moreover, for students to be actively engaged in the assessment process, they need to know what they are learning, why they are learning it, how to learn it, how well they are learning it, and how to take the next steps to advance their learning. These are the skills of lifelong learners that can positively contribute to their performance now and into the future (Adie and Willis, 2015). This process, however, is more easily said than done. Supporting students to develop these skills is a start, and for this teacher can provide feedback to the students for further improving their skill of questioning. By involving students during an ongoing dialogue, teachers can share understanding of the standard of performance. For instance,

- Sharing learning intentions and success criteria with students;
- Sharing the examples and case studies with the students; and
- Involving students in annotating work samples against the pre-defined criteria and standards.

This would also enable the students to self-assess the quality of their work as well as that of their classmates. Students can identify their weaknesses and strengths and that of their peers, and hence focus on improving their own skills. Black and William (Black and William, 1998) note that feedback is most beneficial to students when it focuses on strengths and weaknesses, rather than individual marks. Teachers can also award students appreciation letters, certificates or grades for their active involvement in the assessment process.

References

Black, P. & William, D. (1998). Assessment and Classroom Learning. *Assessment in Education*: *Principles, Policy & Practice,* 5(1), 7-74.https://www.gla.ac.uk/t4/learningandteaching/files/.../BlackandWiliam1998.pdf

Black, P. & Wiliam, D. (1998). Inside the Black Box: Raising Standards Through Classroom Assessment. *Phi Delta Kappa*, 1-13. https://www.rdc.udel.edu/wp-content/uploads/2015/04/InsideBlackBox.pdf

Slamecka, N. J., & Graf, P. (1978). The Generation Effect: Delineation of a Phenomenon. *Journal of Experimental Psychology: Human Learning and Memory*, 4, 592-604. http://dx.doi.org/10.1037/0278-7393.4.6.592

https://www.bera.ac.uk/blog/involving-students-in-assessment-conversations

PEER REVIEWERS

Prof. Amit Kauts
Dean, Faculty of Education
Guru Nanak Dev University
Amritsar

Prof. Deepa Sikand Kauts
Head, Department of Education
Guru Nanak Dev University
Amritsar

Dr. Bhagwan Balani
Principal, Bombay Teachers' Training College
Mahakavi Bhushan Marg, Colaba
Mumbai

Prof. Lokesh Verma
Prof. & Head, Department of Education
Jammu University
Jammu (J & K)